DATE DUE

SEP 0 1 2010			
NOV 0 2 2010			
NOV 1 3 2010			
NOV 3 0 2010			
OCT 2 9 2013			
GAYLORD			PRINTED IN U.S.A.

THE SONGS OF HOLLYWOOD

THE SONGS OF

HOLLYWOOD

PHILIP FURIA

AND

LAURIE PATTERSON

OXFORD
UNIVERSITY PRESS
2010

OXFORD
UNIVERSITY PRESS

Oxford University Press, Inc., publishes works that further
Oxford University's objective of excellence
in research, scholarship, and education.

Oxford   New York
Auckland   Cape Town   Dar es Salaam   Hong Kong   Karachi
Kuala Lumpur   Madrid   Melbourne   Mexico City   Nairobi
New Delhi   Shanghai   Taipei   Toronto

With offices in
Argentina   Austria   Brazil   Chile   Czech Republic   France   Greece
Guatemala   Hungary   Italy   Japan   Poland   Portugal   Singapore
South   Korea   Switzerland   Thailand   Turkey   Ukraine   Vietnam

Published by Oxford University Press, Inc.
198 Madison Avenue, New York, NY 10016

www.oup.com

Oxford is a registered trademark of Oxford University Press.

Library of Congress Cataloging-in-Publication Data
Furia, Philip, 1943–
The songs of Hollywood / Philip Furia and Laurie Patterson.
p.   cm.
Includes bibliographical references and index.
ISBN 978-0-19-533708-2
1. Motion picture music—United States—History and criticism.
I. Patterson, Laurie.   II. Title.
ML2075.F87 2010
782.421640973–dc22   2009014846

1 3 5 7 9 8 4 6 2

Printed in the United States of America
on acid-free paper

CONTENTS

ACKNOWLEDGMENTS

We would first like to thank the archivists and librarians who, over a period of fifteen years, helped us locate, screen, and research rare films at the Motion Picture, Broadcasting and Recorded Sound Division of the Library of Congress, the Wisconsin Center for Film and Theater Research at the University of Wisconsin-Madison and the State Historical Society of Wisconsin, and the UCLA Film and Television Archive. Our editor at Oxford University Press, Norman Hirschy, has worked with us on this project from the start with imagination and dedication. He selected three excellent scholars—Geoffrey Block, Steven R. Swayne, and Richard Crawford—to review our proposal for this book, each of whom offered astute criticisms, wise cautions, and helpful suggestions. Richard Barrios read the completed draft of the manuscript and shared his extensive knowledge of musical film to save us from errors he alone could have caught and to help us clarify and strengthen the argument of the book. Our copy editor, Patterson Lamb, and our production editor, Joellyn Ausanka, brought their rigorous and felicitous skills to bear on our manuscript.

The following colleagues, friends, and acquaintances have helped us in other ways, ranging from explaining technical aspects of filmmaking to recommending a particular film or song: Les Block, Cynthia Buckley, Sharon Cummings, Frank Capra Jr., Ray Evans, Howard Green, Chip Hackler, Tony Hill, Robert Kimball, Michael Lasser, Miles Kreuger, David Monahan, David Oppenheim, and Jim Patterson. Our friend and colleague Todd Berliner read the manuscript with the same rigor he brings to his own scholarship, challenging us on many points, recommending that we consider additional films and songs, and providing advice and encouragement as we wrote about what is in many ways for us a new area of research. In addition to his considerable help with the manuscript, he did us the great favor of introducing us to his friend Richard Sherman, who gave a gracious and illuminating interview about his long career writing songs for Disney films.

We also want to thank Lacey Chemsak of SONY/ATV Music Publishing, Kara Darling of Williamson Music, Daniel Peters of the Hal Leonard Corporation, and Troy Schreck of Alfred Publishing for their help with copyright permissions for the song lyrics listed on page 253.

Finally, we want to express our gratitude to the College of Arts and Sciences, the Graduate School, and the Department of Creative Writing at the University of North Carolina Wilmington that supported this project in so many ways over so many years.

THE SONGS OF HOLLYWOOD

I

You Ain't Heard Nothin' Yet

Songs written for Hollywood movies have always had to play second fiddle to those from Broadway musicals. We think of Jerome Kern, Irving Berlin, the Gershwins, and Cole Porter as writers of Broadway shows—*Show Boat, Annie Get Your Gun, Girl Crazy, Kiss Me, Kate*—but they wrote some of their best songs for Hollywood movies. Berlin, for example, wrote "Cheek to Cheek," "Puttin' on the Ritz," and, of course, "White Christmas" for films. Other songwriting teams, such as Al Dubin and Harry Warren, Johnny Mercer and Harold Arlen, and Sammy Cahn and Jimmy Van Heusen, worked almost exclusively in Hollywood. In more recent years, the Sherman brothers (*Mary Poppins*), Marilyn and Alan Bergman (*Yentl*), and other Hollywood songwriters have continued to create wonderful songs for films.

Yet songwriters themselves regarded writing for the stage more highly than writing for the screen. As lyricist E. Y. "Yip" Harburg, who worked with equal success on Broadway (*Finian's Rainbow*) and in Hollywood (*The Wizard of Oz*), put it: "Broadway was the literary Park Avenue...and Hollywood was Skid Row." Still, Harburg went on to say that "for a while, especially during the Astaire-Rogers era, Hollywood was turning out some great songs." In fact, Hollywood songwriters created great songs well before and long after the heyday of Fred Astaire and Ginger Rogers in the mid-1930s. Beginning in 1929, lyricists and composers such as Leo Robin and Richard Whiting wrote sophisticated songs for Paramount operettas that usually starred Maurice Chevalier and Jeanette MacDonald under the direction of Ernst Lubitsch or Rouben Mamoulian. At Warner Bros., Al Dubin and Harry Warren wrote jazzy numbers for films such as *42nd Street* (1933) that were spectacularly choreographed by Busby Berkeley. At RKO, the songs of Irving Berlin, Dorothy Fields and Jerome Kern, and Ira and George Gershwin were superbly rendered by Fred Astaire and Ginger Rogers. In the 1940s, MGM, under the leadership of producer Arthur Freed (a lyricist himself), created such films as *Meet Me in St. Louis* (1944), *The Harvey Girls* (1946), and *Easter Parade* (1948), where songs were as integral to

3

character and dramatic narrative as they were in the best Broadway musicals of the decade. MGM continued to produce such wonderfully "integrated" musical films throughout the 1950s, from *An American in Paris* (1951) through *Singin' in the Rain* (1952), *The Band Wagon* (1953), *Seven Brides for Seven Brothers* (1954), and culminating in *Gigi* (1958).

By the late 1950s, however, original film musicals were being displaced by screen adaptations of Broadway musicals such as *Oklahoma!* (1955), *The King and I* (1956), and *South Pacific* (1958). That displacement accelerated over the next decade with film versions of *West Side Story* (1961), *The Music Man* (1962), *My Fair Lady* (1964), and *The Sound of Music* (1965). By 1970, the Broadway takeover was virtually complete as films of *Fiddler on the Roof* (1971), *Cabaret* (1972), and *Grease* (1978) outnumbered and, in box-office terms, outperformed such original film musicals as *Nashville* (1975), *New York, New York* (1977), and *Yentl* (1983). Today, most musical films, such as *Chicago* (2002), *Dream Girls* (2006), and *Sweeney Todd* (2007), are screen versions of stage shows. While some Broadway adaptations made for wonderful films, many were overly faithful reproductions of their Broadway originals, "stagey" rather than cinematic. Their songs, moreover, are not the songs of Hollywood but Broadway "theater songs" (or as they are sometimes dubbed, "show tunes").

In addition to writing for original film musicals, Hollywood lyricists and composers created great songs for dramatic films as well. What could be more sultry than Johnny Mercer and Hoagy Carmichael's "How Little We Know"— more whispered than sung by Lauren Bacall in *To Have and Have Not* (1944)? Or more winsome than Mercer and Henry Mancini's "Moon River" in *Breakfast at Tiffany's* (1961) as performed by Audrey Hepburn in her own fragile voice, not dubbed, as she was by the operatic Marni Nixon in the filmed version of *My Fair Lady* ? Equally touching is Jackie Gleason's rendition of Sammy Cahn and Jimmy Van Heusen's "Call Me Irresponsible" in *Papa's Delicate Condition* (1963), where he plays an alcoholic husband and father in a role originally offered to Fred Astaire. Standing unsteadily before his wife's dress mannequin, Gleason slurs his way through polysyllabic phrases ("Call me irresponsible,/ Call me unreliable,/ Throw in undependable, too...") as he expresses his love for a woman for whom, he knows, he has been a lifelong frustration.

Some of the greatest "songs of Hollywood" were not actually written for a film but presented in it so movingly that our impression of the song is indelibly associated with that movie. Herman Hupfeld wrote "As Time Goes By" in 1931 as an independent ballad that, despite a recording by Rudy Vallee, quickly faded into oblivion. But when Humphrey Bogart implored Dooley Wilson to "Play it!" (not "Play it again, Sam") in *Casablanca* (1942), "As Time Goes By" was transformed into a "standard" that has taken its rightful place in what has been called "The Great American Song Book." "As Time Goes By" may thus be considered one of the "songs of Hollywood" by a process of adoption.

Still other songs were originally created for one film but more memorably presented in another. Irving Berlin wrote the title song for *Puttin' on the Ritz* (1930), where it was given a lifeless rendition by smarmy nightclub singer Harry Richman. Since then, "Puttin' on the Ritz," one of Irving Berlin's most rhythmically intricate songs, has been revived in several films. The most spectacular rendition was in *Blue Skies* (1946), where Fred Astaire danced with seven reflections of himself. The most hilarious revival came in *Young Frankenstein* (1974), when Gene Wilder introduced Peter Boyle on stage as, not a monster, but a "cultured, sophisticated man about town," then joined him—both attired in top hat, white tie, and tails—in a duet of "Puttin' on the Ritz."

Least interesting of the songs of Hollywood are those that were merely sung over the opening or closing credits of a film. Such "theme" songs, even when they are superb, often bear only a titular relation to the story and characters of a film. Johnny Mercer and Henry Mancini wrote the theme song for *Days of Wine and Roses* (1962) without even looking at the script for the movie. Its haunting images of days that run away "like a child at play,/ Through the meadowland/ Toward a closing door, A door marked 'Nevermore,'/ That wasn't there before" evoke the loss of youth but have little to do with the film's searing portrait of an alcoholic marriage. Mercer later admitted that he thought *Days of Wine and Roses* was a costume epic set in the medieval Wars of the Roses. Even when such title songs resonate with a film's narrative, the fact that they are not presented on screen makes the connection tenuous. At the end of *The Way We Were* (1973), Robert Redford rushes across the street to hold his former lover, Barbra Streisand, in a futile embrace. At that moment, the title song, with its ruefully nostalgic lyrics by Marilyn and Alan Bergman and its plangent melody by Marvin Hamlisch, comes up on the soundtrack but immediately the film concludes, and the song continues playing over the closing credits.

Songs that *do* figure in films are presented in one of two ways. From the very beginning of sound films and continuing to this day, the majority of songs are presented as "performances" by actors portraying singers, dancers, songwriters, or other theatrical characters. In such roles, they have a realistic excuse to sing because they are demonstrating, auditioning, rehearsing, or performing a song in a nightclub, in vaudeville, in a Broadway revue or musical, on the radio, or some other theatrical venue. The very earliest films to incorporate songs, such as *The Jazz Singer* (1927) and *The Singing Fool* (1928), told stories about singers who sang popular songs of their day before an audience who reacted to the performance with applause. This performance convention avoided the problem studios worried about from the outset of sound films: how would an audience respond to an ordinary character suddenly moving from dialogue into song then back to dialogue without even the applause that cushions such a transition in a stage musical. The performance convention for presenting a song solved the problem: in a movie, performers *perform*.

Yet such presentations threatened to rob song of its greatest power. In opera, operetta, and musical comedy, characters express their deepest feelings in songs at heightened dramatic moments. What they sing is not a preexisting popular song but what purports to be an original, spontaneous song that is integrally related to their character and situation. One thing Hollywood tried to do was to capture some of that dramatic power by having "performance" numbers at least resonate with character and story. In *Rose of Washington Square* (1939), for example, Alice Faye plays a singer closely modeled on Fanny Brice. Just as Brice in real life was in love with gangster Nicky Arnstein, Faye's character is enthralled by a crook played by Tyrone Power. When Power is arrested, Faye tells fellow-singer Al Jolson she's quitting show business. Jolson dissuades her by showing her a new song, "My Man," and telling her it expresses her stalwart love for Power and she should sing it for all the world to hear: "This is your song and you sing it and they'll never forget it or you." As Faye sings the song from the stage, Power watches from the wings, but when he sees a stagehand reading a newspaper whose headline predicts he'll be sentenced to ten years in prison, he jumps bail and flees. While Power is "on the lam," he wanders, dirty and unshaven, into a diner where he again hears Faye singing "My Man" on the jukebox. The scene then cuts back to Faye singing "My Man" on stage in another performance, and the camera finds Power in the audience, listening to her one more time before he turns himself in to the police.

While songs done as performances can resonate with character and story, another, more expressive convention for presenting songs developed more gradually. This convention derived from stage musicals where characters broke into songs that expressed what they were feeling at particular dramatic moments. Such "integral" songs were not done as performances by actors portraying singers but as spontaneous emanations of emotion. Initially, only a few characters could sing without a realistic "excuse": cartoon figures (since they were already stylized, what did it matter if they broke into song?); children (who uninhibitedly burst into song); and, in a strange racist twist, blacks, who, stereotypically, were thought to be full of "natural rhythm." The convention of breaking into song gradually extended to Europeans in films Maurice Chevalier made at Paramount in the early 1930s. Then, with the Astaire-Rogers films at RKO in the mid-1930s, ordinary Americans could move from dialogue into song as easily as they moved from walking into dancing, though in most of their films

Astaire and Rogers portrayed professional singers or dancers, so that their forays into song put less strain on verisimilitude. By the late 1930s, the convention was finally established that characters could sing songs that were an integral expression of what they felt at a particular dramatic moment. The studio that capitalized on this new convention was MGM, which, under the supervision of producer Arthur Freed, created musical films where characters broke into integral song as easily as did characters in Broadway stage musicals. And, again as in stage musicals, other characters take no notice of the fact that a fellow performer has just moved from talking into singing.

The way many songs were presented in Hollywood movies, either as performances or integral expressions of character, was different from the way songs were presented on Broadway. As Busby Berkeley was one of the first to demonstrate, cinematography and editing could render a song more spectacularly on the screen than would be possible in even the most lavish stage production. Berkeley filmed dancers from overhead in kaleidoscopic patterns that could never have been seen from the perspective of a theater audience. His camera also tracked through the outspread legs of gorgeous chorines in his patented "crotch shots." When the sequences were edited, shots were juxtaposed in montages that would be impossible to present in a live stage performance.

Cinematography and editing could also render a song more intimately than any stage production. In *Swing Time* (1936), Fred Astaire sits at a piano in Ginger Rogers's apartment and sings Dorothy Fields and Jerome Kern's "The Way You Look Tonight" to himself as she washes her hair in the bathroom. The camera cuts back and forth between him and her as she becomes increasingly enthralled by the song. As she wanders out of the bathroom to be near him, her hair still smothered in shampoo, the camera moves in on her in an extreme close-up. Her slightest facial movements, movements that would not be visible to the audience of a stage production, register how deeply she is touched by the song while her shampooed hair adds a delightfully comic counterpoint to her rapture.

Just as songs in film could be presented in ways that outshone stage productions, they were often crafted differently from Broadway songs. A song such as "The Way You Look Tonight" is more understated, musically and lyrically, than ones created for stage performance—more casual, nonchalant, conversational; less florid, less operatic, less, well, "theatrical." In writing for a Broadway musical, in days when performers weren't "miked" as they now are, composers had to create "singable" melodies with plenty of long notes that performers could sustain and project to the back of the balcony. Lyricists then set such long notes with equally long open vowels—"oohs" and "aahs"—and tried to avoid ending a phrase with a word that had a terminal consonant that could not be sustained by a singer (Oscar Hammerstein once fretted about concluding a line with "and all the rest is *talk*!")

In the early 1930s, however, Hollywood devised the "playback" system, which changed the rules of songwriting. In this system, performers first recorded a song in a sound studio by singing into a microphone. Then, during shooting, they would lip-synch to a playback of their own recording. For songwriters, the playback system meant that composers need not worry about providing long notes to give a melody "singability"; because singers were using a microphone, every note, even the shortest, was picked up clearly and amplified. For lyricists, the microphone provided even more flexibility: instead of concentrating on long open vowels, they had a wider palette of short vowels and consonants—not just the more singable "*l*s," *m*s," and "*n*s" but dental "*t*s" and "*d*s," guttural "*k*s" and "*g*s"—even plosive "*p*s" and "*b*s" (though these could sometimes "pop" the mike). Since, as a Germanic language, English is rich in such consonants, lyrics that used them liberally—"Isn't It Romantic?" "Cheek to Cheek," "Let's Call the Whole Thing Off"—sounded more like everyday conversation.

The playback system also offered new opportunities for the way songs were performed in film. Because singers merely had to lip-synch to their own pre-recording, they could seem to be singing while performing the most athleti-cally demanding dances, as Donald O'Connor does with "Make 'Em Laugh" in *Singin' in the Rain*. On the other hand, prerecording enabled them to render the most intimate songs with casual nonchalance. Some of the best performers in musical film, such as Maurice Chevalier, Fred Astaire, and Gene Kelly, never sang out bombastically but rather presented a song as if they were talking rather than singing. "The one advantage that nonsingers like myself have on good singers," Kelly observed, "is that we can almost talk what we have to say." More gifted singers, such as Judy Garland, learned to deliver songs more informally and understatedly than she had from the vaudeville stage.

Given the fact that Hollywood movies could showcase songs much more spectacularly, as well as more intimately, than Broadway stage productions and that the prerecording and playback system gave composers and lyricists so much more freedom as they crafted words and music, it might seem strange that song-writers would compare writing for Broadway to "Park Avenue" and working in Hollywood as "Skid Row." Part of the discrepancy simply reflected the songwrit-ers' sense of disruption as they moved from the East to the West Coast. While some songwriters gladly left New York for Hollywood with the advent of sound films, the major Broadway songwriters—Kern, Porter, the Gershwins—trekked westward only because the Great Depression darkened so many Broadway the-aters. As Broadway songwriters migrated to Hollywood in the early 1930s, they found film a very different venue for their work.

In a Broadway musical, lyricists and composers were central to the production from the very beginning, working with producers and playwrights on where to place songs in the story. Their songs had what songwriters called "particularity," for they were integrally tailored to certain characters and dramatic situations. Musically, such songs could be intricate and daring, for stage singers often had trained voices that could traverse three octaves and change keys in the course of a melody. Lyricists, many of whom had started out as writers of *vers de société*, wrote witty, literate lyrics that were appreciated by sophisticated Broadway audiences. During rehearsals, songwriters collaborated with directors and choreographers to revise songs to suit the abilities of singers and dancers. Before a show opened in New York, songwriters rewrote or replaced songs based on the reactions of audiences at out-of-town "try-out" performances. On opening night on Broadway, their names appeared on the theater marquee, often above even the title of the show—Oscar Hammerstein and Jerome Kern's *Show Boat*, Richard Rodgers and Lorenz Hart's *A Connecticut Yankee*, George and Ira Gershwin's *Strike Up the Band*.

In Hollywood, by contrast, the compartmentalized, assembly-line production of movies had long been established by 1927 and was not about to change when songwriters arrived. They were told to write songs—period. Since the songs were usually presented as "performances," they need have little relation to character or dramatic situation. Usually, the lyricist and composer were given a screenplay—sometimes only a narrative treatment and occasionally even less than that—and sent off to a bungalow on the lot to crank out songs, songs that were expected to become *hits*. They seldom had any say in how their songs were presented and frequently were berated by producers who were wary of music or lyrics that departed from the simplest of formulas. As film historian Richard Barrios notes, "the film spectator was deemed on a lower plane than the more sophisticated Broadway equivalent, and songs had to be tailored accordingly. Simpler and more accessible modes of current pop tunes were held as the prototype for film use. In this formula, lyrics were kept plain and often repetitive, rhyme schemes obvious, melody and harmony nonadventurous." Sam Goldwyn once ordered George Gershwin to write more like Irving Berlin. Richard Whiting had to endure the scorn of a producer who, after listening to the composer demonstrate a new melody, tore the sheet music from the piano, threw it on the floor, and shouted "Phooey!" When a movie came out, the names of the songwriters were buried in the middle of the credits, and even the most successful Hollywood composers and lyricists were virtually unknown compared to their Broadway counterparts. Composer Harry Warren, who had written almost as many hit songs as Irving Berlin, was bitter that his name was unfamiliar to most people because he had not written a successful Broadway show. "In Hollywood," he grumbled, "a songwriter was the lowest form of animal life."

In effect, writing songs for Hollywood was less like writing for a Broadway musical and more like working on Tin Pan Alley. To understand the songs and songwriters of Hollywood, therefore, one needs to know something about Tin Pan Alley and its long-standing link to the movies. Before Tin Pan Alley, there really was no popular song industry in America. The relative affordability of factory-built pianos in the latter decades of the nineteenth century made the sing-a-long around the parlor piano the center of middle-class home entertainment in the days before the phonograph or radio. The new pianos created a demand for sheet music, but traditional music publishers did not try to meet that demand. Such publishers were spread across the country, and, while they might publish popular songs, they first waited until a song had *become* popular, through such venues as minstrel shows, before they would publish the sheet music for sale. Their mainstay was in church hymnals and music instruction books, so the publication of a song was a sideline. When one of Stephen Foster's songs, "Massa's in de Cold, Cold Groun'" (1852), sold 75,000 copies of sheet music, it was considered a phenomenal hit.

But in the 1880s a new breed of sheet-music publishers set up shop, first around Union Square in New York, then off Broadway and West 28th Street, where, so the story goes, the din of so many tinny pianos cranking out new songs struck a newspaper reporter as sounding like clanging tin pans and earned the area its sobriquet. These publishers, most of them Jewish immigrants who had started out as salesmen, believed that if you could sell corsets and neckties, you could also "sell" songs. They specialized exclusively in popular songs and tried to make songs to order for the public taste by following simple musical and lyrical formulas. Once manufactured in the publishing office, a song could then be *made* popular through what came to be called "plugging." Plugging could range anywhere from bribing a vaudeville performer to work your company's new song into her act to sending "pluggers" out to a busy street corner with a piano mounted on a truck. In 1892, a Tin Pan Alley song, "After the Ball," sold more than a million copies of sheet music, demonstrating the popular music industry's power to create and plug its songs far beyond the success of even Stephen Foster. By 1910, the sheet-music publishers of Tin Pan Alley were producing virtually every popular song in America.

With the emergence of the film industry at the turn of the century, Tin Pan Alley saw another avenue for plugging songs. Although, as film historian Rick Altman has established, "many early films were shown in silence," popular songs still found their way into the earliest storefront nickelodeons. As reels were changed, which had to be done every ten minutes, slide photographs, along with song lyrics, would be projected on the movie screen by a machine called a "magic lantern projector." The slides were tinted photographs of live models superimposed against background images that depicted scenes from a song's lyric. As slide after slide flashed on the screen, a Tin Pan Alley plugger would lead the audience in a sing-a-long to help popularize his publisher's latest song. Slide songs were shown in most of the country's 10,000 movie houses in 1910 and were one of Tin Pan Alley's most successful means of plugging its songs.

Such song slides largely disappeared by 1913, replaced by live musical accompaniment of the film itself—by a pianist or violinist in small-town theaters or by a huge Wurlitzer organ or even a full symphony orchestra in big-city music palaces. By the 1920s, Tin Pan Alley had found another way to use films to plug songs. With the emergence of "star" performers, such as Douglas Fairbanks, Charlie Chaplin, and Mary Pickford, Tin Pan Alley began "dedicating" new songs to such stars by placing their photographs on sheet music covers. "As the songs sold, producers slowly began to notice how the music connection gave the star an attractive new facet and how a music store could be a salutary place in which to plug an upcoming movie." By the mid-1920s, Tin Pan Alley publishers and Hollywood producers were working together to create "theme" or "title" songs for a movie. The songs would be played in movie theaters as part of the musical accompaniment for the film, then sheet music would be sold in the lobby. Some theme songs, such as "Charmaine" for the 1926 silent film, *What Price Glory?,* became enormously popular, the film plugging the song, the song, in turn, plugging the movie in what nowadays would be called "synergy" between a film and a range of commercial products. In 1928, the title song of *Ramona,* in a gimmick that employed the new medium of radio, was sung on a coast-to-coast broadcast six weeks before the film was released. Dolores Del Rio, the film's star, sang it in a Hollywood radio station while Paul Whiteman's Orchestra accompanied her from New York. The plug was so successful that "Ramona" became a hit before the release of the film, drawing crowds to theaters where Del Rio herself sometimes appeared to sing for the opening night audience. With the development of talking pictures, Tin Pan Alley was ready to hawk its wares directly on the screen.

Hollywood, however, was at first not quite ready for songs—or even sound. After decades of attempts to wed sound to film, including failures by the great Thomas Edison himself, studios were wary when engineers claimed to have solved the nagging problems of synchronization and amplification. One of the few that even entertained the possibility of sound pictures was Warner Bros. Sam Warner, the visionary in the family, was the first to embrace the prospect of talking pictures. "I worshipped Sam," Jack Warner later said, "because he was a dreamer who could grab a handful of clouds and weave them into a magic rug. Sam never talked big, but his mind was like a periscope. He could look around corners and see things coming." Sam argued that making talking films—before any other studio—could help the brothers realize their ambition to break out of the ranks of second-tier studios and compete with the giants of the industry, such as Famous Players-Lasky (Paramount), First National, Fox, and Loew's (MGM). Going into sound pictures would have been a move similar to that of their innovative father, Benjamin, who upon arriving from Poland, set up his cobbler shop in Baltimore with a gimmick— shoes repaired "while you wait."

But Jack, Albert, and Harry Warner would have foreseen the enormous problems involved in making talking pictures. Soundstages would have to be built to shut out noise from the outside world. The entire process of filming would undergo a sea change; no longer would the director shout instructions through a megaphone to actors who mimed their roles. Before "Lights! Camera! Action!" would come a chilling new phrase, "All quiet on the set!" Quieting the set would involve muffling everything from the whirr of the camera to the sputtering of arc lights. Filming scenes outdoors, as silent films did so beautifully, would have seemed insurmountable in sound.

Even if sound films could be made, what theaters could show them? Would the owners of the 14,637 theaters across the country install sound equipment at a cost of between $16,000 and $25,000? As film historian Douglas Gomery points out, "one-half of America's movie theaters were in towns with a population of 5,000 or less" (only 22 percent were in towns of more than 100,000). How could those theater owners recoup such an investment in sound equipment? Then there was the problem of foreign distribution. In 1925, foreign sales constituted 25 percent to 30 percent of the gross for a film. How could a talking picture—in English—play in France, where 70 percent of the films shown were made in Hollywood? Or Germany, where 60 percent were Hollywood films? With silent films, all that was required for foreign distribution were translated title cards; what would it take to make foreign language versions of sound films?

On top of these problems, there was the clichéd wisdom, "If it ain't broke, don't fix it." The movies were surely not broke. In 1926, Hollywood made more than 400 feature movies. They did great business and not only attracted a huge middle-class audience but the working-class, immigrant population who, ever since the early twentieth century had flocked to storefront "nickelodeons" to see the novelty of moving pictures. One of the appeals of silent films to such immigrants was that there was no dialogue spoken in a language that was still foreign

first theater to be acquired by the studio and one of only two theaters in the country that could show sound films. Although tickets cost $10—then a record for a motion picture premiere—all 1,208 seats were sold. The short opened with a speech by Will Hays, head of the Motion Picture Producers and Distributors of America, Inc., Hollywood's newly created self-regulatory body. Hays's speech extolled the power of sound film to carry great classical music "to the town halls of the hamlets" of America and preserve—forever—performances in the face of the truism that "the art of the vocalists and instrumentalists is ephemeral." After Hays spoke, the 107-piece New York Philharmonic played Wagner's Prelude to *Tannhäuser*, then a parade of concert, vaudeville, and opera stars performed. The highlight of the Vitaphone program was Giovanni Martinelli's rendition of "Vesti la giubba" from Leoncavallo's *I Pagliacci*. The successor to the great Caruso, Martinelli was not only a superb tenor but a consummate actor, one who had a "keen ability to seize upon the crucial point in opera where music and drama intersect.... In a very real way Martinelli was the first musical film star, demonstrating more than a year before *The Jazz Singer* the power resulting from the meeting of amplified voice and projected image."

The success of the Vitaphone program, along with that of *Don Juan* with its synchronized soundtrack, justified Warner Bros. $3 million investment. It also prompted other theaters to install sound projection equipment, and within the year 230 theaters could show sound films by Warner Bros. as well as William Fox's newsreels, which carried a spoken soundtrack on the "Movietone" sound-on-film process. Their success prompted Warner Bros. to create another "Vitaphone Program" but instead of classical performers, this second short (which actually ran an hour) featured vaudeville stars such as Willie Howard, George Jessel, and, most stunningly, Al Jolson, who sang three songs from his repertory of hits. It was, in effect, "canned" vaudeville, but the fact that audiences were not seeing a live performance was offset by the novelty of sound film and that they were seeing and *hearing* renowned performers in their own local theater.

It may have been Jolson's show-stealing performance in the Vitaphone short that prompted Warner Bros. to expand its experiments with sound. The studio combined its two-front sound experiment into a hybrid—a silent feature film with not only a synchronized soundtrack but several song sequences in sound. The problem was how to present such songs. It might seem ludicrous for an actor, in an otherwise silent film, to suddenly burst into song then revert to mime acting without even the applause that cushions the transition from song back to spoken dialogue in a stage musical. A more sensible way of presenting a song on the screen would be to have it sung by an actor who was playing the role of a singer and thus had a realistic "excuse" to sing. Thus was born the "performance" convention of presenting song in film.

For Sam Warner, a logical choice for such a film about a singer was a play by Samson Raphaelson that was having a successful run, financially if not critically, on Broadway. Ironically, *The Jazz Singer* starred George Jessel, who was initially slated to star in the film version after he finished touring with the play. But negotiations between Jessel and Warner Bros. broke down over the recordings of songs Jessel would make as part of the filming process and for which, on the advice of Eddie Cantor, he demanded extra compensation. Warner Bros. replaced him, perhaps gladly, with Al Jolson, even though they had to pay Jolson the then staggering fee of $75,000. Filming began in June, first in New York for location shots, then in Hollywood in July for interior scenes. For the song scenes, Warner Bros. had erected the first soundstages. Under Sam Warner's supervision, their walls were lined with felt, the camera was enclosed in a soundproof wooden box with one glass wall, and the sputtering arc lights were replaced with incandescent lamps. Musicians, just out of camera range, accompanied the performers. Fifteen feet above the floor, sound engineers monitored the recordings of songs from a glass-walled booth. Under such conditions, the first songs in a feature film were recorded.

What kinds of songs were they? Not original songs written specifically for *The Jazz Singer*. There was no need for that. Since Jolson and Bobby Gordon, who played Jolson's character as a boy, would be performing songs in saloons, nightclubs, and vaudeville, the film could use existing pop songs. The songs, moreover, need not be integral to the story since they would be presented purely as performance numbers. What such songs could do, as many later films such as *Alexander's Ragtime Band* (1938) and *Goodfellas* (1990) have also demonstrated, was underscore the passage of time in the narrative through the historical progression of changing styles in popular music. Filming of *The Jazz Singer* ended in early September, and the film premiered in New York on October 6, 1927. The man most responsible for the film, however, was not there. In his relentless drive to create a sound film, Sam Warner's health broke down, and he died of a brain hemorrhage, at age thirty-nine, a day before the opening of *The Jazz Singer*. Harry, Jack, and Albert also missed the historic occasion to take a train back to Hollywood when they got word of Sam's imminent death. "There is no doubt that *The Jazz Singer* killed him," Jack Warner later wrote, "Sam brought it into the world and gave his own life in exchange."

What now seems a bizarre hybrid of a movie, with its abrupt transitions from a silent film to song sequences in sound, then back to silent film, enchanted 1927 audiences. After starting out like any other silent film, but with a synchronized orchestral score made up of a pastiche of Tchaikovsky melodies, there suddenly comes a moment when Bobby Gordon, playing Jolson as the thirteen-year-old son of a cantor, performs a song, "My Gal Sal" (1905), in an East Side saloon.

Written by one of the great songwriters of the early days of Tin Pan Alley, Paul Dresser, brother to novelist Theodore Dreiser, "My Gal Sal" was typical of the kind of song formula Tin Pan Alley relied upon at the turn of the century. With its portrait of a small-town girl who has gone astray in the big city but is still fondly remembered by her first sweetheart, "My Gal Sal" was a sentimental waltz ballad that told a story in verses that alternated with a more lyrical refrain or chorus, much in the "strophic" style of most nineteenth-century song. While the lyric, in diction and sentiment, would have been deemed proper by middle-class standards, that a cantor's son was singing it in a saloon would have been shocking in the dramatic context of the film.

And shock it does. As cantor Rabinowitz and his wife fretfully wonder why their beloved "Jakie" (short for "Jacob") is not home as the Sabbath draws nigh, the film cuts to a man having a beer in a tavern. Beguiled by a sweet voice emanating from the adjoining saloon, he wanders to the swinging doors to find Bobby Gordon singing "My Gal Sal." Aghast, the man, who turns out to be a neighbor of the Rabinowitz family, rushes to their home, and, as the film reverts to silence, "tells" them (through title cards) what their son is doing. The film then cuts back to the saloon—and sound—where Gordon sings a very different kind of early Tin Pan Alley song, "Waiting for the Robert E. Lee" (1912) by L. Wolfe Gilbert and Lewis F. Muir. Such a song would have been even more reprehensible for a cantor's son to sing, for it is a syncopated, ragtime song that would have been dubbed, in the parlance of the day, a "coon" song.

Coon songs became popular in the mid-1890s after ragtime was introduced to the general public at the Chicago World's Fair of 1893 (officially the "Columbian Exposition," which celebrated the five-hundredth anniversary of the voyage of Columbus). Born in the brothels of New Orleans, ragtime could take the form, in the hands of such composers as Scott Joplin, of an elegant piano solo built on classical principles, the left hand providing a stately *oom-pah* beat derived from brass bands, the right hand "ragging" the melody by coming in slightly before or after the beat. On Tin Pan Alley, however, ragtime became the basis for songs that caricatured blacks (even though some the songs were written by black songwriters, such as Ernest Hogan's "All Coons Look Alike to Me").

Despite their demeaning racist caricatures, ragtime coon songs introduced sprightly new two-beat rhythms that set them apart from such lugubrious three-quarter-time waltz ballads as "My Gal Sal." Coon songs also had passionate, vernacular lyrics, often with erotic overtones that would have been deemed improper in a waltz ballad. Thus a black could exult "Hello! ma Baby,/ Hello! ma honey,/ Hello! ma rag-time gal/ Send me a kiss by wire/ Baby, my heart's on fire" or lament "'Member dat rainy eve/ dat I drove you out,/ Wid nothing but a fine tooth comb?/ I know I'se to blame;/ well, ain't dat a shame/ Bill Bailey, won't you please come home?" The crude humor of these lines was compounded by the sheet-music cover that depicted racist caricatures of bug-eyed, thick-lipped blacks with wooly hair that would seem impervious to a "fine tooth comb."

For all its syncopated, rhythmic energy, "Waiting for the Robert E. Lee" has the same strophic form as "My Gal Sal"—verses that narrate a story about blacks rejoicing at the arrival of the "good ship Robert E. Lee that's come/ To carry the cotton away" alternating with refrains that punctuate that narrative with vernacular exclamations:

> *Watch them shufflin' along,*
> *See them shufflin' along.*
> *Go take your best gal, real pal,*
> *Go down to the levee,*
> *I said to the levee and*
> *Join that shufflin' throng*
> *Hear that music and song.*

It is this chorus that Gordon sings, moving rhythmically and sensuously—foreshadowing of the kind of songs Jolson will later sing in nightclubs and vaudeville—when his father enters the saloon.

Over the protests of the accompanying piano player, Warner Oland (later of "Charlie Chan" fame) drags his son home for a whipping despite the fervid pleas of his wife, played by Eugenie Besserer. After tearfully taking leave of his mother, Jakie runs away from home to pursue his singing career. Thus the first two songs in *The Jazz Singer* are presented as performances of Tin Pan Alley songs. While they are not integral to the characters or story of *The Jazz Singer*, the performances themselves propel the narrative by provoking responses, first by the neighbor of the Rabinowitz family, then by the cantor himself.

While "My Gal Sal" and "Waiting for the Robert E. Lee" typify two major developments in the early history of Tin Pan Alley—and thus correspond to the era of Jolson's character's childhood—the most important song in *The Jazz Singer*, Irving Berlin's "Blue Skies," exemplifies the kind of song that would dominate American popular music in the 1920s. Despite the fact that "My Gal Sal" is a waltz ballad and "Waiting for the Robert E. Lee" is a ragtime coon song, both cling to the nineteenth-century pattern of *strophic* song—that is, they consist of verses, which narrate a story ("In a cavern, in a canyon, excavating for a mine/ Lived a miner Forty-niner, and his daughter Clementine…"), and alternating eight- or sixteen-bar refrains, which repeat the same lyrical exclamations ("Oh, my darlin,' Oh, my darlin,' Oh, my darlin' Clementine…").

Beginning in 1910, with such songs as Shelton Brooks's "Some of These Days," however, a new song form took hold on Tin Pan Alley. The verse, instead of carrying the narrative weight of a song, merely served as an introduction to an enlarged version of the refrain, now called the chorus, which expanded to thirty-two bars. That chorus, moreover, was divided into four eight-bar sections that alternated among two, three, or even four melodies in patterns that ranged from ABAB, where two different eight-bar melodies alternate with one another, to ABCD, where four different eight-bar melodies follow each other in sequence. The most common pattern was AABA, where an initial eight-bar "A" melody was heard, repeated, then varied with a different "B" melody, also called the "bridge" or "release," before the "A" melody returned for the final eight bars. The AABA pattern is a supremely effective way to structure a song: give the listener an engaging eight-bar melody (A); repeat the same phrase (A); then, in the third set of eight bars, the "bridge" or "release," vary the pattern with a different eight-bar melody (B); but in the final eight bars, return to the same initial strain (A). Slick, streamlined, and catchy, this musical formula typified the Tin Pan Alley song, then the Broadway song (where songwriters such as Jerome Kern would handle it with subtle sophistication), and finally the Hollywood song.

Just as this new thirty-two-bar chorus was establishing itself as the dominant popular song form, a dance craze took hold of America. At its forefront, a new dance, the fox-trot, provided a four-beat alternative to the three-step waltz of "My Gal Sal" and the two-step of ragtime and marches that set the tempo of "Waiting for the Robert E. Lee." The foxtrot's alternation of slow gliding steps with quick ones opened up new possibilities for composers. As theater historian Mark Grant observes, "The foxtrot combines slow and fast, rhythmic flexibility and downbeat regularity, in a unique way. It can be made to swing or syncopate, yet it gives off a subtle lilt even when the rhythm is four-square and unswinging. It can be elegant and romantic or peppy and jazzy with a simple alteration of the basic tempo. It can be equally swank or earthy because it mixes courtly and folk dance elements in a way that no other dance ever has."

The Jazz Singer presented "Blue Skies" as the kind of thoroughly up-to-date, thirty-two bar AABA foxtrot that "Jackie Robin" sings as he finally achieves success on Broadway in the 1920s. Jolson's character does not, however, perform the song on stage but instead sings it to his mother as a demonstration of how, after running away from home, he has finally attained stardom. Although Berlin did not write the song for the film—it was a big hit from the previous year—it has dramatic resonance with this dramatic moment in *The Jazz Singer*. "Blue Skies" is a love song for a singer who has suddenly found romance after many years of sadness. That passage from sadness to joy is underscored musically as each A-section starts in the melancholy key of E minor but then shifts to a buoyant G major. The fact that the singer has known sadly blue days in the past will, as the song unfolds, tinge his present joy over being in love. The first two A-sections exult in that current happiness with parallel lyrical images:

> *Blue skies*
> *Smiling at me*
> *Nothing but blue skies*
> *Do I see.*
> *Bluebirds*
> *Singing a song,*
> *Nothing but bluebirds*
> *All day long.*

It is in the release or bridge that the song undergoes a transformation as the singer's awareness of past unhappiness—and of the possible transience of his current joy—overshadows his exultation:

> *Never saw the sun*
> *Shining so bright,*
> *Never saw things*
> *Going so right,*
> *Noticing the days*
> *Hurrying by—*
> *When you're in love,*
> *My, how they fly!*

As the release ends and we shift to the final A-section—usually the pivotal point of an AABA song—the minor key returns and the lyric departs from its parallelism with the previous A-sections:

> *Blue days,*
> *All of them gone—*
> *Nothing but blue skies*
> *From now on.*

While "Blue Skies" and "Bluebirds" are joyous images, the phrase "Blue days" refers back to the time when the singer had the "blues." Though it rejoices that those days are gone, the lyric, in the release, realizes that time rushes by "when you're in love" and those "blue days" may return. That realization, coupled with such negative words as "never," "gone," and "nothing," undercuts the lyrical affirmation as subtly as do the minor-key passages.

"Blue Skies" thus resonates with the dramatic moment in *The Jazz Singer* when Jolson, after many years of missing his beloved mother, is reunited with her. Before he sings, the scene is silent. Jolson enters his parents' apartment, surprising his mother, and we see his father giving Hebrew lessons in another room. After a few moments of title-card dialogue, Jolson offers to demonstrate one of the songs in his new Broadway show. As synchronized sound comes up again, Jolson strides to the parlor piano and launches into "Blue Skies." While he renders the song as a performance, his hammy, flourishing rendition portrays him as a kid showing off for his mother.

After one chorus of "Blue Skies," however, Jolson did something extraordinary—he *talked*. He had spoken a few lines earlier in the film. After Jolson sang "Dirty Hands, Dirty Face" in a scene set in a San Francisco nightclub, the audience of extras broke into applause. Jolson, seemingly forgetting he was in a movie, spoke to the on-screen audience as he frequently did in his stage performances: "Wait a minute. Wait a minute. You ain't heard nuthin' yet. Wait a minute, I tell ya.... You wanna hear 'Toot Toot Tootsie'? All right, hold on." As Jolson finally sang the song, director Alan Crosland looked through the glass wall of the soundproof box that enclosed the camera. When he caught Sam Warner's eye, he signaled "Cut?" by sliding his fingers across his throat. Sam, who was in charge of the production, smiled, shook his head, and mouthed, "Leave it in."

After the take, Crosland asked Sam if they should reshoot the scene without Jolson's banter. Although he was suffering from a painful headache, Sam Warner had sensed the power of spoken words wedded to song.

"The lines should stay."
"You sure?"
"Yeah, they stay."
"You're the boss."
"I've got another idea," Sam added, "but I've got to talk to Jolson about it."

The idea that Sam presented to Jolson was to give an even longer speech in conjunction with a song in another scene. The scene Sam had in mind had already been shot; in it, Jolson returns to his family home and accompanies himself on the piano as he sings "It All Depends on You" to Eugenie Besserer, his on-screen mother. Sam wanted to reshoot the scene but have Jolson sing Irving Berlin's "Blue Skies" and insert a monologue between two choruses of the song.

> "I could get the script people to write in a few lines on title cards to bridge from your entry to the song," Sam suggested.
>
> "Nah," Jolson replied, "no need to do that. I'll just kinda make it up as I go along…like I always do."
>
> "Right," Sam said, "You do it, Jolie, just like you always do."
>
> "Leave it to me. I'll knock 'em on their asses."

After singing one chorus of "Blue Skies" to Eugenie Besserer, he starts the kind of spiel he improvised on stage, telling her that he is going to buy her an apartment in the Bronx, deck her out in a new pink dress, and take her to Coney Island where he will kiss her in the Tunnel Love. That the monologue is so ludicrous strengthens the impression that it came off the top of Jolson's head, but what really suggests the sense of improvisation is the reaction of Besserer. While at first she manages to stay in character, the actress is obviously ruffled as Jolson's patter goes on and on. "What is this guy doing?" she seems to be thinking. "This is a silent movie—and he's *talking*!" Besserer has no dialogue of her own and can

only mutter an "Oh, no, Jakie" as Jolson rambles on. At one point, she leans over and grabs him as if sheer physical force could make him stop talking but then stoically resigns herself to waiting him out. Finally, he sings a second chorus of "Blue Skies" in an even "jazzier" and more flamboyant performance style.

It may be that Jolson's lengthy spiel between the two renditions of "Blue Skies" was an attempt to make the song more integral to the dramatic context of his performance. Jolson's banter about kissing his mother in Coney Island's Tunnel of Love—and his actual kissing Besserer on the lips—turns the song from a demonstration of his talent to an expression of his happiness at being reunited with her. To add to the Freudian overtones of the

scene, Jolson's second chorus is interrupted by his irate father, who yells "Stop!" At which point the sound stops altogether for several seconds, then, as the movie returns to being a silent film, all we hear is the musical soundtrack. Dialect cards reappear as the father demands to know why his estranged son has brought "jazz" into his house,

Jackie defends his choice to live in the modern American world, and Eugenie Besserer, comfortably back in the mime acting style of silent film, portrays a woman torn between her duty as a wife and her love as a mother.

It's easy to overstate the crucial importance of the "Blue Skies" sequence in prompting Warner Bros. and other studios to shift from silent movie to "talkies," but the expressive power of the song and Jolson's talking is manifest in the scene. The combination of talking and singing, dialogue and song, makes "Blue Skies" not just a performance number but a song that resonates with Jolson's feelings at a particular dramatic moment. As such, it is far more integral and expressive than any of the other songs in the film. "It was a shock to the audience," director Frank Capra recalled, "to see Jolson open his mouth and hear words come out of it. It was one of those once-in-a-lifetime experiences to see it happen on screen. A vision…a voice that came out of a shadow." Another contemporary viewer of the film, playwright Robert Sherwood, saw the scene as the harbinger that would transform an industry:

> Al sits down at the piano and sings "Blue Sky" [*sic*] to his mother…His father enters the room and realises that his house is being profaned with jazz and shouts "Stop!" At this point the Vitaphone withdraws…Such is the moment when I for one suddenly realised that the end of silent drama is in sight.

Attendance, critical reviews, and profits of $3 million on a film that cost $500,000 to make forced other studios sit up and take notice of the possibilities of sound—and song—in film.

None, however—not even Warner Bros.—plunged into the production of talking pictures. "The effect on the overseas market would be disastrous," Adolph Zukor intoned at Paramount, "Only a small part of the world speaks English." "Studios would have to be rebuilt," added Jesse Lasky. "We have too big an investment in the silent picture," pronounced Universal head Carl Laemmle. At MGM, Louis B. Mayer was content to let Warner Bros. make the next move: "Let them develop it if they can. Then we'll see about it."

It was the next movie Warner Bros. made with Al Jolson, *The Singing Fool*, in 1928, that really precipitated the sound revolution. Still essentially a silent movie with a musical soundtrack, it had enough singing—and talking—sequences to qualify as a "part-talkie." As such, it is even more of a mongrel than *The Jazz Singer*, going from silent film stretches into segments of talking and singing, then reverting to silence. Nevertheless, *The Singing Fool* represented certain advances on *The Jazz Singer*, even if its story was an equally hackneyed tale about a singing waiter who achieves stardom but gives it all up when his gold-digging wife runs off with another man, taking with her Jolson's beloved child.

One advance was that some of the songs for the film were new, specifically written for *The Singing Fool* by the songwriting team of Buddy DeSylva, Lew Brown, and Ray Henderson, one of the most successful of the 1920s. Where *The Jazz Singer* inserted existing Tin Pan Alley songs into the story, DeSylva, Brown, and Henderson created several new songs tailored to C. Graham Baker's screenplay for *The Singing Fool*. While it still adhered to the "performance" convention for presenting songs in film, *The Singing Fool* refined that convention by making Jolson a singing waiter who writes the songs he performs. Thus the songs express his character's feelings.

The song that really made the movie was one that DeSylva, Brown, and Henderson wrote almost as a joke. In the film, Jolson's little boy is all that holds the marriage together for as long as it does. Jolson wanted a song he could sing as he cradled the toddler, so he called the songwriters from California to ask them to come up with a number about "a little kid that's dyin' and his daddy's cryin' his heart out."

Buddy DeSylva, who was in Atlantic City, asked "How old is the boy supposed to be?"

"He is about three, and is standing at my knee," Jolson replied.

"That's fine, DeSylva said. "I have two lines ready, 'Climb upon my knee, sonny boy; although you're only three, sonny boy."

While some accounts have DeSylva suggesting to Jolson, "Why don't you take it from there?" others tell of DeSylva, Brown, and Henderson setting out to write the most mawkish, maudlin number they could concoct, sure that even Jolson would be appalled at its sentimentality. When they sang "Sonny Boy" to him over the phone from New York, trying to keep from convulsing in laughter, the songwriters were flabbergasted to find that Jolson loved it.

The song is a clear echo of Berlin's "Blue Skies":

> *When there are gray skies,*
> *I don't mind the gray skies,*
> *You make them blue, Sonny Boy!*

Whereas "Blue Skies" is sung only once in *The Jazz Singer*, "Sonny Boy" is reprised several times in *The Singing Fool*. The first time Jolson sings it the toddler, played by Davey Lee, is awakened by a quarrel between Jolson and his wife, played by Josephine Dunn, over her lavish expenditures. Lee waddles into their bedroom to ask that Jolson sing "Sonny Boy" to help him get back to sleep.

On the one hand, "Sonny Boy" is done as a domestic performance, but since the song was "written" by Jolson's character, inspired by the child he cradles in his arms, it is also an "integral" song that expresses his paternal love.

The presentation of the song is also striking because the music that accompanies Jolson's singing has no realistic source on screen. Every time Jolson sang in *The Jazz Singer*, the music that accompanied him was realistically "accounted for" by on-screen musicians, or, in the case of "Blue Skies," Jolson's own piano accompaniment (though his piano-playing was dubbed, just out of camera range, by Bert Fiske). When he sings "Sonny Boy" to Davey Lee, however, the music that accompanies him is only on the orchestral soundtrack. Since that musical soundtrack plays throughout the film, the break with verisimilitude is barely noticeable, but the moment establishes an important convention in the presentation of song in film—that, when a character sings, the music that accompanies the performance need not be realistically represented by on-screen musicians.

The way "Sonny Boy" is reprised through the rest of the film is even more expressive, even though each presentation is a performance of one kind or another. Because DeSylva, Brown, and Henderson were experienced Tin Pan Alley songwriters, they knew that to "sell" a song you plugged it as often as possible. The first reprise comes after *The Singing Fool* has reverted to a silent film, so the music of the song is heard only on the soundtrack as Jolson bids farewell to Lee before his estranged wife, along with her lover, take the child with them to Europe. A maid brings Davey Lee to Jolson in Central Park and insists he make it brief. The contrast between Jolson's first singing "Sonny Boy" as he nestled the child comfortably in the security of his home and this reprise, where the song plays as the child is being taken from his arms, gives "Sonny Boy" additional poignancy.

The next reprise comes after we have seen Jolson, demoralized by the loss of his son, abandon his career and hit the dregs, only to be pulled back together by his old boss at the speakeasy, as well as by the faithful cigarette girl who has always secretly adored him. His decline and fall, as well as his comeback to stardom, all occur without presenting a single new song; the latter part of the movie is dominated by reprises of "Sonny Boy." Just as he has regained the pinnacle of acclaim, a phone call comes from the hospital to tell him that his son is gravely ill. Rushing out of the theater, he arrives at the hospital in time to lift the child into his arms and, at the boy's faltering request, sing "Sonny Boy" again. Although he thinks the song has only put the child to sleep, Jolson learns after he leaves the hospital room and hears the mother shriek—a dramatically effectively use of

sound—that the child died in his arms. As he rushes back to the room, he sees the doctor and nurse pull the sheet over Davey Lee's head.

Jolson returns to the theater, distraught but determined to go on with the show, despite the pleas of the cigarette girl and his black valet. With the valet beside him, Jolson applies blackface makeup, then goes to the wings where he stands beside the stage manager. The music the orchestra strikes up, however, is "Sonny Boy," and Jolson pleads with the manager to have them play something else. "But that's your big hit," the manager counters, adding he thinks Al will feel better if he sings it. Jolson agrees to go on, asks the conductor, "Please play that again, will ya?" and bravely launches into "Sonny Boy." As he sings, he sees a vision of Davey Lee's face, beaming, above the audience. Suddenly that vision injects new vitality into his performance, and his voice becomes jubilant. At the climax of the song, in the last eight bars he improvises, "songwriter" that he is, a new lyric:

> *The angels, they grew lonely,*
> *And they took you because they were*
>   *lonely,*
> *I'm lonely too, Sonny Boy.*

The song bowls over the on-screen audience with a performance that, unbeknown to them, simultaneously expresses and assuages Jolson's grief. These various reprises wed the song integrally to the dramatic context of the film so that "Sonny Boy" resonates with different emotional meanings each time it is heard.

What seems bathetic today wrung the hearts of the opening-night audience—including most of the critics—when *The Singing Fool* premiered on September 19, 1928, at New York's Winter Garden. It was at this theater that Jolson had performed many of his Broadway shows, and it had recently been wired to show Vitaphone pictures. Jolson was in the audience and, like most everyone else, wept helplessly after the film as he took bow after bow from the stage. "Sonny Boy" demonstrated how powerfully even a song done as a performance could be if it resonated with what a character felt at the dramatic moment when he sings it. As such, it represented an important advance over *The Jazz Singer*.

"Sonny Boy," as well as several other songs in the score, became a huge hit. Jolson's recording of "Sonny Boy" and "There's a Rainbow 'round My Shoulder" became the first million-selling phonograph record of the talkie era, and both songs sold more than a million copies of sheet music. *The Singing Fool* grossed $5.9 million, a staggering sum that would not be eclipsed by another sound feature film until *Gone with the Wind* in 1939. Profits for Warner Bros. went from $2 million to more than $4 million between 1928 and 1929. With such profits, it could expand. Warner Bros. acquired First National, a much bigger studio with a huge production lot in Burbank and a string of theaters around the country. By 1930, Warner Bros. owned 525 theaters in 188 cities and brought in profits of $12 million. It was such financial success, based more on the presentation of song in *The Singing Fool* than in *The Jazz Singer*, that made Warner Bros. a giant and brought the era of silent film to an end.

2

THAT'S THE BROADWAY MELODY

By 1930, Hollywood had made the conversion to sound. Paramount released its first all-talking picture in January of 1929, and in March Fox announced its decision to produce only sound films. By the end of the year, 9,000 theaters were equipped to show sound films, as opposed to only 400 at the end of 1928. Most films were made with at least some sound sequences and many featured songs, if only a title or theme song. As film historian John Kobal notes, "Will Hays, Czar of Hollywood, could announce in 1930 that attendance at picture showings in the USA had increased 15,000,000 weekly in 1929, due to the enormous popularity of sound films." Given such a drastic shift, it is surprising that the biggest studio, MGM, was one of the last to produce sound films, not even making part-talkies until 1929. Perhaps the reticence of MGM is a reflection of the studio's *wunderkind* producer, Irving Thalberg—twenty-eight at the time of *The Jazz Singer* but already the intimidating, artistically rigorous, and idealistic head of production at MGM—who initially saw sound as merely an adjunct to silent film. In 1928, Thalberg, with his brother-in-law Douglas Shearer, a brilliant technician, added a synchronized score as well as sound effects to the otherwise silent film *White Shadows in the South Seas*. In the same year, he ordered the reshooting of two reels of the completed silent, *Alias Jimmy Valentine*, renting sound facilities from Paramount so that Lionel Barrymore and William Haines could repeat their final scenes by speaking into concealed microphones. Although in hindsight it is tempting to see Thalberg as an innovator in all things cinematic, his initial attitude toward sound was conservative.

While Irving Thalberg had been slow to appreciate the significance of sound, "his talent as a head producer," biographer Bob Thomas notes, "came into full flower in the sound era; all that had gone before seemed only a rehearsal. He had perfected the visual mechanics of film during the silent period; now he was prepared for the vastly more complex challenge of combining dialogue with action, of bringing sophistication and immediacy to the screen." Thalberg realized how profoundly sound could transform movies, and he spared no expense in reshooting footage, earning MGM the nickname "Retake City." "Movies aren't made," he said, "they're remade." After seeing a preview of one movie that was enthusiastically received by the audience, Thalberg asked the director if one scene would be funnier if the actor's shoes squeaked. "Yes," the director replied. "But that set has already been struck. It would cost thirty-five to forty thousand dollars to shoot a retake of that scene." "I didn't ask you what it would cost," Thalberg snapped. "I asked you if it would improve the picture." The scene was reshot.

Once Thalberg did realize the appeal of sound in film, however, it was not song but dialogue that intrigued him. Always alert to story ideas and deeply involved with script development, Thalberg read a story by Edmund Goulding called "Whoopee," about a sister act in vaudeville loosely based on the real-life Broadway headliners, the Duncan Sisters. One of the sisters, the short and feisty Hank, is engaged to a songwriter and performer, Eddie Kerns, who falls in love with her soft and willowy sister Queenie. Intrigued by its backstage romantic triangle, Thalberg said, "This is good; let's do it as a half-talkie." Then playwright Jimmy Gleason was brought in to spice up the dialogue, particularly for the brassy character of Hank. When Thalberg read dialogue that bristled with the argot of Broadway, he said, "Let's make this an all-talkie."

Thalberg may have sensed that Americans had come to relish their own slang. In 1919, H. L. Mencken published his dictionary, *The American Language*, in which he argued that American English, particularly in its slang and vernacular catchphrases, was more colorful and vital than British English. By the late 1920s, radio and syndicated newspapers were bringing colloquial voices such as Walter Winchell, Ring Lardner, and Damon Runyon to the public ear. "Winchell proclaimed Broadway," as historian William R. Taylor notes, "'the slang capital of the world,'" adding that "it is difficult to imagine any other spot on the globe where the citizenry take so readily to slang." Among the terms Winchell cited as emerging from Broadway that have since become part of the American vernacular were *click, hit, flop, bimbo, baloney, cinch, turkey, phoney, racket, squawk, squeal,* and *gyp*, as well as phrases such as "wow 'em," "take somebody for a ride," and "you're all wet." Thalberg must have sensed that audiences would relish such gritty dialogue as "Ya big sap," "Ain't it swell?" "Don't lose your nerve," "It's in the bag," and "Are you trying to crab our act?" in an "all-talkie" movie. Even the title of Goulding's story, "Whoopee," was Walter Winchell's euphemism for sex.

Song lyricists, too, had been using such vernacular idioms throughout the decade. Many popular songs of the 1920s took their titles from colloquial catchphrases—"Ain't We Got Fun?" (1921), "Toot, Toot, Tootsie! (Goodbye)" (1922), "Who's Sorry Now?" (1923), "(I've Got the You-Don't-Know-) The-Half-of-It, Dearie, Blues" (1924), "Yes, Sir! That's My Baby" (1925), "Breezin'

Along with the Breeze" (1926), "My Heart Stood Still" (1927), "She's Funny That Way" (1928), "Ain't Misbehavin'" (1929). Some song titles were based on phrases, such as "What'll I Do?" (1924), which did not even seem distinctively American until British listeners asked Irving Berlin what a "wattle" was. Ira Gershwin once explained that he took his lyrics "out of the air" by listening to the way Americans conversed. By turning colloquial idioms to romantic ends, he described falling in love with the phrase "I hit the ceiling" (normally an expression of anger), had a man react to his first passionate kiss with the question "How Long Has This Been Going On?" (a catchphrase usually associated with finding that one's partner has been unfaithful), and concluded a romantic paean with "the world will pardon my mush/ But I have got a crush, my baby, on you." The movies began to talk—and sing—at the moment when Americans were, as Winchell might have put it, "ga-ga" over their language.

As his enthusiasm grew for making an all-talkie out of "Whoopee," Thalberg decided to add original songs to the film. He considered several established composers and lyricists, including Billy Rose and Fred Fisher, New York–based writers of such hits, respectively, as "Barney Google" (1923) and "Chicago" (1922). Rose, with his characteristic flamboyance, hired a full orchestra to accompany him as he demonstrated his songs to Thalberg. By contrast, two young California songwriters, Arthur Freed and Nacio Herb Brown, sang their songs at a piano. "I like your songs better," Thalberg announced, perhaps hearing in them the more informal and casual air that distinguishes film songs from songs written for the Broadway stage. Before Thalberg made his final decision, however, he wanted to hear the Freed and Brown songs with a full orchestra. At radio station KFI, the studio orchestra backed the songwriters, but it was still Brown at the piano and Freed singing the numbers in his untrained baritone. Thalberg gave the neophyte Californians the nod over the Broadway veterans, and since the title of Goulding's story had already been used for the Broadway musical *Whoopee* (1928), Thalberg used one of Freed and Brown's songs, "The Broadway Melody," as the title for the film. Freed and Brown went from earning $250 a week to making half a million dollars a year. In another dozen years, Arthur Freed would become MGM's major producer of musicals, overseeing such classics as *Meet Me in St. Louis*, *An American in Paris*, and *Singin' in the Rain*, the film that showcased many of his own hits with Nacio Herb Brown.

The title song for *The Broadway Melody* is presented at the very beginning of the film as a performance in the office of a Tin Pan Alley publisher. That setting reflects another major historical development in the relationship between Hollywood and the popular song industry. Although MGM was the last major studio to make a musical sound film, it was the first to realize the importance of acquiring a Tin Pan Alley publishing firm along with its catalogue of songs.

In September of 1928, MGM purchased the majority share of the Robbins Music Corporation, one of the largest sheet-music publishing houses in New York. Warner Bros. would soon follow MGM's lead by paying $5 million dollars for the publishing house of Witmark, and Paramount would take over the T. B. Harms firm and rename it Famous Music.

Once Hollywood studios owned these publishers' catalogues, they had a vested interest in keeping the songs alive. By inserting old songs into new movies, studios could collect additional royalties from songs that had proven their mettle. A song such as Gus Kahn and Isham Jones's "It Had to Be You" (1924), for example, has been featured in more than half a dozen movies, most recently in *When Harry Met Sally* (1989) and *A League of Their Own* (1992). Such continued recycling enabled many songs to do what popular songs are not supposed to do—*stay* popular. The very notion of popular song is based upon ephemerality: a song is popular for a while then fades away so that new songs can take its place. Contemporary songwriters such as Jerry Lieber and Mike Stoller referred to their own songs, such as "Hound Dog" and "Poison Ivy," as "disposable" music. But Hollywood's acquisition of the song catalogues of Tin Pan Alley publishing houses helped many songs transcend popularity and become what we now call "standards."

Along with acquiring the songs of Tin Pan Alley, Hollywood studios brought songwriters, arrangers, and other staff members from the cramped quarters of their New York publishing house cubicles and nestled them in cozy bungalows on the studio lot—sometimes with windows that gave a view of the mountains ("just the atmosphere for the composition of melodies," cooed one executive). The publishers themselves, who had once been instrumental in helping lyricists and composers develop ideas for songs, remained in New York, complaining that all they did, now that the songwriting business had migrated westward, was collect royalties. For songwriters, however, the move to Hollywood was a boon. On Tin Pan Alley, they were paid royalties only on sheet-music and recording sales of their songs—usually a penny each for the lyricist and composer, with the publisher keeping the rest of the profit. In Hollywood, songwriters were paid a regular salary in addition to royalties. As *Photoplay* reported in an article entitled "Westward the Course of Tin Pan Alley" in September 1929, "The new arrangement has made Hollywood brighter than any blue heaven for the composer and lyricist." Soon most popular songs had their origins in the movies rather than on Tin Pan Alley.

The opening scene of *The Broadway Melody* gives us a glimpse into the world of Tin Pan Alley that was already becoming a thing of the past. As the camera moves briskly from one little cubicle to another, where different songs are being created, demonstrated, and practiced, we hear a cacophony that illustrates why the sounds emanating from Broadway and West 28th Street sounded like clanging tin pans. There is an element of sound *design* in the scene, because one song, however faintly, stands out amid the din. Charles King, playing Eddie Kerns, composer and performer, is instructing a piano player (played by the real composer, Nacio Herb Brown) on the proper tempo for "The Broadway Melody." When the publisher strolls by to hear the song, King asks him to quiet the performers in the surrounding cubicles. Gradually the noise dies down; the performers leave their cubicles and crowd around King and Brown to hear them demonstrate "The Broadway Melody."

By making the lead character both a songwriter and a singer, *The Broadway Melody* gives the songs King sings an expressive power and an "excuse" for him to reprise them as he demonstrates, rehearses, and performs them. The title song, for example, is presented three times in quick succession, each time in a different dramatic context. In King's initial rendition of "The Broadway Melody" in a Tin Pan Alley office, the audience focuses its attention on this one song after the bewildering array of earlier melodics. Other musicians pick up the accompaniment with a clarinet and guitar, providing King with an on-screen orchestral combo rather than just Brown's piano accompaniment, then singers snap their fingers and sway to the syncopated rhythm. The song is clearly going to be a hit, and when two flappers beg for the chance to put the song over in vaudeville, King's response provides several pieces of exposition—that the song has already been taken by the great Zanfeld (read Florenz Ziegfeld) for his new Broadway show, where King will perform it himself with two new arrivals in New York, the Mahoney Sisters.

Thus, while *The Broadway Melody* followed *The Jazz Singer* and *The Singing Fool* by presenting songs as "performances," it was a more comprehensive "backstager" that traced not simply the career of a singer but the mounting of a Broadway show. That wider narrative framework made it possible to involve more characters and more dramatic situations in the presentation of a song. After King demonstrates the song on Tin Pan Alley, he calls upon the Mahoney sisters, "Hank" (Bessie Love) and "Queenie" (Anita Page), who have just arrived at their New York hotel. King assures them he can get them roles in Zanfeld's show where they will accompany him in a performance of his new song. Naturally, the sisters clamor to hear it, and King gets to reprise the song for their eager ears. As he does so, an orchestral accompaniment swells up behind him—with no visible orches-tra on-screen. When he performed "The Broadway Melody" in the Tin Pan Alley office, the accompanying pianist, clarinetist, and guitarist were there in full view. But in this reprise of "The Broadway Melody," the accompaniment is blatantly not "there," without explanation, though near the end of their rendition, in a mild nod to realism, Hank picks up a ukulele and strums it as she dances to King's singing. This reprise of "The Broadway Melody" furthered the convention, established by Jolson's singing "Sonny Boy" in *The Singing Fool*, that characters could break into song without the visible presence of accompanying musicians on screen.

The next reprise of "The Broadway Melody" occurs during a dress rehearsal of the Zanfeld show, so the orchestra again is plainly visible on screen, and the song is done as a pure performance. Even then, however, it becomes the focus of the drama as Eddie argues with the conductor over the volume of the orchestral accompaniment, Queenie frets nervously about appearing on a Broadway stage, and Zanfeld stops the rehearsal to cut a full chorus of the song. That cut obliterates the Mahoney sisters from the number, prompting a feisty protest from Hank to Zanfeld's face. Only after those dramatic conflicts are resolved does the number get its full reprise, and it is at this point that the song's lyric resonates ironically with character and dramatic situation. We have seen during rehearsals how fiercely competitive, heartless, and even back-stabbing show business can be, but the song's upbeat, syncopated melody and its jaunty lyrics are determinedly optimistic: "Your troubles there are out of style/ For Broadway always wears a smile." The song thus comes across as a "performance" in every sense of the word—one that masks the grim and gritty showbiz world it celebrates.

This sequence of reprises of "The Broadway Melody" propels the first few scenes of the film in a way no previous song had done. The song is central to each major scene—in effect, *telling* the story of the film. Although that song-driven narrative flags over the rest of *The Broadway Melody*, these early scenes show how song, even done as a performance, can be integral to story and character.

The Broadway Melody's big ballad, "You Were Meant for Me," is also integral to the film's story and characters. Although King is engaged to Bessie Love,  he falls in love with Anita Page. Finding himself alone with Page in her hotel room, he sings it in what at first seems like an expressive emanation of his love. Her reaction, however, is far from the clichéd "swooning" to his "crooning": instead she is bewildered, distraught, and torn between her affection for King and her fidelity to her sister. She retreats from his advances, horrified that she is being serenaded by her sister's fiancé. Only then do we learn that "You Were Meant for Me" is not the spontaneous expression of King's feelings for Page but one of his own recent hits. Still, King tries to make the song integral and expressive by insisting, "I wrote it for you, Queenie....I wrote it about you....It's you....Don't you know what I mean?"

"You Were Meant for Me" gets a reprise as a pure performance song when Page, in her confusion over King's overtures, accepts the invitation of stage-door playboy "Jock Worriner" to a fashionable party. When he asks Page to dance, the orchestra strikes up "You Were Meant for Me," and Worriner starts to sing the lyrics. Page, however, complains that she hates such "sentimental" songs, so Worriner orders the orchestra to play something else, and they switch to, as if it were the only other song in the world, "The Broadway Melody."

Such plugging of songs in movies was a boon for Tin Pan Alley. As *Variety* reported:

> The picture song, from the music men's viewpoint, is the millennium. It's the quickest, easiest and least expensive means of song hit making ever known....From the picture producer's standpoint, the song hook-up is invaluable. It gives their celluloid product a new form of plugging and exploitation over the radio, on the records and in the streets, through mass whistling and harmonizing, which no amount of paid advertising could accomplish.

As an example of the power of movies to sell a song, "MGM/Loew's New York Capitol Theatre sold 1,500 copies of sheet music for 'The Pagan Love Song,'" the theme song for *The Pagan* (1929), in a mere four days. *Variety* noted that the sales transpired "without undue exploitation effort whereas formerly it would take a number of acts and much painstaking plugging to attain a turnover of any one song like that."

When filming began on *The Broadway Melody* in October 1928, Thalberg told his staff, "This is an experiment; we don't know whether the audience will accept a musical on film. So we'll have to shoot it as fast and as cheaply as we can. I want quality, but I don't want to spend too much money." The film was produced in secrecy in the event the results were disastrous. As Bessie Love explained, many years later, "to get the film out before anybody else could beat them to it, we worked day and night. The film had a four-week shooting schedule, and we would have to be on the set ready and made-up to shoot at 9 AM, and we wouldn't finish until about 9 or 10 at night."

Despite the pressure, technical problems were handled with characteristic MGM expertise and ingenuity. As at other studios, the camera was enclosed in a wooden booth to muffle its whirr, but MGM used three such cameras to film the action from different angles so that the illusion of movement could be created in the process of editing. For some shots, director Harry Beaumont and camera operator John Arnold put the camera booth on wheels so that it could move around the set with some of the fluidity of camera work in silent film. Thalberg was impressed enough by the quality of the work that he approved the filming of one production number, "The Wedding of the Painted Doll," in color, an expensive process. When he saw the footage, however, Thalberg sensed the danger always inherent in making a movie about putting on a Broadway stage musical: "That's not a motion picture," he said. "It's not a movie at all; it's a stage presentation. We'll have to do it all over again. This time arrange the cameras so we can get some different angles, instead of making the audience look at it from the front, as if they were in a legitimate theater."

Just as plans for the massive retake got under way, Douglas Shearer struck upon an innovation that would eliminate the expense of bringing back the orchestra for the retake. "We don't need the orchestra," he told Thalberg. "We've got a perfectly good recording of the music. Why not just play the record and have the dancers go through the number? Then we can combine the film and the sound track in the lab." When Thalberg was assured the process would work, he gave his okay and thus inaugurated the "prerecording" and "playback" system whereby most songs would be filmed thereafter. The performers would prerecord their songs in the sound studio to get the finest vocal performance and sound quality. Then, during filming, they would lip-synch to their own prerecorded song.

After four weeks of hectic filming, *The Broadway Melody* was ready for distribution early in 1929. At a total cost of $379,000, it was expensive but still within the normal range for an MGM feature. It premiered at Grauman's Chinese Theatre on Friday, February 1, 1929, then ran at New York's Astor Theatre for more than a year and had long runs at theaters in other major cities. The film took in $2,808,000 in the United States and $1,558,000 overseas for a total gross income of $4,366,000. Although that was still less than the profit on *The Singing Fool, The Broadway Melody* was, technically and aesthetically, far superior to the Warner Bros. feature. To crown the MGM achievement, *The Broadway Melody* received the Academy Award for Best Picture of the 1928–29 season, only the second film to receive the accolade and the first "talkie" to do so.

Such success, following upon that of *The Jazz Singer* and *The Singing Fool*, firmly established the performance convention for presenting song in films whose dramatic narrative followed the lives of the performers offstage. For the next few years, Hollywood made scores of these "backstagers," as they came to be called, more than fifty such films in 1929 alone. Most are barely distinguishable from *The Broadway Melody* as even their titles—*Broadway Babies* (1929), *Broadway Scandals* (1929), *Gold Diggers of Broadway* (1929)—would indicate. *It's a Great Life* (1929), for example, featured the Duncan Sisters (the real-life vaudeville team upon whom Bessie Love and Anita Page's roles were based in *The Broadway Melody*). "Babe" and "Casey" aspire to play the Palace with their rendition of "I'm Following You," but their piano player, played by Lawrence Gray, breaks up their act by falling in love with Babe. On the road with Gray, Babe becomes ill, lapses into a coma, and deliriously dreams she and Casey are playing the Palace. Casey rushes to her bedside, and as Babe awakes to see that, indeed, her sister has "followed" her, they reprise "I'm Following You" as a "performance" number but one that also expresses their renewed fidelity to each other.

All that distinguished such backstagers from one another were the performers and the entertainment venues that were portrayed in the film. In *The Great Gabbo* (1929), for example, Eric von Stroheim plays a vaudeville ventriloquist who only sings through his dummy. In *Dance of Life* (1929), the setting is the seedier world of burlesque, where Hal Skelly plays a comedian whose pratfalls leave him in such pain that he resorts to drink, but Nancy Carroll, his dancer wife, stands by her man, for which she earns the paean "True Blue Lou," by Leo Robin and Richard Whiting. *Close Harmony* (1929) takes place in a New York nightclub, *Roadhouse Nights* (1930) in a Chicago speakeasy, and *Mammy* (1930) in a traveling minstrel show. While characters and settings changed, however, the presentation of song as onstage performance remained drearily the same.

A few films of the late 1920s and early 1930s managed to present songs in innovative ways despite the constraints of the backstager formula. No studio adhered to the backstager more ardently than Warner Bros., but it enlivened that formula in *Show Girl in Hollywood* (1930), which portrayed the making of a film version of a Broadway show. Alice White, playing a Broadway performer who goes to Hollywood, sings "I Got My Eyes on You" before a camera, and one shot shows us the cameraman's perspective, enclosed in his soundproof box amid the whirr of the camera. In various other shots we see the live orchestra accompanying the song just out of camera range, three cameras recording the scene from different angles, the crew working lights, and sound engineers recording the number on a Vitaphone disc. At the end of the song, the sound man triumphantly signals "Okay!" as an affirmative response to both White's performance and the combined efforts of the film crew to obtain a good recording of her song. Although the song is not at all integral to character or situation, it provides a welcome variation on the usual convention of filming a song as a stage performance. More integral is "There's a Tear for Every Smile in Hollywood," which a has-been star (at thirty-two!) sings to White as a warning that the movies are all about youth: "You can't fool the camera."

Warner Bros. tried another innovative approach to the backstager with *On with the Show!* (1929), which was the first talking picture to be shot entirely in color. Along with that technical advance, the film presented two stories in counterpoint: the backstage story concerned a producer trying to keep his musical show afloat during an out-of-town tryout; the second story was that of the musical show itself. Unlike most backstagers, *On with the Show!* had songs, by Grant Clarke and Harry Akst, which were an integral part of the show-within-a-show, so that the audience could follow the stage musical's plot as well as the film's behind-the-scenes story. Despite that weaving of onstage song with backstage story, the best song in the film was a pure performance number that had little relation to either the backstage story or the story of the musical show-within-a-show. At the very opening of the film, as the onscreen audience enters the theater, one woman exults that they are going to hear Ethel Waters sing "Am I Blue?" and there are other allusions to the number throughout the early part of the movie. Eventually, Waters trudges on stage carrying a bale of cotton and wearing a gingham dress and a bandana around her hair. After singing the verse, she puts down the cotton bale and launches into the chorus. Although the song is not really a twelve-bar blues but a standard Tin Pan Alley 32-bar chorus, Waters's delivery, replete with improvised lines, gives it the feel of genuine blues. For the second chorus, she is joined by several black men dressed as sharecroppers, and, as they sing, she chants her lines in a kind of call-and-response that furthers the feel of the blues. At only one point does the film cut away from Waters to view the backstage story, but the cut is brief and there is no dialogue to distract us from Waters's performance. Louise Fazenda merely puts her finger to her lips to shush a man who has come to repossess the scenery.

A much more innovative backstager, Paramount's *Applause* (1929), was directed by Hollywood newcomer Rouben Mamoulian, fresh from a Broadway stage triumph in 1927 with an adaptation of Dubose Heyward's novel, *Porgy*. The film starred Helen Morgan, who recently had had her own stage success as Julie in *Show Boat*, in a gritty backstager about the world of burlesque. Mamoulian gave himself a five-week crash course in filmmaking by observing a production at the Astoria Studios in New York. Then, having "learned what not to do" he set about breaking all the rules that bound early talking pictures. "In those days," he recalled, "a scene was shot with three cameras, two for close-ups, one for a long shot. And then into the cutting room to intercut the three. I insisted on a fluid camera, which would pan freely, as well as move in and out of a scene."

Such deft camera work enlivens the first production number in *Applause*, which presents three different songs against a dramatic backstage narrative. The first song, "Give Your Little Baby Lots of Lovin,'" by Dolly Morse and Joe Burke, is performed by a chorus line of seedy burlesque dancers. The camera pans across their overweight bodies and homely faces then turns to the equally garish faces of leering men in the audience. Meanwhile, backstage, Helen Morgan, who willingly put on some thirty extra pounds for the role of "Kitty Darling," collapses as she goes into childbirth. When the lead comic rushes on stage and calls for a doctor, the camera tracks through the theater and finally locates one in a curtained box, embracing a girl. The camera then follows him from overhead as he goes backstage, obviously stagestruck as he gawks at the world behind the cur-

tain. When he beckons one of the chorines to help him with the delivery of Morgan's baby, the other women resume their onstage performance with "Waiting for the Robert E. Lee." Soon the missing chorine rejoins them to announce that Morgan has just delivered a baby, and the girls excitedly whisper the news down the line. After the number, they rush backstage to Morgan's dressing room to view her newborn daughter, while those remaining on stage break into Irving Berlin's "Everybody's Doin' It Now." As the suggestive song is heard in the background, the camera makes two more innovative moves—first filming overhead as the chorines look down on Morgan and the baby, then, reversing perspective, shooting from Morgan's point of view as she looks upward at their circle of faces.

Mamoulian was equally imaginative in filming "What Wouldn't I Do for That Man?" a bluesy lament by Yip Harburg and Jay Gorney, in which Morgan voices her helpless enthrallment to Fuller Mellish ("Hitch Nelson"): "He's not an angel or saint/ And what's the odds if he ain't"). Instead of presenting the song on stage as a performance, Morgan sings the song softly to herself as she sits on the floor of her hotel room, gazing fondly at a photograph of Mellish. As she sings, the screen splits diagonally and in the upper half we see Mellish embracing one of the chorines in another room in the hotel. He then takes leave of the girl with a wisecrack and goes down to Morgan's room, as she completes the song, to greet her with a smarmy "Hello, beautiful!"

By this point in the film, Morgan's baby daughter has grown to a teenager and is about to leave the convent where she has been sent to school. Mamoulian sets up a powerful musical contrast by filming the idyllic setting in the convent where the daughter, "April" (Joan Peers), silently takes leave of the nuns as "Ave Maria" plays on the soundtrack. Peers then arrives in New York and goes to the burlesque theater where she sees Morgan reprise a raucous rendition of "Give Your Little Baby Lots of Lovin.'"

Sitting in the audience, Peers is horrified as she looks back and forth from her mother and the other burlesque dancers on stage to the rowdy men who ogle them from the audience. After a brief meeting with her mother backstage—and an introduction to "Hitch," who takes in Peers's youthful figure with a leer of his own—she witnesses an encore of the song from the wings where she sees only the looming shadows of her mother and the chorines flung on a huge scrim.

Mamoulian then used the same song in an utterly different dramatic context as Morgan puts Peers to bed in her apartment. Now Morgan sings "Give Your Little Baby Lots of Lovin'" as a gentle lullaby—"Close your pretty eyes/ And close your pretty lips"—while Peers mutters a prayer to herself as she clutches a crucifix under

the pillow. Mamoulian wanted the song and prayer recorded simultaneously, to counterpoint each other. Here he ran into opposition from the technicians and crew. "But, they said, we couldn't record the two things—the song and the prayer—on one mike and on one channel. So I said to the sound man, 'Why not use two mikes and two channels and combine the two tracks in printing?' Of course it's general practice now, but the sound man and…the cameraman said it was impossible. So I was mad. I threw down my megaphone (all directors still used megaphones in those days) and ran up to Mr. Zukor's office.… 'Look,' I said, 'Nobody does what I ask…' So Zukor came down and told them to do it my way; and by 5:30 we had two takes in the can. Next day I went to the studio very nervous. But as I went in, the big Irish doorman, who'd always ignored me before, raised his hat and bowed. It seemed they'd had a secret 7:30 view of the rushes in the studio, and were so pleased with the result that they'd sent it off to a Paramount Sales Conference. After this, what Mamoulian said, went."

Fox's *Sunnyside Up* (1929) also enlivened the backstager formula by dealing with amateur rather than professional performances, giving the songs a more informal and casual presentation than the usual "socko" Broadway or vaudeville renditions. The songs were written by Buddy DeSylva, Lew Brown, and Ray Henderson, who had moved from New York to Hollywood, the first major Broadway songwriting team to make a move that soon virtually every other composer and lyricist would follow. On Broadway, DeSylva, Brown, and Henderson had a lighter touch than other theatrical songwriters—less soaring than Kern and Hammerstein, less sophisticated than Rodgers and Hart, less driving than the Gershwins (George Gershwin's mother once asked her son why he couldn't write more like DeSylva, Brown, and Henderson). Fox had them write the screenplay for *Sunnyside Up* as well so they could interweave their songs more tightly with the story and characters. The first of these, "I'm a Dreamer (Aren't We All?)," is done as a performance but one that resonates with the character's feelings. Janet Gaynor, who has been gazing at a newspaper photo of Charles Farrell on the society page announcement of his engagement, says to her friend and roommate, played by Marjorie White, "You know, Bea, there's a song that expresses my feeling exactly." She then takes a zither from the wall, looks directly into the camera, and sings the song, primarily to herself—"He's ideal, but then he isn't real,/ I'm a fool"—but addressing the viewer as well—"Aren't we all?" On the second chorus, the camera moves in from a medium shot to a close-up, and Gaynor renders the song, half-talking, half-singing, to make it even more intimately expressive. The fact that Gaynor, a silent film star, has only the tiniest of voices adds to the impression that this is an ordinary girl singing to herself—not a professional singer "delivering" a song from the stage.

In a sequence that has songs drive the narrative and, in effect, tell the story, the film cuts from Gaynor's apartment in a working-class neighborhood of New York to a Southampton mansion. There Charles Farrell and his fiancée, played by Sharon Lynn, demonstrate a song for their society friends, "You Find the Time, I'll Find the Place," which they are going to perform at an annual charity show. While the song portrays them as devoted lovers, they quarrel afterward, and after knocking back several martinis, Farrell jumps into his roadster and heads for the city. Driving through Gaynor's neighborhood, he swerves to avoid a child playing in the street, crashes, and winds up recuperating in Gaynor's apartment. Telling him to rest, she joins the Fourth of July block party where she and others put on a show. When Gaynor's turn comes to perform "Sunnyside Up," the camera pulls back to show Farrell climbing out on the fire escape to watch her. Gaynor gives the song a rousingly amateur performance, including a brief, equally amateurish tap dance, and then gets the crowd to join her in a second chorus. While done as a performance, the song binds the community together as we see couples, who had earlier quarreled, embracing and dancing. Just before the second chorus, Gaynor says that the song's buoyant optimism expresses the collective spirit of the neighborhood, and one line in the lyric—"If you have nine sons in a row,/ Baseball teams make money you know"—is exemplified by a beaming mother with her brood of children. As the number closes, the camera returns to Farrell's aerial view of Gaynor's performance. Inspired by her rendition of the song, he invites Janet and her friends to participate in his society charity show.

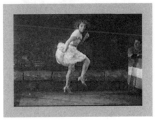

As in so many other backstagers, putting on that show takes up the bulk of the latter half of the film, but in *Sunnyside Up* some of the songs performed in the show are integral to the story. When Gaynor and Farrell do a duet, "If I Had a Talking Picture of You," the song sparks gossip among society matrons in the audience. "They sang that song as if they were really in love," whispers one dowager, and soon word spreads that Gaynor is his "kept woman." Before Gaynor goes on to do her solo, a reprise of "I'm a Dreamer," she learns of the gossip, and as she gamely tries to get through the song we see a montage of leering, whispering matrons gazing at her contemptuously—just the opposite of her adoring working-class neighbors at the block party. The song becomes all the more poignant as she sings it in humiliation, knowing her dreams of marrying Farrell are now hopeless—"I'm a fool" indeed. She barely makes it offstage before she collapses, and her friends whisk her back to the city. Thus songs, even though they are done as performances, advance the narrative.

A reprise of "If I Had a Talking Picture of You" brings Farrell to the realization that he has fallen in love with Gaynor. Distraught at her departure, he

stares at her photograph—as Gaynor did at his photo in the newspaper when she sang "I'm a Dreamer" at the beginning of the film—and suddenly Gaynor's image comes to life in the frame and begins to sing to him. Her song prompts him to seek her out and propose to her, but she rejects his proposal as a token of his pity. Only when she comes upon him, unseen, as he sits at the piano, staring at her photograph and singing "If I Had a Talking Picture of You," does Gaynor realize his love is sincere and join him in song. Even though songs are rendered as performances in *Sunnyside Up*, they advance, complicate, and finally resolve the narrative. The film also was a box-office success, taking in $3.5 million and appealing to small-town audiences with its amateur-based, working-class variation on the backstager formula.

Although it still rendered songs as performances, one of the films furthest removed from the backstager formula of *The Broadway Melody* was MGM's *Hallelujah!* (1929), one of several all-black musicals produced in the early years of talkies. Because of racial stereotypes about blacks as more "spontaneous" than whites, musicals could be made about blacks in which characters burst into song without having to have the realistic excuse that they were professional—or even amateur—performers putting on a show. The popularity of black spirituals and jazz in the late 1920s added to the appeal of making all-black musical films. It was the era of the "Harlem Renaissance," or as Langston Hughes later cynically described it, "When the Negro Was in Vogue." Beginning with the success of Noble Sissle and Eubie Blake's all-black *Shuffle Along* on Broadway in 1921, white audiences embraced black performers such as Louis Armstrong and Duke Ellington. They traveled to Harlem to see revues at the Cotton Club and the Plantation Inn, where black casts played to white audiences, and the strictures of Prohibition were considerably loosened. Paul Robeson popularized spirituals such as "Sometimes I Feel like a Motherless Child" and "Deep River" in concert performances, and *Show Boat* was the Broadway smash of 1927 with its racially mixed cast, themes of racism and miscegenation, and hits such as "Ol' Man River" and "Can't Help Lovin' Dat Man." A novel (albeit by a white poet from Charleston) about a crippled black man became a best seller, went on to become a stage success in 1927, and inspired George Gershwin to write the opera *Porgy and Bess* in 1935. Even in Hollywood, in the wake of sound pictures, studios could venture a musical film about blacks. The very racist stereotypes about blacks having "natural rhythm" would actually make their bursting into song less a strain on the credulity of white audiences.

In Fox's *Hearts in Dixie* (1929), which was the studio's first musical film, songs such as "Carry Me Back to Old Virginny," "Deep River," and "Swing Low, Sweet Chariot," were woven through the film, sometimes only on the soundtrack but at other times spontaneously sung by the characters. It was in MGM's *Hallelujah!* (1929), however, the first all-talking, all-singing, all-black film that black performers sang songs specifically written for the film. Director King Vidor, who had grown up in rural Texas, wanted to do a movie about blacks in the South using African American music. He took the idea to Irving Thalberg, who approved it, but the final okay had to come from the president of Loew's, Nicholas Schenck. When Schenck listened to Vidor and Thalberg's proposal, he nixed the idea, saying "It's not practical....A picture like that will attract too many Negroes to the theaters, and the whites will stay away." Vidor then offered to make the film without salary and bank on a share of its profits. "I'll put my salary into the picture's cost," he told Schenck, "dollar for dollar with everything you spend. I'm willing to gamble my money with yours." "If that's the way you feel about it," Schenck said, "I'll let you make a picture about whores." Schenck gave his okay but added a stipulation—some of the songs used in the film had to be written by his old friend from New York's Lower East Side, Irving Berlin. Vidor resented having to use Berlin's songs but realized it was the only way to make the picture.

A song Berlin wrote for *Hallelujah!*, "Waiting at the End of the Road," came as close as any performance song did in this period to being expressive of what a character feels at a dramatic moment. As Daniel L. Haynes, playing "Zeke," a sharecropper, unloads his family's wagonload of cotton at the gin, he and his younger brother hear other sharecroppers walking down the road singing what purports to be an old African American folk song. The brother reminds "Zeke" that he knows the song and asks him to join in. At first protesting that it's been a long time since he's sung that song, Haynes bursts into a rendition that is an informal "performance" but one

that also expresses his joy at the family's good harvest. As he sings, the film cuts away from him (one of the first times the camera did not focus on the singer of a song in film) to a montage of workers in the gin processing the cotton, so that the images on the screen do not suggest performance so much as heartfelt, "folk" expression. The fact that the film was shot outdoors, with sound added later, gives the song even less of a "backstager" performance quality. The only problem is that "Waiting at the End of the Road," despite its homespun lyric,

is a Tin Pan Alley fox-trot—the furthest imaginable kind of song for southern blacks to sing as a purportedly traditional song.

Despite strong critical reviews and an Oscar nomination for Vidor, Schenck's prediction had been right: theater owners balked at booking a film that might alienate white audiences, and *Hallelujah!* lost money. "MGM can afford it," Thalberg said, in one of his characteristic commitments to artistic quality over commercial success.

Another variation of the song-as-performance convention was short-lived and almost brought an end to song in film. Movies such as MGM's *The Hollywood Revue of 1929*, Warner's *The Show of Shows* (1929), and *Paramount on Parade* (1930) made no attempt to weave a backstage story, however flimsy, around the presentation of song. Instead, they were simply filmed versions of stage revues that featured a studio's roster of stars in musical numbers as well as comical and dramatic skits. *The Hollywood Revue of 1929*, for example, was a cross between a minstrel show and a vaudeville revue, with Conrad Nagel as "interlocutor" and Jack Benny as "master of ceremonies," as well as a trio of children carrying poster boards announcing the various acts as was the practice in vaudeville. The absence of a live audience is painfully apparent throughout; with no laughter, no applause, Joan Crawford lamely tries to flirt with her invisible listeners. Camera movement is a dreary series of long, medium, and close-up shots. There are a few cinematic tricks, such as Conrad Nagel's response to Charlie King's taunt that, like most silent screen stars, he can't sing: Nagel serenades Anita Page by lip-synching to a recording by King himself. *The Broadway Melody's* other star, Bessie Love, in miniature, climbs out of Jack Benny's pocket—his wallet pocket, of course—then "grows up" next to him until she assumes her real-life size and sings a lament about the awful sound effects in talking pictures. Marion Davies, also miniaturized, enters through the spread legs of a line of Buckingham Palace guards—an anticipation of Busby Berkeley's "crotch shot"—then the camera speeds up to show her hurled from one guard to another across the ranks. So faithful to the stage performance model is the film that the curtain closes for an intermission, and we watch the musicians amble back into the orchestra pit to strike up an overture for Act II.

Perhaps the film's dullest moment is the presentation of one of Hollywood's most jubilant and infectious songs, Arthur Freed and Nacio Herb Brown's "Singin' in the Rain." "I'll never forget how Herb and I got around to writing 'Singin' in the Rain,'" Freed recalled. "He came to me one afternoon with the news that he'd just written a great tune for a coloratura soprano. He sat down and played it with all the classic trills. All I could think of was that a vamp in the bass and a few minor changes would give it the zip for some lyrics I had written." While the song had zip, its presentation did not. In *The Hollywood Revue of 1929*, Gus "Ukulele Ike" Edwards stands stock still on a theater stage and sings into a microphone obviously concealed behind a tree to his left. As he sings chorus after chorus, dancers cavort silently up and down staircases amid obviously simulated rain. Perhaps it is because Gene Kelly, twenty-three years later, would do the song so integrally and dynamically that Edwards's stiff "performance" rendition epitomizes all that was bad about the way songs were presented in early sound movies. Little wonder that *Variety* ran a report under the headline "Revue All Cold, Say Film Men" and *Billboard* echoed, "Picture Audiences Turning Thumbs Down on Revues." Other musical films advertised themselves as "Not a Revue," and by the end of 1930 the film revue was a dead genre. The revue, ironically, had tried to solve the problems of the backstager formula by presenting songs without a realistic "excuse." What audiences wanted, clearly, were films with a narrative structure and songs that resonated with character and dramatic situation.

The film revue was the last straw for audiences—as well as critics—now that the novelty of sound had worn off. One critic in 1930 lambasted "the present Hollywood craze for plots dealing with stage life" as a reflection of the fact that "Hollywood finds in stage life the easiest formula for making a song and dance show realistically plausible." "To make singing and dancing expressly cinematic," the critic argued, "requires a little thinking and a little imagination, whereas aping the stage requires none." *Billboard* noted that "the public is beginning to feel just a little disgruntled with the numerous stories of this type that are being thrown at them." *Variety* reported that by 1930, people were going to theater box offices, asking, "Is this film a musical?" and walking away if it was.

Hollywood studios responded by cutting back on musical production and even deleting songs from completed films of 1930 such as *Reaching for the Moon*, *The Life of the Party*, and *Are You There?* The cuts resulted in bizarre moments when a dramatic scene builds up to a song only to shift to a non-musical scene. Song, which had helped bring sound to film, was now an albatross around its neck. Combined with the effects of the crash of 1929 and the ensuing Great Depression, the failure to think beyond the backstager formula and the performance convention for song left Hollywood studios reeling, financially as well as aesthetically. Talking pictures had boosted movie attendance from 65 million in 1928 to 110 million in 1930. By 1932, however, attendance had dropped to 60 million. Even Warner Bros. suffered a loss of $8 million in 1931. Song, the very thing that had ushered in the "talkies," seemed about to disappear from the screen.

3

THAT'S THE SONG OF PAREE

Movie musicals fell out of favor just as major technical problems with sound were being solved. By the early 1930s, the whirr of the camera was silenced so that it could be taken out of its soundproof booth and move again with the fluidity it had in silent film. While shooting *The Wild Party* in 1929, Dorothy Arzner, Hollywood's only major female director at the time, placed a microphone on a fishing pole and suspended it over actors' heads just out of camera range. From then on, microphones on booms could follow actors as they moved, again as freely as they had in silent film. Arc lights, their sputtering silenced, returned, and portable recording equipment made it possible to film outdoors.

Yet for the movie musical to make a comeback from the disastrous revues where songs were presented as performances, characters would need to sing without the realistic excuse that they were rehearsing or presenting songs in a stage musical. In other words, films would have to learn to present songs in the way opera, operetta, and musical comedy had always done. The simplest way to do that was to make a film version of a stage musical. Beginning with Warner's *The Desert Song* in 1929, Hollywood studios began adapting Broadway operettas. In 1930, film adaptations of stage shows included *The Vagabond King, Song of the Flame, Golden Dawn,* and *New Moon.* In such films, the backstager formula of presenting songs as performances was dropped in favor of rendering songs just as they were presented on stage—characters giving voice to their feelings in songs created expressly for a particular dramatic moment. Movie audiences, studios reasoned, would suspend their disbelief when a character broke into integral song without a realistic excuse—if they knew they were watching a filmed version of a Broadway show.

Operetta was particularly adaptable to film because the foreign settings, characters, and stories were remote from the everyday world of the audience. What did it matter if characters in such settings burst into song? In fact, it was easier for performers in filmed operetta to move from dialogue into song and back again than it was for those in musical comedies. "Operettas tended to place their songs far more ponderously than in most musical comedy. In *Good News* and its fellows, lead-ins to songs were mostly light, often self-mocking, funny, and fun. In *The Desert Song* and *New Moon* they were often deadly serious." Audiences should have been appalled by the cinematography and editing of operetta films, which often amounted to no more than a canned version of the stage performance. They should have guffawed at such stentorian lines as those by John Boles when, as the Red Shadow in *The Desert Song*, he sings to Carlotta King, "Didn't you say you like romancing?/ Have you changed your mind?" Perhaps the most absurd moment in these early filmed operettas came in *Golden Dawn*, a 1930 musical set in Africa, when Noah Beery booms out "The Whip Song" as he lashes prisoners:

> *When I crack my whip, that's my call,*
> *In this hell-hole they call Africa,*
> *I'm the biggest man of them all.*

In such filmed operettas, camera close-ups of melodramatic performers with huge open mouths singing bombastic lyrics to lush melodies should have had theatergoers rolling in the aisles. Instead, the public embraced these movies. *The Desert Song* drew in more money than any previous Warner Bros. film except for *The Singing Fool*.

Critics, however, were appalled. "The Warners, whether wisely or not remains to be seen, threw aside motion picture technique entirely," wrote Maurice D. Kann in *Film Daily*. "If those who see it are willing to accept the picture for what it is, *The Desert Song*, by virtue of its music and optical appeal, is an attraction. That means, however, that what until now has been the accepted form of celluloid entertainment has to be forgotten, which is asking a good deal." Creighton Peet in the *New York Post* was more adamant: "Before musical plays are done into celluloid they must be completely rewritten, and their new producers must put far behind them the paint and canvas illusions of the stage."

Perhaps audiences initially loved such films because they provided, albeit in a "canned" version, the spectacle of integral song. Rather than presenting preexisting songs as performances in a backstager, these filmed operettas gave audiences the thrill of seeing—and hearing—characters express what they were feeling in what purported to be original song. A performance of an existing popular song by a professional singer seldom can be as moving as a song that seems the spontaneous outpouring of a character's emotion at a heightened dramatic moment. As audiences wearied of backstagers, they embraced film adaptations of stage operettas.

Spurred by the success of such adaptations, several studios, most notably Paramount, created original screen operettas. Paramount had several European directors, such as Ernst Lubitsch and Rouben Mamoulian, who could present operetta with a light touch that made it more suitable for film than the bombastic stage operettas of Rudolf Friml and Sigmund Romberg. Paramount also had performers such as Maurice Chevalier, who could present song in a casual style. The gravelly voiced musical hall star talked rather than sang his way through a song. He had grown up in a working-class district of Paris, and "his upbringing made him the French equivalent of a Cockney, with the innately mocking manner and lack of concern for the future of the poor Parisian." In Chevalier's first film at Paramount, *Innocents of Paris* (1929), he played a junk man, albeit one who aspires to a career in the theater. Along with several of his music hall signature songs, Chevalier sang several new songs written for the film by the team of Leo Robin and Richard Whiting. As the songwriters watched Chevalier rehearse one of their songs, "Louise," Robin was concerned that Chevalier used the same hand gestures to illustrate the lyric as he sang both choruses. He said to Whiting, "Dick, that's wrong, doing the same gestures in both choruses. The second chorus isn't an anticlimax. It should be the climax."

Whiting told Robin that if it bothered him that much, he should tell Chevalier himself. Overcoming his trepidation before the great international star, Robin, who had grown up in the steel-mill district of Pittsburgh, where he had directed amateur theater, suggested Chevalier withhold his hand gestures until the second chorus. At first, Chevalier scoffed at the suggestion. But a few moments later, he called Robin aside and said, in his French accent, "Rob*an*, you are *right*." In effect, Robin had sensed that the presentation of song should be less "theatrical" and more understated in a film than on stage. When the *Innocents of Paris* was released, Chevalier was amazed that the tune audiences were humming as they left the theater was not one of his interpolated French music-hall hits but "Louise."

When Ernst Lubitsch saw *Innocents of Paris*, he was determined to have Chevalier star in *The Love Parade* (1929), the first operetta to be written for the screen. Before he came to Hollywood in 1922, Lubitsch, as biographer Scott Eyman notes, had already become the master of "the comedy of manners and the society in which it transpired, a world of delicate *sang-froid*, where a breach of sexual or social propriety and the appropriate response are ritualized, but in unexpected ways, where the basest things are discussed in elegant whispers." Chevalier recalled being stopped in the studio hallway by "a small round figure" who "looked a little like a droll, cigar-smoking cherub." Lubitsch told him, "I am walking around with a film musical in my head, Maurice. Now I will put it on paper. I have found my hero." But Chevalier balked when Lubitsch told him he would be playing a prince. "'You see me as a prince?' asked the bewildered Chevalier. 'I'm sorry, I'm flattered, but that's impossible. A fisherman, yes, I could play, or any other kind of man from a simple background. It's what I am and it's in the way I talk and the way I walk and everything I like and understand. But an aristocrat? Believe me, in royal uniform I would make the most ludicrous-looking prince on the screen.'" Still, Chevalier agreed to do some costume stills for the part, and when Lubitsch saw the results, he exulted, "'Splendid, Maurice, marvelous. You are a prince!'"

In *The Love Parade*, Lubitsch planned to cast Chevalier opposite Bebe Daniels, who, as she would demonstrate when she sang "You're Getting to Be a Habit with Me" in *42nd Street* (1933), had a nonchalantly sultry way of delivering a song. But after seeing Jeanette MacDonald's screen test for another Paramount film, Lubitsch changed his mind. "If she can sing and dance," he said, "I'd give her the part." He soon learned she could indeed sing, but her vocal style was much more operatic. Still, the contrast between her style and Chevalier's informality would serve as a musical reflection of their different social rank—she the Queen, he a mere count and a civil servant to boot—as well as *The Love Parade*'s mixture of operetta and conversational film song. In their next films together, Chevalier would plunge further down the hierarchy until, in *Love Me Tonight* (1932), MacDonald would still be a princess, but he would be a mere tailor.

With his co-stars in place, Lubitsch set about making *The Love Parade*, his first sound film, a "crossbreed" between European operetta and American film, where "the songs were partly sung, partly spoken, in a casual, humorous manner." While songs were presented informally rather than in the booming, fervid style of swashbuckling operetta, they are not done as "performances" but as integral numbers that define character and propel the narrative. *The Love Parade* opens, for example, with a song by Chevalier's servant, played by Lupino Lane, who sings as he sets the table in Chevalier's Paris apartment, where Chevalier resides as a diplomat for his native country of Sylvania. Lane sings nonchalantly as he works, winking slyly as he sets out "brandy" and "a little bottle of champagne" for Chevalier and his date for that evening. The evening goes awry, however, when a man barges in on the couple (in what would become one of his cinematic trademarks, Chevalier breaks the dramatic illusion by turning directly to the camera and informing the audience, "Her husband!"). After a comic encounter, husband and wife leave but not until the wife has turned away from the husband, whose clumsy fingers cannot button up the back of her dress, and walked to Chevalier, who manages the sartorial task with ease. At that point the head of the Sylvanian Embassy enters to inform Chevalier that his amorous antics in Paris have finally gone too far and that he is summoned back to Sylvania.

This turn in plot sets up the next informally integral song as Chevalier takes in the news that he must leave his beloved Paris. He flings open the windows, steps out on the balcony, and sings "Paris, Stay the Same," a lilting fox-trot that functions expressively to register his regret. He stoically bemoans the fact that "I've lost my station and my reputation" but beseeches Paris to remain impervious to such changes. The comic number is enlivened cinematically, first by cutting away from the singer to lovely young ladies around the city, sitting in

the windows of their apartments, and sadly listening to the news of Chevalier's departure. The joke is heightened when Lupino Lane then sings his own chorus of farewell and, in another cut away from the performer, maids and other servant girls also appear at their windows to lament the valet's departure. Then the joke goes over the top as Chevalier's dog barks out a chorus, and the camera cuts to female dogs around town howling in lamentation. The comedy, the casual performances, and the cinematically innovative cuts away from the singers make the song a far cry from film operettas that were based on stage productions.

With the next song in *The Love Parade*, we revert momentarily to the style of operetta. The scene shifts to Sylvania and the royal castle, whose pastoral remoteness is belied by a busload of tourists who perk up at their guide's historical litany only when he mentions that the castle and its art collection are worth "a hundred and ten million dollars." The bus even sports a modern advertising banner—"SEE SYLVANIA FIRST"—and

the operetta-land locale is invaded by airplanes, telephones, movie newsreel cameras, and radio announcements and commercials. Lubitsch then presents us with a sight—and sound—gag as the royal guards march up to the castle but then are ordered to tiptoe off quietly so as not to awaken the still-sleeping queen.

As Jeanette MacDonald awakens, her ladies-in-waiting ask about her dreams, and, when she replies that she's had a delightful dream, one lady expresses her wish that it will come true, reflecting all Sylvania's longing that she will marry and produce an heir. "I'm afraid it will always have to remain a dream," MacDonald sighs, then launches

into "Dream Lover," a lilting waltz, in counterpoint to Chevalier's urbane foxtrot for "Paris, Stay the Same." Also in contrast to his chattily nonchalant delivery of a song, she sings with operatic opulence, joined on the second chorus by her ladies-in-waiting as she coyly undresses for her bath.

MacDonald is won over to Chevalier's singing style, however, in their first duet, prompted by her reading of the official report on his behavior in Paris (which she clearly finds fascinating as she reacts to it in a stretch of wonderfully silent comedy). He suggests that as a punishment he should have to attend to her every wish, sliding into rhymed and rhythmic dialogue as he imitates her issuing a command: "From morning till *night*, never dare to leave my *sight*." She at first is outraged that attending her would be a punishment and, in a sound cue, rings the bell for her butler. By the time he enters, however, music comes up on the soundtrack, and she informs him that "Count Albert" will be her guest for dinner. MacDonald and Chevalier then sing—or rather talk-sing—the patter duet "Anything to Please the Queen" with its many double entendres such as his offering to be "cold" or "hot" at her command. While she is ostensibly in charge of the situation, the fact that she adopts his nonchalant singing style underscores the fact that she is under his sway musically as well as romantically.

In their next duet, after dinner, they retire to her boudoir. As the strains of "Dream Lover" come up, she asks Chevalier to forget that she is a queen. "What would you do?" she says, if she were a "mere" woman. He kisses her hand, but when he tries to kiss her lips, she asks, "If you do this on first meeting, what could be left for later?" "Plenty," he says and breaks into "My Love Parade," where he compares her to famous women—"charms of Josephine," "beauty of Camille." She joins him in the song, again, not in her operatic style but in a charmingly informal delivery, trading lines back and forth with him. The duet binds them together, and they kiss, though she recovers herself enough to order him to leave but not without sharing another kiss and calling him "Alfred" rather than the formal "Count Alfred." He responds by calling her "Louise" (an in-joke, since the song "Louise" from *Innocents of Paris* had already become one of his signature numbers).

After he leaves, she sits at the piano and accidentally strikes a key that sends her into a reprise of "Dream Lover." As she sings, reverting to her operatic style, her ladies-in-waiting, other servants, soldiers, and members of parliament, who have been watching through windows and keyholes, listen to learn if she has at last found her lover. As they join her in singing, the song brings the community together. She, in turn, hears them and smiles that her people are pleased with her newfound romance. The song then moves the story ahead to their wedding day.

At the wedding, however, dark clouds gather as Chevalier has to vow to be "obedient" and "docile" to the queen. The marital strain such a relationship entails is expressed in song but not between the newlyweds. Instead, as they retire to their bedroom, Chevalier's valet and one of the palace maids sing "Let's Be Common," a knock-down, drag-out combative song where they vow, "You thrash me and I'll thrash you." The maid, who is taller than Lane, whacks him around and, when he follows her to her bedroom, throws him out the window, shaking her fist at him and shouting "Don't do it again!" Funny in itself, the song reflects the conflict already emerging in Chevalier's marriage to MacDonald.

That conflict deepens when he awakens the next morning to find himself alone in bed and a note saying MacDonald has arranged for him to play tennis in the morning and bridge in the afternoon, while she, of course, attends to affairs of state. Her superior role is then given voice in song as she, attired in military regalia and astride a horse, reviews the palace troops and sings  the rousing "March of the Grenadiers." The crowning indignity comes when Chevalier learns that he cannot even be served breakfast unless the queen is present. As he storms off to watch others eating breakfast, he sings, "Nobody's Using Them Now," nonchalantly but with understated passion as he complains "Nobody takes me seriously."

The Love Parade is thus thoroughly driven by song right to its conclusion as Chevalier and MacDonald reprise several of their numbers in dramatic fashion. After Chevalier announces he is returning to Paris, MacDonald tearfully sings "Dream Lover" but then rouses herself with "March of the Grenadiers" and goes out to review her troops. As Chevalier packs his bags, he hums "Paris, Stay the Same" but when MacDonald promises to surrender authority and addresses him as "My king," they join together in song with a brief reprise of "My Love Parade." Throughout *The Love Parade*, songs are as integrally woven into story and characters as they are in a stage operetta, yet there is nothing "theatrical" about their presentation; most songs are rendered intimately and informally. Such deft integration and presentation of song in film was met with critical acclaim, commercial success, and a then-record six Academy Award nominations. Recognizing that the film broke new ground in presenting songs integrally rather than as performances in a backstager, *Variety* observed, "It can be said that this is the first true screen musical."

That success prompted Lubitsch to plan another original film operetta for Chevalier and MacDonald, *Monte Carlo* (1930), but Chevalier opted for a concert tour that would put him back in touch with the live audience he loved.

He was replaced by British musical star Jack Buchanan, who rendered songs with Chevalier's same nonchalant ease, but the chemistry between him and Jeanette MacDonald was nowhere as electric. Still, *Monte Carlo* inspired Lubitsch to present one song more spectacularly than anything heretofore seen in the movies. Near the beginning of the film, MacDonald runs away from her wedding to a foppish nobleman, and with her lady-in-waiting, played by Zasu Pitts, boards a train without knowing where it is heading. When MacDonald learns the train is bound for Monte Carlo, she tells Pitts that she will gamble her last ten thousand francs and win enough money so that she won't have to find a wealthy husband.

The prospect of winning thrills her, and to express that joy in visual terms, Lubitsch cuts to a dazzling montage of close-up shots of the train— the bullet-like nose of the engine, the churning wheels, and the smoking steam whistle. As the camera returns to MacDonald sitting in her compartment, the sound of the whistle launches her into the verse of "Beyond the Blue Horizon"— "Blow, whistle! Blow away!/ Blow 'way the past./ Go, engine,/ Anywhere./ I don't care how fast." As she sings, the song's soaring melody and exultant lyrics express her newfound joy. With its long vowels—"I see a new horizon./ My life has only begun."—the lyric is wonderfully singable, and its deft internal rhymes—"Beyond the blue hor*izon*/ *Lies* a *ris*ing *sun*"—give it what lyricists called "memorability," that subtle pattern of repetition that drives a lyric into the listener's subconscious. On the second chorus, MacDonald flings open her train window and leans out as the camera pans across fields where peasants join her in song. As the song concludes, the train pulls into Monte Carlo so that

she has traversed the journey during the course of the song.

Monte Carlo introduced Lubitsch to the work of the lyricist Leo Robin, who would work with him on four other films. Robin had started out as a playwright, but when fellow-Pittsburgher George S. Kaufman read some of his work, he advised Robin that he faced a long apprenticeship to break into the competitive world of Broadway theater. Trying to soften the blow, Kaufman asked him if he wrote anything else beside plays. When

Robin showed Kaufman some song lyrics he had written, Kaufman exclaimed, when he saw Robin's lyric for "My Cutey's Due at Two to Two Today," "That's it—that's what you should be doing!" After writing for a few Broadway shows, Robin moved to Hollywood where he wrote lyrics for most of the rest of his career. In Hollywood, Robin found that the art of the songwriter was hardly appreciated. He recalled one day when Aldoph Zukor, head of Paramount, told him "I like your lyrics very much." "And that's the first time I heard the word 'lyrics' in Hollywood," Robin said, "because nobody there knew what the hell a lyric meant. They'd refer to *the words*. And I was very pleased to know that Zukor was knowledgeable enough about show business to use a word like that."

Robin was even more impressed by Lubitsch. "He was the first director that ever wanted the songs integrated into the picture, rather than having them just 'spotted' here and there without any real connection with the story. In those days all the producers wanted were hit songs. They realized a hit was great for exploiting a picture and contributed to its success. But Lubitsch wanted his songs to *come out* of the action of the plot or the situation." Robin especially relished one compliment from Lubitsch. "I work with you," he told the lyricist, "because you do not make performers out of my characters." "He felt," Robin said, "that with my style of integrating the lyrics with the book and everything, the character remained the same, instead of suddenly becoming a performer and walking out of the picture.... Pictures [generally] weren't written that way, [but] I wrote it as if it were a show, with all the songs integrated." Clearly this understated, integrated style that did not render song as a "performance," as had been commonplace in previous films, was exactly what Lubitsch needed to fuse European operetta and American musical film.

Although not directed by Lubitsch, Paramount's *Playboy of Paris* (1930) featured "My Ideal," one of Robin's most integral and expressive lyrics. The film opens with Chevalier as a waiter in a Paris restaurant, cleaning up after hours, dreaming of the woman he will someday find. In the chatty verse of the song Chevalier imagines a woman who, as he sweeps the floor, will "sweep me off my feet," and, as he turns chairs from off the tops of tables, will "turn me upside down." The verse also reflects the restaurant setting with lines such as "the idol of my heart/ Can't be ordered a la carte." In the chorus of "My Ideal," Richard Whiting's melody had unusual leaps that gave it a winsome plangency, and Whiting captured that quality in casually colloquial phrases:

> *Will I ever find the girl in my mind*
> *The one who is my ideal.*
> *Maybe she's a dream and yet she might be*
> *Just around the corner waiting for me.*

The "just around the corner" was Robin's lyrical riposte to President Hoover's assurance to Americans in the Depression that "Prosperity was just around the corner," an assurance Robin wittily again sent up in "Love Is Just around the Corner" (1934). While there had been many songs where women long for the man of their dreams—"The Man I Love," "Someone to Watch over Me"—Chevalier gives a man's expression of the same romantic daydream in "My Ideal."

Chevalier, MacDonald, Robin, and Whiting were reunited with Lubitsch in 1932 in *One Hour with You*, where songs were again presented as expressions of characters' feelings that were integral to the story. In addition to such songs, the film employed rhymed and rhythmic dialogue, sometimes as a lead-in to song but also as delightful stretches of patter. The film also let Chevalier indulge his penchant for looking into the camera and talking directly to the audience. In a Paramount operetta, it had become acceptable for ordinary characters to sing, talk in rhyme, and even address the audience.

In addition to his songs with Richard Whiting, Robin wrote lyrics to melodies by Oscar Strauss. With both composers, his lyrics set a new standard for sexiness in film song. At the beginning of the film, a policeman catches Chevalier and MacDonald necking on a park bench, but Chevalier, in his first direct address to the camera, assures the screen audience that they are married. As the scene cuts to their bedroom, they sing the duet, "What a Little Thing Like a Wedding Ring Can Do," which makes marital sex seem steamy: "I can squeeze you here/ I can squeeze you there," Chevalier sings as he moves his hands from MacDonald's waist to her hips, "And I'm never told to handle with care."

Their marital Eden is disrupted by MacDonald's friend Mitzi, played by Genevieve Tobin, who has recently arrived in Paris and, bored with her current marriage to a professor of "Ancient History," sets her sights on Chevalier. Since he is a doctor, Tobin feigns illness and telephones MacDonald, who insists Chevalier attend to her friend. As he reluctantly sits by Tobin's bedside, Chevalier chants, "If I have to examine you, let me see your tongue" but she coyly retorts, touching her breast, " 'No, that's not the way to start—put your head against my heart." They then segue into "Three Times a Day":

Maurice: Let me take a look at your mouth. Say, "Ah."
Tobin: "Aaaahhhh"

Chevalier reveals he is succumbing to her
charms as he picks up on her seductive "Ah":

Ah—I know it can't be chronic,
But if you feel this way
Perhaps you need a little tonic
Three times a day.

As she coos, "I know a sweeter way," he staunchly resists with internal rhyme:
"Oh, no, Madame, I couldn't *see* you *three* times a day."

The title song, too, advances the plot as it is sung by Tobin, MacDonald,
Chevalier, and Charles Ruggles (a friend enamored of MacDonald) as they
dance at a party. Lyrical phrases are tossed from one character to another as they
in turn change partners:

Tonight when all our dancing is through,
And moonbeams fall on roses and dew,
Perhaps you may even say that you love me too,
And let me stay one hour with you.

As Jeanette cuts in on Tobin to dance with her
husband, Maurice's resolve strengthens; as she sings
"How I would love one hour with you," he grate-
fully responds, "I'm tired of all this hullabaloo."

Yet through the usual comic confusions, she
suspects him of flirting with a different woman,
and Tobin, seizing her opportunity, invites him back to her apartment for an
assignation. Chevalier then expresses his dilemma in song:

I love Colette, I haven't weakened yet,
But, oh, that Mitzi!
Some girls are slow,
Some even answer "No."
Some girls are cool,
And others only "fool,"
But, oh, that Mitzi!

After a quarrel with MacDonald, Chevalier climbs into Tobin's car and heads off toward her apartment.

The next day, served with divorce proceedings by Tobin's husband, who has had her followed by a private detective, Chevalier confesses his guilt to the screen audience by again singing into the camera. Thus the song, "What Would You Do?" cleverly handles the adulterous affair by implicating the screen audience through direct address:

If her head were on your shoulder
And she grew a little bit bolder,
Oh, I ask you what would you do with a girl like that?
Do you think you could resist her?
Do you think you wouldn't have kissed her?
Would you treat her like your sister?
Come on, be honest, mister.
If you saw her turn her light out,
Would you get your hat and get right out?
Now I ask you what would you do?
That's what I did too!

We have indeed come a long way from the presentation of song as a performance. Here it is not only expressive of a character's thoughts and feelings but directly addressed to the film audience.

The plot reaches comic resolution when Chevalier confesses his adultery to MacDonald, begs her forgiveness, then, in a turn that could only have been allowed before the 1934 Production Code, permits her to save face by claiming that, while he spent the night with Mitzi, she has had a liaison with their friend Charlie Ruggles. Instead of closing with a song, both Chevalier and Macdonald address the screen audience as "Ladies" and "Gentleman." As their dialogue goes back and forth, they explain that even though they have strayed as husband and wife, they still are madly in love with each other. "What would you do?" MacDonald asks the audience and Chevalier closes with a rhyme, "That's what I'd do too." As they kiss, the strains of "What Would You Do?" come up on the soundtrack.

Several other Paramount films took their cue from Lubitsch's cinematic operettas, the best of which was *Love Me Tonight* (1932) whose director was Rouben Mamoulian. Born in Russia, Mamoulian directed stage plays, operas, and operetta in Europe before coming to America and developed a style that would be well-suited to musical drama. "I discovered I had no affinity for naturalism on the stage," he said. "My aim always was rhythm and poetic stylization." His first American stage success came in the Theatre Guild's 1927 production of *Porgy*, the dramatic adaptation of Dubose Heyward's novel about a crippled black man who fights the brutal Crown for the love of the sensuous Bess. Sensing the wealth of music that lay behind this story, which was set in Charleston's Gullah community, Mamoulian brought his quest for "a truly dramatic theatre, a theatre that would combine all the elements of movement, dancing, acting, music, singing, décor, lighting, colour and so on." As he later described the opening of the play, Mamoulian stressed the musical character of his direction:

> The curtain rose on Catfish Row in the early morning. All silent. Then you hear the Boum! of a street gang repairing the road. That is the first beat; then beat 2 is silent; beat 3 is a snore—zzz!—from a Negro who's asleep; beat 4 silent again. Then a woman starts sweeping the steps— whish!—and she takes up beats 2 and 4, so you have:
>   Boum!—Whish!—zzz!—Whish!
> and so on. A knife sharpener, a shoemaker, a woman beating rugs and so on, all join in. Then the rhythm changes: 4:4 to 2:4; then to 6:8; and syncopated and Charleston rhythms. It all had to be conducted like an orchestra.

Mamoulian used the same technique for the opening of *Love Me Tonight* as the city of Paris awakens from silence into sound—a shoemaker pounding nails, a grinder sharpening knives, a woman shaking out laundry—all of it set to the rhythm of a metronome.

To write the songs, Mamoulian was blessed with the recently arrived Broadway team of Richard Rodgers and Lorenz Hart. Deeply committed to integration of song and story, Rodgers and Hart had revolutionized popular song with their first Broadway hits, "Manhattan" (1925) "Mountain Greenery" (1926), and "Thou Swell" (1927) which sported brilliant double and triple rhymes, literate wit, and intricately syncopated rhythms. *Variety* compared them to Gilbert and Sullivan and credited the pair with sparking a renaissance in popular song. Although the Depression forced Rodgers and Hart to follow the westward migration of songwriters from Broadway to Hollywood, they saw in movies an exciting new venue for song—more casual, colloquial, and "American" than the stage musical. The combination of their lyrics and music with Mamoulian's stylized sense of musical drama made for one of Hollywood's greatest presentations of integral song.

For "That's the Song of Paree," the opening number of *Love Me Tonight*, Rodgers and Hart matched Mamoulian's rhythmic scene of Paris awakening with a clever patter song for Chevalier. Roused by the various sounds outside his window, his first words of dialogue rhyme:

Lovely morning song of Paree,
You are much too loud for me.

From rhymed dialogue, he slides easily into the talk-song of the verse with its clever rhymes:

It's not a sonata by Mozart,
The song of Paris has its faults.
It has less than a poor nanny goat's art,
But at least it's no Viennese waltz.

After that slam at Viennese operetta, Chevalier sings a chorus about the sounds he hears as he dresses:

It has taxi horns and klaxons
To scare the Anglo-Saxons,
That's the song of Paree.
It has men that sell you postcards
Much naughtier than most cards,
That's the song of Paree.

As the song continues, Chevalier strolls through the streets of Paris on his way to his tailor's shop, greeting people in more rhymed and pun-filled dialogue:

Chevalier: How's your bakery?
Girl: I need a beau.
Chevalier: Where's your husband?
Girl: He kneads the dough!

The flow from rhymed dialogue through verse to chorus and back to rhymed conversation propels *Love Me Tonight* by song from the very outset.

Even more dynamic was the presentation of "Isn't It Romantic?" one of the first songs in film that was reprised over and over in an extended dramatic sequence. The song starts in Chevalier's tailor shop where a customer, Emile, has just tried on his new wedding suit. The splendor of the outfit inspires both men to rhymed dialogue:

Chevalier: The tailor's art
                    For your sweetheart.

Emile: It's like poetry in a book!
How beautiful I look!

Chevalier then launches into the verse and chorus of "Isn't It Romantic?" but conjures up a practical, unromantic vision of marriage:

Isn't it romantic?
Soon I will have found
Some girl that I adore.
Isn't it romantic?
While I sit around,
My love can scrub the floor.
She'll kiss me ev'ry hour
Or she'll get the sack,
And when I take a shower
She can scrub my back.

His catalogue of down-to-earth marital bliss goes on to envision a "moonlight night" but one where "she'll cook me onion soup." Even the prospect of children is not so much a result of romance but a "duty that we owe to France" to increase the population diminished as a result of the loss of so many young men in World War I.

Emile then picks up the song as he leaves the shop but substitutes nonsense syllables for lyrics:

Isn't it romantic?
Da, da, da, da, da,
A very catchy strain!

As he declines an offer of a ride from an importunate taxi driver, the cabbie picks up the song, and, when a long-haired composer enters the cab, the driver exults:

Da, da, da, da, da
At last I've got a fare!

As the cabbie sings, the composer joins in the song, taking out a pencil and paper:

Da, da, da, da, da
I think I'll take that down.

Then he writes down, as he sings, the precise notes of Rodgers's melody:

A-B-A-G-F-E-D
C-C-A-A-B-flat

As the composer gets out of the cab at the train station, a street vendor accidentally spills lemonade on him. In an exchange that did not make it into the final
print, Hart tried to slip one past the censors:

Composer:	You fool!
	You've soiled my pants!
Vendor:	Isn't that romance?

On the train, the composer decides, "I'll write
some words as well" and vows, "This song has got
to sell!" On board the train is a troop of soldiers who also pick up the song, one
singing, "Hey, Henri, pass the bottle!" and another shooting back, "This is rotten beer!" As the soldiers debark and march off across the countryside, they sing
a lyric that is about as far from romantic as a song can get:

Isn't it the right foot?
Isn't it the left!
That town is full of dames.
So we lift a light foot!
Marching full of heft
And don't give your right names…
We'll fool 'em and forget 'em
And we'll march away!

As they march, a gypsy boy hears them sing and plays the melody on his
violin. Once he's memorized it, he rushes to his band's campfire to play it
rapturously as darkness descends. From the gypsy camp, the song wafts up
to Jeanette MacDonald, standing on the balcony of her castle, and she bursts
into a lyric that sharply contrasts her idyllic vision of romance with Chevalier's
practical one:

Isn't it romantic?
That a hero might appear and say the word.
Brought by a secret charm or
By my heart's command,

My prince will ride in armor
Just to kiss my hand....
He'll be strong and tall
And yet a slave to me.

Thus in the course of a single song, we have traversed from bustling Paris to a castle in the bucolic
countryside, united a practical-minded, middle-
class tailor, who sings in a chattily informal style,
with an aristocratic princess who expresses herself with operatic opulence, and established
both character and imminent dramatic conflict

as Chevalier and MacDonald sing of their very different expectations for an
ideal mate. "Isn't It Romantic?" thus reveals how wonderfully song could be
presented in film, using the power of cinema to cut from one scene to another,
moving from characters in one locale to other characters and other places in a
fluid sequence united by a song.

Hart's lyric for the sequence is a tour de force, but the song could not sustain
so many repetitions if Rodgers's music were not so constantly surprising, the
melody moving with "charming unexpectedness" through unusual leaps and
descents, culminating in what composer Alec Wilder terms "superb writing" as
Rodgers restates "the opening notes in the final cadence an octave higher." The
problem of writing a song so integrally tied to character and dramatic situation
was that it could not easily stand alone for pop singers who wanted to perform
or record it. Hart solved this problem resourcefully by writing an additional,
more generic lyric that could be published as sheet music and sung on recordings and radio:

Isn't it romantic?
Music in the night,
A dream that can be heard.

He did the same for "Lover," another hit song from *Love Me Tonight*, which
in the film is sung by Jeanette MacDonald as she rides on horseback across the
castle grounds, interrupting her daydreams of an ideal lover with commands to
her horse:

Lover,
When you find me,
Will you blind me

With your glow?
Make me cast behind me
All my…
WHOA!

But for the sheet music, Hart wrote a romantic rather than a comic lyric:

Lover, when I'm near you
And I hear you speak my name
Softly, in my ear you
Breathe a flame.

It was this version that was popularized by Frank Sinatra, Peggy Lee, and other cabaret singers.

While *The Love Parade* filmed its songs on the set in the old-fashioned way—with an orchestra accompanying the performers out of camera range—*Love Me Tonight* took advantage of the prerecording and playback technique developed in the filming of *The Broadway Melody*. That technique had singers prerecord songs into a microphone then lip-synch to their own prerecording on the set. Rodgers and Hart instinctively realized they could write a song that bristled with triplets and eighth-notes, short vowels, and crisply alliterative consonants. The very title itself, "Isn't It Romantic?" would be difficult to sing from the stage without a microphone. Soon other songwriters would create similarly abrupt songs as "Let's Call the Whole Thing Off," "Cheek to Cheek," "(I've Got) Beginner's Luck," "They All Laughed," "Stiff Upper Lip," and "Nice Work If You Can Get It." Such songs, because their lyrics were closer to everyday speech, made Hollywood songs even more colloquial, further distancing them from songs written for the Broadway musical and strengthening Rodgers and Hart's hopes that the musical film would offer a new avenue to make musicals more informal, more casual, more American.

The innovations in presentation of song at Paramount should have inspired other studios to abandon the backstager song-as-performance convention and create musical films where characters gave voice to their feelings in integral, expressive, spontaneous song. But one of the few studios that followed Paramount's lead, United Artists, produced a major flop in *Hallelujah, I'm a Bum!* (1933). The film starred Al Jolson as the leader of a group of hobos who live in Central Park during the Great Depression. Rodgers and Hart, following their success with *Love Me Tonight*, wrote a score that consisted of rhymed dialogue and song. As Lorenz Hart explained, "The dramatic action, the flow of photography and the humor and pathos of the characters in the story will be inherent in the music. We wrote lyrics and music especially for the camera." Unfortunately, such an attempt to create a thoroughly integrated film musical, which, as John Kobal notes, "might have developed into a type of originality totally indigenous to film" was a dismal failure.

By 1933, the Depression had taken its toll on Hollywood, and no studio was harder hit than Paramount. From profits of more than $18 million in 1930, Paramount slipped to $8.7 million in 1931, then saw a deficit of more than $15 million in 1932 and went into receivership in 1933. At the same time, the contracts of Maurice Chevalier, Jeanette MacDonald, and other big stars were up, and most of them went to MGM. With their departure, Paramount's brilliant experiment with original film operettas, beginning with *The Love Parade* and culminating in *Love Me Tonight*, came to an end.

4

HIP HOORAY AND BALLYHOO

Although it was not driven to bankruptcy as were Paramount, RKO, and Universal, Warner Bros. was hit hard by the Great Depression. While 110 million people went to the movies each week in 1929, attendance declined to 80 million in 1930 then to 50 million in 1932. Profits for the studio paralleled that decline in attendance: from earnings of $14 million in 1929, Warner's profits for 1930 dropped to $7 million, then in 1931 the studio lost nearly $8 million and another $14 million in 1932. Their response was to cut back on production, particularly the production of musicals. From making twenty musicals in 1930, Warner Bros. made only four in 1931 and the same number in 1932. Instead, under production chief Darryl F. Zanuck, second-in-command to studio head Jack Warner, the studio concentrated on realistic films that reflected the Depression, especially gangster films such as *Public Enemy* and *Little Caesar*, which made stars out of James Cagney and Edward G. Robinson, respectively, in 1931.

But then Zanuck came across *42nd Street*, a novel by Bradford Ropes that told the story of the mounting of a Broadway musical that was as gritty as any of Warner's crime features. The dialogue crackled with the same show-business argot that had drawn Irving Thalberg to *The Broadway Melody*, with lines such as "She's just a good mattress for some tired business man," "She only said 'No' once, an' then she didn't hear the question," and "She thinks she's the Broadway lily—and of course you an' me know that dame's slept in more beds than George Washington ever did." Zanuck assigned a team of screenwriters to adapt Ropes's novel, but even in this pre-Code era they had to tone down a story that involved a homosexual affair between director Julian Marsh and juvenile lead Billy Lawler, another liaison between the nymphomaniac star Dorothy Brock and gigolo Pat Denning, and the crumbling marriage of lecherous dance director Andy Lee, whose wife blackmails him by threatening to expose his affair with an underage chorine.

But Zanuck knew that more than a tough-nosed story was needed to revive the backstager musical. Having seen the choreography of Busby Berkeley in several films produced by Samuel Goldwyn, Zanuck signed him to a seven-year contract. Berkeley had started out arranging military drills in World War I, worked as the assistant to Sammy Lee, choreographer of the *Ziegfeld Follies*, then directed several Broadway musicals in the late 1920s. In Hollywood, Berkeley choreographed musical numbers for such Goldwyn films as *Whoopee!* (1930) and *The Kid from Spain* (1932) that featured Eddie Cantor. Berkeley took advantage of the newly mobile camera and the playback system of pre-recording songs to present musical numbers more spectacularly yet also more intimately than was possible on the stage.

"I quickly realized," Berkeley later reflected on his first days on a movie set, "that the camera had only one eye; I felt the camera intuitively. I said to myself, 'Buzz, there are unlimited things you can do with a camera, so you might as well start now—in your first picture!' When I arrived on the set, I saw that four cameras had been set up for shooting, placed in different locations, to give a variety in angles. After you've shot the action you wanted, the cutter would take the sequences and put them together. Well, this isn't the way I'm going to do it. I told the assistant cameraman that I only shoot with one camera. That was a bit daring, because everybody knew I had only just arrived from New York and I'd never worked in films before! But I told them that I did my editing IN the camera, and I always have ever since. I only use one camera in anything I have ever done."

That single camera became the "surrogate for the average male out front in the stalls" as Berkeley satisfied the audience's prurient wish to get closer to the girls but then teasingly pulled back or overhead to render them in sexless, geometric patterns. In filming *Whoopee!*, for example, Berkeley told Goldwyn, "We've got these beautiful girls, why not let the public see them?" In *Whoopee!'s* opening scene, the camera moves in to show the chorus girls in close-ups. Then we get a glimpse of what would become another of Berkeley's hallmarks—the "crotch shot," where the camera moves intimately through the outspread legs of a line of dancers. But the camera then views the girls from overhead where we see a young Betty Grable at the center of a kaleidoscopic pattern in which the bodies of the other girls form an abstract geometric composition. In the intimate close-ups and crotch shots, as well as the overhead abstractions, the camera gave movie audiences perspectives on a production number that no theater audience could possibly have in a live performance.

To provide the songs for such spectacular numbers, Zanuck brought together a new songwriting team: composer Harry Warren and lyricist Al Dubin. Warren, born Salvatore Guaragna, was steeped in opera, especially Puccini, but could create jazzy, rhythmic melodies, such as "By the River Sainte Marie" (1931) and

"I Found a Million Dollar Baby (In a Five and Ten Cent Store)" (1931). Warren was a staff composer at Remick's, one of several Tin Pan Alley music-publishing firms bought out by Warner Bros. A diehard New Yorker, Warren resisted the migration of songwriters to Hollywood until the stock market crash of 1929 forced him westward.

His initial assignment in Hollywood was to write new songs for a film version of a Broadway musical, Rodgers and Hart's *Spring Is Here* (1929). "I couldn't figure out why they would buy a movie musical, dump most of its songs, and ask us to write new ones," Warren complained. He soon learned that now that Hollywood studios owned Tin Pan Alley music-publishing houses, they wanted to collect royalties on new songs written for their films rather than pay for the right to use songs that had been written for the original Broadway musical. "It was just that the studios owned the publishing houses, which the public didn't seem to realize, just as they owned chains of theaters and radio stations." *Spring Is Here* "had been only a moderate success on Broadway, so Warner Brothers felt no qualms about dumping much of its book and all but three of its original songs. That left the studio room to create a few new song hits from which it hoped to profit directly." Still, Warren lamented, "I could never understand the business manipulations of the movie business."

The profit-making motive of using movies to sell songs and songs to sell movies put Warren off, as did his dealings with studio people. Hollywood at that time was a series of small villages, and Warren missed the excitement of New York. Returning east, he wrote for Broadway revues, dance bands, and radio performers. Even when he did supply songs for the movies, he remained in New York rather than return to Hollywood. As the Depression deepened, however, fewer backers could be found for Broadway shows, and when Darryl F. Zanuck dangled the prospect of writing a full score of songs for an original movie called *42nd Street—about* putting on a Broadway show—Warren returned to Hollywood. Little did he realize, as Roy Hemming notes, "that this would not be just another short-term trip to the movie capital—that, in fact, the sensational success of *42nd Street* and its musical numbers would revitalize the whole genre of movie musicals and make Harry Warren, at age thirty-nine, the movies' hottest composer."

Lyricist Al Dubin had written primarily with another composer in Hollywood, Joe Burke, and they had had success with "Tip Toe through the Tulips with Me" (1929) and "Dancing with Tears in My Eyes" (1930), both with simple, sentimental lyrics. Teamed with the jazzier Harry Warren, Dubin took his cue from the hard-boiled urban idiom of Warner's gangster movies. The first full number in the picture, "You're Getting to Be a Habit with Me," reflects Dubin's newfound vernacular punch:

Ev'ry kiss, ev'ry hug
Seems to act just like a drug;
You're getting to be a habit with me.
Let me stay in your arms,
I'm addicted to your charms;
You're getting to be a habit with me.

Although the song is presented strictly in the performance tradition, it resonates with the characters and story of *42nd Street*.

It is first sung as a rehearsal number after the exhausted chorus girls have been tap dancing furiously under the dictatorial Warner Baxter, playing director Julian Marsh, who relentlessly drives, berates, and harangues his cast. At the beginning of the film, he is warned by his doctor that directing another show will add to the pres-  sure that is already killing him, but, addicted to show business, he can't resist plunging into a new production. He calls a stop to the frenzied rehearsal, and, as the exhausted dancers take a break, the star of the backstage musical, played by Bebe Daniels, coolly perches on the piano and sings "You're Getting to Be a Habit with Me" in a nonchalant, off-handed fashion. Dubin's lyric smacks of New York streetwise slang with its winking allusion to drugs, though Warren "always insisted that the underground drug culture among musicians in the '20s and '30s had not inspired the song. Instead, he said, the idea came from a secretary on the Warner lot who had remarked to Dubin one day that she was uncertain about a guy she was going around with, but that 'he's getting to be a habit with me.'" The contrast between Daniels's ease and the frenetic rehearsal makes the song seem a cool oasis amid the hullabaloo, but the camera frames Baxter looming in the foreground in front of the singer. As he concentrates on her performance, smoking a cigarette, it is clear that while the song, for her, is merely a performance, it resonates integrally with his addiction to show business. Without even looking at Daniels or complimenting her, the absence of his usual critical rant implies his approval.

42nd Street set the pattern for a new wave of Warner Bros. backstagers. Each would chronicle the mounting of a Broadway show, and, while some songs would be presented early in the film as demonstrations or rehearsals, most would be saved for the conclusion as the show opens and one song follows another like a fireworks spectacle. In fact, the one number we've seen in rehearsal and dress rehearsal, "You're Getting to Be a Habit with Me," is not "performed" in the finale. Since it has been associated with star Bebe Daniels, when she breaks her ankle and must be replaced at the last minute by Ruby Keeler, the cherubic Keeler is not given such a knowing, sophisticated song. It is Keeler's struggle to bring off the role that forms the backstage drama on opening night, for the financial fate of everyone involved hangs on her performance. That pressure elicits a speech from Baxter that culminates in what has become one of the classic lines of Hollywood film:

> Now listen to me—listen hard.... Two hundred people—two hundred jobs—two hundred thousand dollars—five weeks of grind—and blood and sweat depend on you. It's the life of all these people who have worked with you... you're going out a youngster—you've GOT to come back a star!

Powerful enough in the film, where it frames Keeler's songs in dramatic suspense as the audience wonders if she will put them over in the show, Baxter's speech must have been all the more moving to audiences in the worst year of the Great Depression.

With that backstage drama as context, the first of the "Big Three" climactic numbers, "Shuffle Off to Buffalo," is a straight stage performance similar to earlier backstager films. We view the show from the audience's perspective, occasionally moving in for close-ups or panning to show the theater audience. The song's risqué lyric depicts newlyweds off to a honeymoon at Niagara Falls while the other train passengers titter at their awkwardness. In one sleeping compartment, Ginger Rogers, munching an apple, and Una Merkel, eating a banana (as she could not have done after the Code), knowingly comment on their marital bliss by observing that "When she knows as much as we know,/ She'll be on her way to Reno."

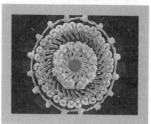

In the next two numbers, however, Berkeley uses the camera in ways that were becoming characteristic of his work. In "Young and Healthy," the camera films the dancers in close-up then moves through their outspread legs. At other points, the camera films the dancers from overhead as they turn on a revolving platform. The dancers, in fact, do little dancing. It's the camera that dances around, beneath, above, and through them, creating an astonishing cinematic presentation of song that could only be done in film.

The final number, the title song, combines the simple stage presentation of "Shuffle Off to Buffalo" with the cinematic innovation of "Young and Healthy." "Forty-Second Street" starts off as a stage performance filmed from the perspective of the audience as Ruby Keeler sings before a closed curtain. As the curtain opens, the camera takes us into close-ups of her face  and tapping feet, then "fools" us—as a theater audience would not have been fooled—by pulling back to reveal that she has been dancing on the roof of a taxicab. The camera then moves rhythmically, relentlessly among the performers, sharing with them the same driving energy that joins the massaging hands of a hairdresser to the palm of a nursemaid spanking an infant. The camera moves through the crowd, then up the side of a building and into an apartment where a man accosts a woman who flees and leaps from the balcony. From another window, Dick Powell, in his lusty tenor, reprises "The big parade goes on for years/ It's the rhapsody of laughter and tears/ Naughty, bawdy, gaudy, sporty/ Forty-Second Street." Returning to a theatrical perspective, a hundred dancers in elegant black-and-white attire take to the stage, holding placards that outline New York's skyscrapers. With one last cinematic trick, we see at their feet a huge skyscraper with Keeler and Powell at the seeming top. But the camera, by panning along the side of the building, makes it seem to rise in the air, lifting Powell and Keeler with it. Berkeley's choreography rendered New York's vitality visually just as Dubin and Warren captured the city's energy in words and music.

The very last scene of *42nd Street* shows Baxter standing outside the theater after the show, smoking, as the crowd pours out. He overhears several remarks about how unfair it is that director "Julian Marsh" gets so much credit that should instead go to Ruby Keeler and the other performers. With a weary, wry smile, he sits on the fire escape stairs, flicks his cigarette away, and, to signal that with this new show he's had his theatrical "fix," we hear the strains of "You're Getting to Be a Habit with Me."

Darryl F. Zanuck made *42nd Street* on a big budget of $400,000, but it netted a huge return, rave reviews, and the sense among critics that musical films had been revitalized—by the very studio that had inaugurated the genre. "In *42nd Street*," *Variety* reported, "there's a legitimate reason for everything. It's a back stage play, but one of the best that has hit the screen." *Motion Picture Daily* stated, "There was never anything wrong with the musical formula any more than there was anything wrong with the gangster film. There were too many rotten ones turned out.... A good film, regardless of how you type it, will carve its own niche." The *New York Times* recognized that *42nd Street* would initiate a new wave of backstage musicals but welcomed the rejuvenation: "There was a time when spectators were satiated with backstage stuff, but here it is pictured brightly and with a degree of authenticity."

What had been revitalized with the backstager formula was its convention that songs should be presented as performances. The integral convention of presenting song, which had been nurtured at Paramount by directors such as Lubitsch and Mamoulian, had no place at Warner Bros., which would make backstagers for the rest of the decade. The success of the film also proved the wisdom of Hollywood's union with Tin Pan Alley. Three of the film's four songs, "Forty-Second Street," "Shuffle Off to Buffalo," and "You're Getting to Be a Habit With Me," became hits, each making *Variety's* Top 10 list for eleven weeks. Why bother with "integral" songs, Warner Bros. seemed to ask, when "performance" numbers garnered such success both within the film and beyond it?

42nd Street set the pattern for a series of Warner Bros. backstagers over the rest of the decade, including *Gold Diggers of 1933*, *Footlight Parade* (1933), *Dames* (1934), and *Gold Diggers of 1935*. These films had similar story lines, characters (including many played by the same actors), songs by Dubin and Warren, and choreography by Busby Berkeley. Songs were presented as performance numbers in a Broadway musical, which usually had its premiere at the end of the film. That structure, however, made the presentation of song early in the film problematic, since it was in the finale that they would get their most spectacular showcase. *Gold Diggers of 1933* solved that problem by opening with Ginger Rogers, in a close-up shot, singing "We're in the Money":

Old man Depression you are through,
You done us wrong!
We never see a headline about a breadline today
And when we see the landlord we can look that guy right in the eye.

As the camera pulls back, we see that she and other chorus girls literally *are* "in the money"— bedecked in silver dollar coin costumes and cavorting against a backdrop of huge silver dollars blazoned with "In God We Trust" and "Liberty." They wear coin hats, boas of coins, and wave large coins as fans as they perform what seems to be a full-scale production number, but one that opens rather than concludes the film.

On the second chorus, Rogers sings the lyric in Pig Latin, where "We're in the money" becomes "Ereway inhay the oneymay." She'd done it as a joke during rehearsals and was at first terrified when she realized direc-tor Mervyn LeRoy overheard her, only to find that he loved the idea. As she rattles off the nonsensi-cal lyrics, the camera, again showing on film what could never have been produced onstage, moves in for an extreme close-up of her mouth as teeth and lips enunciate the syllables. Before the number can finish, however, the sheriff and his men burst in,  and we realize that this has just been a dress rehearsal. The men have come to repos-sess the sets and costumes, shoving the chorus girls aside and removing sections of their coin costumes, ending the song's fantasy of easy wealth.

Where *42nd Street* didn't present most of its songs until the final "perfor-mance," *Gold Diggers of 1933* manages to work most of its songs earlier in the film, as demonstrations or rehearsals, then reprises them at the end. By casting Dick Powell as a socialite who wants to be a songwriter, the film portrays him creating and demonstrating his own songs. First he sings "The Shadow Waltz" to Ruby Keeler, who listens from her apartment window opposite his, and the song fuels their budding romance as they blow kisses to one another. As Powell plays "I've Got to Sing a Torch Song," Ruby and her roommates are visited by a pro-ducer, played by Ned Sparks, who asks her to invite Powell over, where he dem-onstrates the song to Sparks's nodding approval. Later, Sparks overhears Powell playing the music that will become "Remember My Forgotten Man" and gets the inspiration for a Depression anthem that will be the show-within-a-show's grand finale: "He's got it—just what I want. Don't you hear that wailing? Wail-ing? Men marching…marching in the rain…jobs.…Gee, don't it get ya?"

When rehearsals start for the new musical, entitled *Forgotten Melody*, the first of the big production numbers is enlivened dramatically when Powell interrupts Keeler and the "juvenile lead" (Clarence Nordstrom) as they rehearse "Pettin' in the Park." Powell tells Nordstrom that he has to sing "his" song with more pep and demonstrates how the rhythm should be accented (emphasizing Harry War-ren's jazzy, driving melody and Dubin's equally slangy lyric). Nordstrom shoots back, "Now let me tell you something. I've been a juvenile for eighteen years and you're going to tell me how to sing a song?" In a variation of the star's broken ankle in *42nd Street*, Nordstrom will have a lumbago attack on the opening night of *Forgotten Melody*, and Powell will step in for him, overcoming his reluctance to have his distinguished family name associated with show business.

Rather than follow the example of *42nd Street* and present all of its production numbers in an opening night finale, *Gold Diggers of 1933* premieres *Forgotten Melody* in the middle of the film. At that point, moreover, we get only one production number, "Pettin' in the Park," which reprises the rehearsal of the song with a far more lavish stage presentation that shows couples (including a couple of monkeys) spooning, roller-skating, and playing ball in the park as the seasons change. When a shower comes up, the girls run into a bathhouse. Although they pull down a curtain, we can see their silhouettes disrobing, and Billy Barty, a lascivious eight-year-old midget, pulls up the curtain as the girls emerge clad in metal swimsuits that seem impervious to "petting" until Barty hands Powell a can opener.

Rather than go immediately into the next production numbers, as *42nd Street* had done, *Gold Diggers of 1933* follows the backstage drama that ensues after the successful opening night. By appearing in the show, Powell reveals his identity as the scion of a prominent Boston family, and Warren William, as his older brother, and Guy Kibbee, as the family banker, fly to New York to insist that Powell withdraw from the show. Failing to dissuade Powell, William then tries to break up his love affair with Keeler; but after a series of mistaken identities and drunken confusions, William and Kibbee fall in love with showgirls Joan Blondell and Aline MacMahon.

As the romantic complications thicken, we move to the second big number, "The Shadow Waltz," where Berkeley equipped his chorines with lighted violins and formed them into geometric patterns, including an overhead shot of them arranged to form a huge violin, complete with moving bow. A more elaborate fantasy than "Young and Healthy," "The Shadow Waltz" starts off sung on a stage by Powell and Keeler, but then the camera launches us into surreal space that bears no resemblance to a stage as seen by a theater audience. "For this one Berkeley pushed for more and more odd shots, placing the camera sideways against a mirror to show dancers and their reflections gliding from the top to the bottom of the film frame instead of from side to side." While the choreography for such numbers was Berkeley's, the idea, according to Harry Warren, came from Al Dubin: "There was nothing in the script about a Shadow Waltz or a Forgotten Man. Those were Dubin's ideas, and he deserves credit for them."

Before we get the final big production number, "Remember My Forgotten Man," the backstage drama resolves as Keeler and Powell, William and Blondell, and Kibbee and MacMahon pair off. The resolution makes it possible for *Gold*

Diggers of 1933 to end with a song rather than with the return to the backstage story line that concluded *42nd Street*. The film was originally supposed to end with a reprise of "Pettin' in the Park," but once studio executives Jack Warner and Hal Wallis screened a preview, "Remember My Forgotten Man" was made the finale. The number begins when Blondell leaves the other paired lovers in the wings and goes on stage to portray a streetwalker. In solemn declamation rather than song, she laments the fall of her lover from brave World War I soldier to Depression-era bum. Her words are picked up from a tenement window by the black singer Etta Moten, who renders them as a wrenching blues. The stage then explodes as troops march gaily off to war, return battered from battle, then form a grim soup line as the camera rolls incessantly across their moving bodies. At the climax, soldiers march back and forth horizontally through a series of concentric Art Deco arches while hapless men move forward, perpendicular to the soldiers, as another kind of threatening "army" in the Depression. Blondell then reprises the song, backed by everyone on stage, in a bitterly rousing chorus. And on that note the movie ends, without even a nod to the backstage story. Song thus ends  the film as it does the show-within-a-show, underscoring the power of a song's presentation to serve as the culmination of a film's narrative.

Warner Bros. gave the backstager formula a different twist in *Footlight Parade*, the third major musical the studio brought out in 1933. The film, originally entitled *Prologue*, starred Jimmy Cagney, who surprised movie audiences used to his tough-guy gangster persona with his ability to tap-dance with dynamic grace. Cagney portrayed a producer of "prologues"—live musical stage productions that preceded movie features in big-city theaters. Using such prologues as a vehicle for a "backstager" was a shrewd variation on the backstager formula since the songs did not need to bear any relation to a Broadway show or even to one another; each prologue song was an independent number, complete in itself. Desperate for an outlet for his prologues in tough economic times, Cagney comes up with the idea of creating "touring" prologues that will move from one theater to another, using the same scenery, costumes, and performers. In order to win a huge contract with forty theaters, Cagney has to devise three superlative prologues, and the drama that drives the songs involves his frenzied efforts to create the prologues, rehearse them, and get scenery, costumes, and performers to various theaters according to a hectic schedule.

Cagney gets an inspiration for the most spectacular of the prologues when he sees black children playing in the street amid water sprayed from a fire hydrant. "Hey, that's what that wooden-headed prologue needs," he exclaims in what now seems a crassly racist remark, "a mountain waterfall splashing on beautiful white bodies!" To prevent his idea from being stolen by rival producers, he locks his cast and crew in the theater for three days of frenetic rehearsals. The performance of "By a Waterfall," by contrast, is quietly idyllic. It starts with Dick Powell lying beside a stream as Ruby Keeler sings to him. He then goes into a reverie where he envisions her and other chorines diving or sliding into the water to perform synchronized swimming routines that form intricate geometric patterns. For nearly fifteen minutes, they interlace underwater, create patterns of unfolding flowers or snake-like parallels, provide front and back close-up leg shots—do everything but *dance*. (Berkeley always bragged that he himself had never taken a dance lesson but learned what he knew about dancing simply from watching chorus girls.) After the elaborate spectacle, the chorines reprise the lyrics as Keeler splashes water on Powell's ankles to rouse him from his aquatic fantasy. Then cast and crew pack up, board buses, and frantically rush off to the next theater where they mount another prologue.

Recalling "By a Waterfall" as "my toughest number to film," Berkeley said, "With the technicians, I designed the pool and made caverns underneath it with thick plates of glass that I could shoot the camera through.... We rehearsed it for two weeks and shot it in six days.... We had hydraulic lifts in operation that pumped 20,000 gallons of water a minute over the falls, and the set underneath the stage looked like the hold of some enormous ocean liner." Such musical extravagance was highly expensive; Berkeley's production numbers "used to average close to $10,000 a minute of screen-running time, and his average numbers ran from seven to ten minutes. Thus the cost for a production number alone could be anywhere between $75,000 and $125,000.... Berkeley had a reputation as an expensive director, but on the Hollywood theory that money breeds money, as long as his numbers brought in the patrons, there were no complaints from the front office."

"With Berkeley directing," Ruby Keeler recalled, "I never knew whether I'd be sprouting out of a flower or dancing on a piano. One morning I walked onto the set of *Footlight Parade* and was shocked to see a huge pool of water with girls diving into it. I said, 'Buzz, I can swim a little, but I don't like to be underwater. And I can't dive.'

"He said, 'You'll be able to do it. Get in the water with the kids; get used to it.'

"'Yeah, but after that, what do I do?'

"'For the first shot you'll go down to the other end of the pool and do a porpoise dive....

" 'A porpoise dive?'

" 'Well, you dip your hands and you dive, then you swim underwater to this end of the pool with your eyes open because there's a window here with a camera. You have to time it so when you pop out of the water you're smiling.' "

Warner's rejuvenated backstager formula grew increasingly stale over the rest of the decade, but it produced some superb songs and presented them in innovative fashion. "I Only Have Eyes for You" was featured in *Dames* (1934). Warren's "step-wise" melody, according to composer Alec Wilder, is "a very lovely melody, beautifully and dramatically fashioned" with surprising cadences that are "in a class with the best of theater writing." Dubin's lyric keeps pace with internal rhymes that push words into subtle patterns: "*I* don't *know* if *I*'m in a garden/ Or on a crowded ave*nue*/ *You* are *here, so* am *I*,/ Maybe millions of people *go by*/ But they all disap*pear* from *view*." It is first presented, almost expressively, by Powell as a song he wrote about his love for Keeler. When he reprises "I Only Have Eyes for You," however, he plays a theater ticket agent in a stage production number. After closing the window of his booth, he joins Keeler and sings the song as they enter a subway car. Here Berkeley's cinematic surrealism takes over. Powell dozes off and dreams he sees Keeler's face on all the advertisements in multiple images that float against black space in geometric

patterns. The camera then cuts to the chorines, all attired and coiffed as Keeler, as they parade up and down stairs, around Ferris wheels, finally lifting their ballerina dresses over their heads to form a huge jigsaw-puzzle image of Keeler's face

Berkeley's personal favorite among his numbers was "Lullaby of Broadway," from *Gold Diggers of 1935*, where he also served as overall director. It was one of Dubin and Warren's best songs, one that had originated in a characteristically dynamic melody by Warren that alternates deftly between driving, rhythmic repeated notes and snatches of gentle lullaby-like phrases. When Dubin added a lyric, he told his perpetually homesick collaborator "that he had written it especially for him because the melody just seemed to say 'New York.' " Jack Warner, however, did not like "Lullaby of Broadway" because of its lyric. Warren insisted Dubin's lyric stay with his melody, even offering to write a new melody rather than separate Dubin's lyric from

it. "I'll write you a new song, but I won't divorce this lyric from the melody," he told Warner. When Jolson heard the song, he went to Jack Warner and said he wanted to use it in his film, *Go into Your Dance*, but Berkeley insisted that

"Lullaby of Broadway" had been written for *his* picture, and Warner finally okayed it for *Gold Diggers of 1935*.

As the song opens, we see Wini Shaw's face, singing the first chorus of "Lullaby of Broadway," grow larger and larger until it fills the screen. As she turns her head and puts a cigarette in her mouth, the outline of her face becomes the Manhattan skyline. We then move into the city with a montage of images of people rushing to work in the morning set against those of partygoers heading home after a night on the town:

> *When a Broadway baby says "Good night,"*
> *It's early in the morning.*
> *Manhattan babies don't sleep tight*
> *Until the dawn:*
> *Good night, baby,*
> *Good night, milkman's on his way...*
> *"Hush-a-hye, I'll buy you this and that,"*
> *You hear a daddy saying.*
> *And baby goes home to her flat*
> *To sleep all day.*

The "babies" return to their flats to go to sleep only to awaken in the evening and resume their night life

That partying culminates in a huge production number, involving more than a hundred dancers on an Art Deco nightclub set. Berkeley's camera moves throughout the number, photographing the dancers from a multitude of angles—overhead, close-up, even from under the floor. The number ends as Shaw, pursued by the dancers, accidentally falls to her death from a balcony. Then, in a reverse of the opening of the number, the camera shows her face, in close-up, fade into the background. Berkeley's pride in the choreography is

understandable, for it combines dance, drama, and cinematography in a more complex way than any of his other numbers. It also justified Dubin and Warren's faith in "Lullaby of Broadway," earning them an Oscar for Best Song.

Even with the success of such songs and such films, Warner Bros. still struggled to pull itself out of the red. The studio's net loss for 1934 was more than $2.5 million, and a huge fire at the Burbank studio added another half-million in damages. Finally, in 1935, there was a profit of $674,158. After that point, however, musical production at the studio began to flag. For one thing, the backstager formula had been stretched to the limit. How many ways can you portray the gritty behind-the-scenes story of the mounting of a Broadway musical with songs presented as auditions, rehearsals, or onstage performances before an on-screen audience?

Another factor in the demise of the Warner backstager was the sheer exhaustion of its creative personnel. Between 1933 and 1935, Al Dubin and Harry Warren were called upon to write songs for seventeen musical films. Warren pleaded with the studio to hire other songwriters, but when Mort Dixon and Allie Wrubel were brought in to help out with *Dames* (1934), Warren was embarrassed that his friends' songs were relegated to the sidelines while Berkeley chose songs by Dubin and Warren for the big production numbers. By 1936, Dubin began to show the strain of studio pressure to produce hit songs. A huge man, he grew more and more obese and more dependent on drugs and alcohol. His marriage began to crumble, and "he would disappear for days, with no one having any idea where he was. Then he would turn up, well within a picture's production schedule, with his lyrics in hand."

The last straw came when they were to begin work on *The Singing Marine* (1937). Up until now, Warren had stood by his collaborator. As Dubin's daughter recalled, they "were loyal to one another, accepted each other's faults, foibles, eccentricities, and peculiarities…neither of them ever spoke a bad word about the other, and, although they did not meet much socially, they stood tight against the injustices and inequities of the studio and quickly learned to defend themselves as best they could." But when Dubin failed to show up for work, Warren suggested that Berkeley bring in Johnny Mercer to write the lyrics. Warren had succeeded in getting Warner Bros. to add Mercer and composer Richard Whiting to the staff to share the burden of songwriting. When Dubin learned that Mercer had stepped in, he was professionally chagrined and agreed to go to the Mayo Clinic for treatment of his overeating and alcoholism.

Dubin and Warren worked together on half a dozen more films in 1937 and 1938 but then parted company. Dubin pleaded with Warner Bros. to let him out of his contract. Returning to New York, he wrote lyrics for several Broadway shows and revues. One of his songs, "South American Way" (1939), with music by Jimmy McHugh, made a star out of Carmen Miranda who would go on to make Hollywood films, several of which had songs by Harry Warren, who by then was collaborating with lyricist Mack Gordon. Dubin continued to decline, personally as well as professionally, and moved back and forth between Broadway and Hollywood, even returning to Warner Bros. again in 1943 to write lyrics for *Stage Door Canteen*. He never, however, found a collaborator who elicited his best work the way Warren had done with his melodies. Soon Dubin was too dependent on drugs to work at all, and in February of 1945 he collapsed on a New York street and was taken to Roosevelt Hospital where he died of pneumonia. An autopsy found barbiturates in his bloodstream. He was fifty three.

The Code was another factor that contributed to the demise of the Warner backstager. To avoid federal intervention, Hollywood had established its own censorship office, the Motion Picture Producers and Distributors of America (also known as the Hays Office since it was initially headed by Will H. Hays, who had been President Harding's campaign manager). Although it published a list of guidelines in 1927, the Hays Office did not enforce them. In 1930, however, those guidelines were recast as the "Production Code" by Catholic publisher Martin Quigley and Daniel Lord, a Jesuit priest, who laid out strict rules for the presentation of sex, violence, marriage, and other topics. What gave the Code force was the threat by the Catholic Legion of Decency to boycott unsavory films—at a time when the studios were reeling from the drop-off in attendance in the early years of the Depression. In 1934, Joseph I. Breen, a Catholic layman, was appointed to the Hays Office, where he became a stern censor of sex and violence. On June 22, 1934, the Hays office announced "that henceforth it would get tough with suggestive movies, enforcing its directive by levying fines of $25,000 for violations of the Production Code." Soon, all of the major studios submitted film scripts to get Breen's approval before shooting began.

The new guidelines cramped the gritty, sexy style of Warner backstagers. A number Berkeley had planned for Joan Blondell to sing about her pet cat, which culminated in "an invitation to 'come up and see my pussy sometime,'" was cut from the production schedule. The Hays Office also put a damper on his suggestive fantasy numbers. Undaunted, Berkeley continued to stage numbers for the studio, but the films grew increasingly formulaic and tired, and the budgets slimmer and slimmer, forcing him to economize on his innovations. His plans to showcase "September in the Rain," one of Dubin and Warren's most propulsive songs, in a "forest of silver trees that swayed prettily" to the music in *Stars over Broadway* (1935) were overruled by production chief Sam Bischoff, and one of Dubin and Warren's best songs was relegated to background music.

Still Berkeley plodded on to present wonderful songs. *Hollywood Hotel* (1938) was one of his last major films at the studio. "Gone were the spectacular sets, the intricate overhead shots and the battalions of extras. Instead, Berkeley (who directed the entire film) now relied on his unfailing ability to create interest through inventive camera set-ups and through the sheer brilliance of his editing." The film's biggest song was "Hooray for Hollywood," which soon became the anthem of the film capital, despite the fact that songwriters Johnny Mercer and Richard Whiting had had bitter experiences in Hollywood. "Hollywood seemed to me like a big put-on," Mercer said, "and I just tried to make a little fun of it." His lyrics paid such backhanded compliments to Hollywood as "where you're terrific if you're even good" and "see Mr. Factor—he'd make a monkey look good."

> *Hooray for Hollywood!*
> *That screwy bally hooey Hollywood,*
> *Where any office boy or young mechanic*
> *Can be a panic*
> *With just a good-looking pan....*
> *That phony super Coney Hollywood.*
> *They come from Chillicothes and Paducahs*
> *With their bazookas*
> *To get their names up in lights....*
> *Go out and try your luck,*
> *You might be Donald Duck!*

The lyrical phrases are tossed back and forth among members of Benny Goodman's band such as Frances Langford, Johnny "Scat" Davis, and Gene Krupa in rapid-fire, swinging deliveries.

Berkeley's last film at the studio was *Garden of the Moon* in 1938, which had some clever songs by Mercer, Dubin, and Warren, such as "The Girlfriend of the Whirling Dervish" ("While he's doing her a real good turn,/ She gives him the runaround"), but the film was beset with problems from the outset. Bette Davis found the script so awful she refused the part and was placed on suspension by Warner Bros. Under even more stringent budget constraints, Berkeley could not pull off yet one more choreographic miracle. With his departure went the demise of his experiments with cinematic space. While Berkeley would go on to make films at other studios, he would bow to the convention established by Fred Astaire at RKO in the mid-1930s—that dance numbers be presented in long takes that framed the dancers' bodies in real space with few cuts and barely perceptible camera movement.

Also leaving the studio were its musical stars. Ruby Keeler's last film was *Ready, Willing and Able* (1937), where she played opposite Ross Alexander.

Warner Bros. assigned Johnny Mercer and Richard Whiting to write songs for the big production number and told Mercer he would need to write fifteen sets of lyrics. Mercer was incensed. In Dubin and Warren musicals, the lyrics were sung once or twice, but the production number had the Berkeley chorines going through their formations while Warren's melody played over and over, sometimes for more than a dozen times. Now Mercer was put under more pressure than even Dubin had been. He stormed off the set shouting, "I can't do it. I've had it. I'm through!" Whiting, older and more used to studio pressure—though plagued with a weak heart—bought the biggest dictionary he could find, took it to Mercer's house, and tucked in a note that said, "Onward!"

Mercer took inspiration from the dictionary, which even worked its way into his lyric for "Too Marvelous for Words": "You're much too much/ And oh so very, very/ To ever be in Webster's Dictionary." Ross Alexander, who couldn't sing, talked his way through the lyric at a frenetic pace (occasionally breaking into song, where his voice was dubbed by James Newell) as he dictated a love letter to his stenographer that was to be delivered to Ruby Keeler. The stage was a large library where chorines scampered up and down ladders to shelve or retrieve books (displaying their legs). As Alexander dictates, he stumbles, pauses, and takes suggestions from his secretary, so that the lyric comes off as impromptu speech—"So—I'm borrowing—a love song—from the birds." At times, he reaches for polysyllables, rhyming "glamorous" with "amorous," then at other points he throws in some of Mercer's slang: "I'll never find the words/ That say enough, tell enough,/ I mean they just aren't swell enough."

As Mercer moved into the additional choruses he had to write (which turned out to be only two rather than fifteen), he tossed in such neologisms as "tintinnabulous" (borrowing "tintinnabulation of the bells" from Edgar Allan Poe's "The Bells"). Playing off another erudite word, "apothegm," Mercer has Ross complain that words like "magical" and "mystical" "seem just too apothistical!" He concludes the chorus with more learned vocabulary: "The sweetest words,/ In Keats or Shelley's lyric/ Aren't sweet enough/ To be your panegyric." Alexander brings the song off as comic patter, and the letter is dispatched to Keeler, who reads it to her girlfriends as they puzzle over his arcane language. They urge her to call Alexander for a translation, and, as the chorines hold dictionaries in front of him, he launches into a litany of even more extravagant adjectives, from "euphemistical" to "eulogistical."

Ruby Keeler then dances onto a set designed as a gigantic typewriter. As she and dance partner Lee Dixon (Ross Alexander couldn't dance either) tap-dance on the huge keys, we see chorus girls kick up their legs to imitate the movement of the keystrokes of the typewriter. Mercer's lyric, with such rhymes as "possible" and "collosable," appears on a massive sheet of paper at the top

welcomed a diverse group of individualistic creators and provided them…with an extraordinary degree of freedom to express their artistic idiosyncrasies."

One of the most innovative of these artists was Fred Astaire, who extended the convention Paramount had established in its European operettas by showing that an ordinary American could shift from dialogue into integral song as gracefully as he moved from walking to dancing. Born Frederick Austerlitz in Omaha in 1899, he and his sister Adele started as a dancing act on the vaudeville circuit then graduated to musical comedy on Broadway, initially playing romantic couples but then brother-and-sister leads in such shows as *Lady, Be Good!* (1924), *Funny Face* (1927), and *The Band Wagon* (1931). When Adele, considered the star of the duo, broke up the act to marry an English nobleman, Fred Astaire was on his own. He soon had success on Broadway with *Gay Divorce* in 1932. Although Cole Porter's score did not produce many hits, one song, "Night and Day," had audiences humming their way out of the theater, and the production became known as "The 'Night and Day' Show."

On the strength of that number, Astaire garnered an invitation to Hollywood from RKO. Legend has it that his screen test prompted the judgment, "Can't act. Can't sing. Can dance a little. Balding." A more reliable account is that of David O. Selznick, the producer who signed him: "I am tremendously enthused about the suggestion…of using Fred Astaire," Selznick wrote. "He may prove to be a really sensational bet.…Astaire is one of the greatest artists of the day." After he saw the screen test, however, Selznick had second thoughts: "I am a little uncertain about the man, but I feel, in spite of his enormous ears and bad chin line, that his charm is so tremendous that it comes through even on this wretched test."

Astaire was first shipped over to MGM for a cameo appearance with Clark Gable and Joan Crawford in *Dancing Lady* (1933), then paired with Ginger Rogers as the comic subplot couple in *Flying Down to Rio* in 1933. Astaire resisted the pairing, insisting that after a career teamed with his sister Adele, he deserved the chance to make it as a solo performer. Those years of playing opposite his sister had given him a stage persona that, apart from his dancing, was almost sexless. Claire Luce, his co-star in *Gay Divorce*, had to coach him in romantic scenes, saying "Come on, Fred, I'm not your sister, you know." Throughout his career he disdained on-screen kissing, explaining that "Saying 'I love you' was the job of our dance routines."

Ginger Rogers seemed to be an illogical choice as partner to the debonair Astaire. Originally, Dorothy Jordan was to have played the role of "Honey Hale" in *Flying Down to Rio*, but she quit to marry a producer and Rogers was brought in as her substitute. At Warner Bros., Rogers had been a tarty chorine, playing such roles as "Anytime Annie" in *42nd Street* and disporting in skimpy costumes such as the "coin" outfit she wore for "We're in the Money" in *Gold*

Diggers of 1933. With the advent of the Code, however, she too had to subli-
mate her erotic charms into dancing. Astaire and Rogers didn't even kiss on the
screen until *Swing Time* (1936), one of their last films together at RKO. Yet
their sensuality emerged in song and dance. As Katharine Hepburn allegedly
remarked, "He gives her *class*; she gives him *sex*." When Adele saw her brother
on-screen with Rogers, she exclaimed that it was "the first time I realized that
Fred had sex appeal. Wherever did he get it?"

Even though there is no romantic relation between their on-screen characters
in *Flying Down to Rio*, the Astaire-Rogers chemistry is obvious in their only dance
together. They watch Brazilians do a steamy "Carioca," a dance, confected by choreographer Hermes Pan, in which couples press their foreheads together. Fred and
Ginger decide to join in and bring comic relief to the torrid, terpsichorean revel.
The success of *Flying Down to Rio*, along with that of *King Kong* and *Little Women*,
helped RKO stave off bankruptcy in 1933. When Astaire, who had left Hollywood
to appear in a stage version of *Gay Divorce* in London, learned of the success of *Flying Down to Rio*, he said, "I was amazed that the reaction could be so good because
I knew I hadn't yet scratched the surface with any real dancing on the screen."
Astaire's performance with Rogers was enough to prompt twenty-nine-year-old
producer Pandro Berman to fly to London to watch Astaire in *Gay Divorce,* then
buy the film rights to the show. To ward off censorship from the Code office, the
title was changed from *Gay Divorce* to *The Gay Divorcee*. While it might be objec-
tionable to describe a divorce as "gay," a divorcée could be, since, as Franz Lehár's
operetta had long before established, even a widow could be "merry."

In typical Hollywood fashion, Berman threw out all of Porter's score, except
for "Night and Day," and commissioned new songs by the songwriting teams of
Con Conrad and Herb Magidson and Mack Gordon and Harry Revel. Their
songs were presented as performances, but Astaire rendered "Night and Day"
expressively and integrally, as he had done on Broadway. After searching for
Rogers all over London, Astaire finally finds her at a seaside resort. As she starts
to walk away, he says, "Don't go!" then launches, somewhat abruptly, into the
verse of "Night and Day:"

> *Like the beat beat beat of the tom-tom*
> *When the jungle shadows fall,*
> *Like the tick tick tock of the stately clock*
> *As it stands against the wall . . .*

Astaire seems to have sensed that the verse of a song could be used to bridge
the gap from talking to singing. After talk-singing his way through the verse, he
sings more expansively in the chorus:

Night and day, you are the one
Only you beneath the moon and under the sun
Whether near to me or far,
It's no matter darling where you are,
I think of you, night and day.

Rogers manages to turn one of the most difficult challenges for an actor or actress—what to do when someone is singing to you—into a rich portrayal of her character's quandary of being attracted to Astaire but equally determined to leave. That conflict—Rogers trying to escape, Astaire blocking her way—carries over into a dance that finally resolves it. Unlike the few long takes Astaire would insist on for his later dances, the dance for "Night and Day" is filmed in eight shots, one of which views them, voyeuristically, through Venetian blinds. At its conclusion, Astaire gracefully deposits Rogers in a chair and offers her a cigarette, which she declines with an expression of utter satiation. Initially "Night and Day" was overshadowed by another dance production number in the film, "The Continental," which went on for more than fifteen minutes and won the Academy Award, the first for Best Song. It was "Night and Day," however, that defined how song—and dance—could emerge out of a dramatic situation and be presented as the expression of what characters, who are not performing as professional singers, are feeling at a particular moment in the film's narrative.

Even with the success of *The Gay Divorcee*, which did even better at the box office than *Flying Down to Rio*, Astaire wasn't satisfied. "I'm a bit sour on pictures at the moment," he reflected. "Unless I can do something outstandingly important I don't think I want to be bothered with movies." One of the ways he could do something outstanding in film was to insist, now that he was a proven star, on rehearsal time for dance numbers He stipulated—and got—six weeks of rehearsal time. He also resented Berkeley's use of the camera to create cinematic patterns that sometimes involved little actual dancing. Astaire demanded that the camera follow him in full frame: "Either the camera will dance, or I will." He was equally adamant that songs and dances be integral to the story. "Although the plot lines sometimes lurch improbably, Astaire was concerned from the beginning with making sure his numbers were motivated in the script."

Despite their success as the leads in *The Gay Divorcee*, Astaire and Rogers were again cast as the comic subplot characters in their next film, *Roberta* (1935), which featured Randolph Scott and Irene Dunne as the romantic leads. The film was based on a stage show, but it would be the last of Astaire's films for the next twenty-five years to be an adaptation of a Broadway musical. *Roberta* included some of the hits from the stage production, such as Otto Harbach and Jerome Kern's "Yesterdays" and "Smoke Gets in Your Eyes," but the film also sported some new songs by Kern and Dorothy Fields. Where Harbach's lyrics smack of operetta and sometimes even sound archaic ("Joyous, free, and flaming life forsooth was mine"), Fields had done her lyrical apprenticeship with Jimmy McHugh writing for all-black revues at the Cotton Club. There she laced her lyrics, such as "I Can't Give You Anything but Love" (1928) and "On the Sunny Side of the Street" (1930), with slang and vernacular catchphrases so that she could "swing" more easily than Kern's other lyricists.

Fields wrote conversational lyrics for Kern's new, sixteen-bar melody, "Lovely to Look At," and revised some of the lyrics for other songs by making them more colloquial. One of her revisions, "I Won't Dance," made for a great duet between Astaire and Rogers. Oscar Hammerstein's original lyric (for the British production of *Three Sisters*), gives the reason for not dancing as "I'm not very good at dancing," but Fields changed that to the more erotic "If I hold you in my arms— I won't dance....For heaven rest us/ I'm not asbestos." But presenting the song purely as a performance number was still a long step backward from the integrally expressive presentation of "Night and Day" in *The Gay Divorcee*. The one advance represented by *Roberta* is that, as John Mueller points out, "Astaire firmly established his point of view about using the camera in his dances. None of the four major dance episodes has any obstructing or cutaway shots, and all are recorded in a minimal number of shots—between one and three."

Astaire hit his stride with *Top Hat* (1935), which integrated songs closely with characters and story. It was based on *Scandal in Budapest*, a Hungarian play about a country girl who flees to the city to escape an arranged marriage. In the lobby of a fashionable hotel, she slaps the face of a prominent politician, knowing that the incident will scandalously suggest she is his mistress and thereby free her from her dreaded marriage. The story would have been perfect fare for a Lubitsch or Mamoulian operetta at Paramount, but at RKO it was given an American overhaul until barely all that was left of the original Hungarian play was Ginger's slapping of Fred's face. While the story takes place in Europe, first London then Venice, Fred and Ginger have an American forthrightness that stands out against both the stuffiness and the sophistication of their surroundings.

And what better songwriter to capture simple, direct emotion than Irving Berlin? Upon his arrival in Hollywood, fresh from his Broadway triumph with *As Thousands Cheer* (1933), Berlin worked directly from the script of *Top Hat*, tailoring songs to dramatic situations. At the end of six weeks, he had twelve new songs for the film—the first time that an entirely original score was created for an Astaire film. As in a Broadway show, most of these new songs were discarded, and of the five that were used some were "trunk songs"—unused songs from previous Broadway shows—that Berlin reworked to integrate into *Top Hat*.

The film's first song, "No Strings," was entirely
original to the film and emerged dramatically and
integrally from a conversation between Astaire
and Edward Everett Horton in the latter's London
hotel suite. Horton says they are to fly to Italy to
join his wife and a young friend of hers. He warns
Astaire that his wife may be playing matchmaker
but adds his own opinion that it's time for Astaire
to wed. At that suggestion, Astaire responds with
a subtle bit of dialogue that contains an off-rhyme:
"In me you see a *youth*/ Who is completely on the
loose." He follows that with some rhythmic lines,
"No yens, no yearnings,/ No strings, no connec-
tions," then, casually perched on the arm of the

couch, nonchalantly shifts from talking to singing: "No ties to my affections/ I'm
fancy free/ And free for anything fancy." He sings the rest of the song in the same
chatty style, strolling over to a table to fix Horton a drink. The fact that Astaire
is playing the role of a professional dancer partly "excuses" his impromptu song,
and Horton, as his producer, clearly enjoys the performance. Still, the song is an
integral expression of Astaire's delight in bachelorhood, his American sense of
freedom from restrictions, and his openness to romantic encounters. The song
then propels the narrative as Ginger Rogers, who is staying in the room below,
knocks on his door to complain about the noise of his tap dancing. After she
leaves, Astaire scatters sand from the ashtray on the floor and softly lulls her to
sleep with a "sandman" dance to "No Strings."

The next song in *Top Hat* was one of the "trunk songs" Berlin had brought
with him from New York when he shelved plans for a sequel to *As Thousands
Cheer* called *More Cheers*. The original script for *Top Hat* had Astaire pose as a
London horse-cab driver in order to take Rogers to the London Zoo, where he
would sing a daffy number called "In the Birdhouse at the Zoo." When Berlin
hauled out his trunk song, "Isn't This a Lovely Day (to Be Caught in the Rain)?"
the script was changed so that Astaire, still impersonating a horse-cab driver,
takes Rogers to a park where she can go horseback riding until a rainstorm
comes up. In this way, the give-and-take between song and story in *Top Hat* was
closer to that in the creation of a Broadway musical.

To provide a setting for "Isn't This a Lovely Day?" Rogers takes shelter in a
band shell as the rain starts, and Astaire pulls up with his cab, joins her on the
bandstand, and asks, "Hmmm. Charming little spot you have here. When does
the concert start?" His remark establishes the band shell as a performance site, a
connection reinforced by shots of music stands in the shape of lyres. As thunder

starts, music comes up, and he slides from stylized dialogue into the verse of "Isn't This a Lovely Day?" another colloquially casual song that expresses his

feelings about being "caught in the rain" with her. She maintains her hauteur, but, with her face turned away from him—and toward the camera—she reveals a pleased smile. The dance that follows gradually brings them together in a combative but increasingly friendly union that culminates in their leaping off the stage to revel in the rain.

 "Isn't This a Lovely Day?" established what would become the hallmark style of presenting a song and dance for Fred Astaire. At his insistence, the scene was shot in long takes instead of being broken up into multiple shots like Berkeley's dance numbers at Warner Bros. Director Mark Sandrich made his three cameras move with Astaire and Rogers, each of which framed the dancers from head to foot. Unlike Berkeley's single camera, which often moved while his dancers stood still, Sandrich's cameras portrayed Astaire and Rogers in realistic space rather than the overhead kaleidoscopic shots Berkeley used for surreal perspectives. Sandrich, an engineer, even had a special "Astaire dolly" constructed so the camera could track, glide, and turn with the dancers.

 No sooner has Rogers fallen in love with Astaire than she mistakenly believes he is married to her friend, played by Helen Broderick. The misunderstanding leads to her slapping his face and departing for Venice to join Broderick, who turns out to be married not to Astaire but to Horton. Out of this confusion arises the first "performance" song in the film, "Top Hat, White Tie and Tails." Even this song, however, is integrated into the story. After the first act of Astaire's London show, Horton receives a telegram from his wife saying it is unfortunate that he and Astaire can't fly to Venice after the performance to meet her friend, whom she identifies as Rogers. Astaire, ecstatic, tears the telegram from Horton's hand, tells him to charter a plane to Italy, and rushes on stage. Brandishing the telegram, he breaks into the verse, "I just got an invitation in the mails/ 'Your presence requested this evening, it's formal'/A top hat, a white tie, and tails." His personal elation at the prospect of reuniting with

Rogers gives the performance an expressive relevancy. Berlin's melody and lyric move in abrupt rhythmic bursts that underscore Astaire's glee:

> *I'm steppin' out, my dear,*
> *To breathe an at-mos-phere*
> *That simply reeks with class.*

The clash of high and low diction, which reflects Astaire's casual American presence in stuffy London society, continues as Berlin juxtaposes the arch "I trust that you'll excuse" with the vernacular "my dust when I step on the gas."

The visual and aural spectacle of this number shows the advance in film technology during the 1930s. Astaire sings to his own prerecorded playback, and his taps, which ring out like machine-gun bursts, were added later to the soundtrack as he watched himself on film. Like Lorenz Hart, Berlin sensed the new freedom prerecording and playback gave to a songwriter. Using short notes and clipped consonants, he could rely on Astaire's ability to enunciate syllables and follow the trickiest rhythms to make Fred Astaire singing sound more like Fred Astaire talking:

I'm
Dudin' up my shirt front,
Puttin' in the shirt studs,
Polishin' my nails.

"Top Hat, White Tie and Tails" is then heard on the soundtrack as Astaire and Horton fly to Venice.

There Rogers greets Broderick at a table next to a canal and tells her friend that the man she thinks is Broderick's husband flirted with her. Broderick, assuming she is talking about Horton, encourages her to dance with Astaire, confusing Rogers even more by signaling her to dance more closely. Bewildered, Rogers muses, "If Madge doesn't care, I certainly don't," to which Astaire responds, "Neither do I," then launches from dialogue into song with, "All I know is ... Heaven, I'm in heaven ..." "Cheek to Cheek" is a cross between an integrally expressive song and a performance number: on the one hand, Astaire's singing gives voice to his feelings at this dramatic moment; on the other hand, the orchestra that accompanies him is apparently playing an existing popular song. Having established both integral and performance songs in the film's previous numbers, *Top Hat* here draws upon both conventions for "Cheek to Cheek."

Berlin had begun writing "Cheek to Cheek" in New York for *More Cheers*, but he revised it in Hollywood so that it fit into the dramatic setting of *Top Hat*. Because "Cheek to Cheek" has no verse, it opens with an abrupt exclamation: "Heaven, I'm in heaven." Berlin even challenged Astaire's limited vocal range by taking the melody up a full octave, so that Astaire literally has to "speak" rather than "sing" the end of the line, "My heart beats so that I can hardly *speak*."

Not only did Berlin make the opening of "Cheek to Cheek" abrupt but he also structured the song, musically and lyrically, so that it expanded the usual

thirty-two-bar AABA format into seventy-two bars. At the start of their dance, Astaire sings two eight-bar-sections of an A melody. He then stops dancing, puts his arm on a pillar, and talk-sings the first of two eight-bar B-sections: "Oh! I love to climb a mountain and to reach the highest peak." Then, as they dance another turn, he stops again to talk-sing the second B-section: "Oh! I love to go out fishing in a river or a creek." Then Berlin inserts a third C melody that shifts dramatically to a minor key with "Dance with me/ I want my arms about you," which Astaire sings more openly. That C-section carries the couple from the dance floor to an outdoor veranda, where Astaire returns to the initial A-section. The structure of the song thus shapes the shifting scenes of the dance, as Astaire and Rogers pass from a crowded dance floor, through an intermediary space, and onto an enchanting setting where they dance alone. Unlike Dubin and Warren's songs for Warner Bros. production numbers, in which the same thirty-two-bar AABA chorus is repeated over and over, "Cheek to Cheek" develops an intricate lyrical and musical structure that is integrally wedded to the extended dance sequence and the developing relationship between Astaire and Rogers.

The final production number in *Top Hat*, "The Piccolino," which Berlin wrote expressly for the film, sends up the whole Busby Berkeley tradition of presenting song as a performance. Filmed on an Art Deco set, Berlin's song describes itself as something written by an Italian-American ("a *Latin* . . . who *sat in* his home out in Brooklyn") that has caught on in Europe. Dancers swirl, create abstract patterns with ribbons, and are reflected in the water in a parody of Berkeley's lavish production numbers. Writing such a satiric song was not easy. "I worked harder on 'Piccolino' than I did on the whole show," Berlin recalled, adding "I love it the way you love a child that you've had trouble with." Berlin's efforts were matched by the entire cast and crew, who devoted a staggering 125 hours of rehearsal time to the number.

Top Hat cost $620,000 to make—pricey for an RKO film—but it earned more than $3 million. The film was nominated for several Oscars, and, while it didn't win any ("Cheek to Cheek" lost out to "Lullaby of Broadway" for Best Song), *Top Hat* established Astaire and Rogers as top box-office attractions, surpassed only by Clark Gable and Shirley Temple. All five of *Top Hat*'s songs became hits. On the September 28, 1935, broadcast of radio's *Your Hit Parade*, all were among the top fifteen, and on the broadcast of October 5, "Cheek to Cheek," "Top Hat," and "Isn't This a Lovely Day?" held the first, second, and fourth rankings. Once again, Hollywood had proven that songs sold films—and vice versa.

Given the success of *Top Hat*, it is surprising that RKO reverted, in the next Astaire-Rogers film, to the pattern of *Roberta*—casting Astaire and Rogers as a comic-subplot couple while the romantic leads were Randolph Scott and newcomer Harriet Hilliard (later of television's *Ozzie and Harriet* fame). In place of the beautifully integrated songs of *Top Hat*, most of the numbers in *Follow the Fleet* (1936) were done as rehearsal or performance numbers. Finally, Astaire, at his own request, was cast as a regular guy, a sailor attired in an ordinary uniform rather than top hat, white tie, and tails. As John Mueller dryly observed, "No one is taken in."

The performance numbers have only the slightest resonance with the story and characters. "I'm Putting All My Eggs in One Basket," for example, is rendered by Astaire as he sits at a piano, cigarette dangling from his mouth, in a rehearsal for an amateur fund-raiser aboard the ship. Also as part of the fund-raiser is one of the strangest numbers Astaire and Rogers ever did—a hybrid of an integral and a performance song. In the kind of mini-drama Berkeley had created for "Forty-Second Street" and "Remember My Forgotten Man," Astaire and Rogers don their evening garb to portray characters in a Monte Carlo casino. The story, presented without dialogue, shows Fred losing everything at the gambling table and contemplating suicide on the casino balcony. Just as he lifts a gun to his head, he notices Ginger, equally desperate, about to leap from the balcony. To dissuade her from taking her life, he sings "Let's Face the Music and Dance":

Before the fiddlers have fled,
Before they ask us to pay the bill,
And while we still have the chance,
Let's face the music and dance.

The lyric, playing off the gangster idiom of "facing the music"—being sent up to prison—reflects the despair of the Depression as well as the stoical determination to withstand hard times. Like "Cheek to Cheek," "Let's Face the Music and Dance" is a musically innovative song, with sections running to as many as eighteen measures rather than the usual eight bars and with subtle shifts of key at dramatic points. "The wholly unexpected *e* natural in the eighth measure," as Alec Wilder points out, moves the melody from C minor "almost magically into C major." Yet, as Wilder also observes, the song is a "minuscule melodrama....Mata Hari" music. So histrionic a hybrid of the two conventions of presenting song has neither the intimacy of a casually integral song nor the sparkle of a straightforward performance number.

In the next Astaire-Rogers film, *Swing Time* (1936), RKO wisely reverted to the formula of *Top Hat*. Astaire and Rogers are the central romantic leads, Astaire is in formal attire for almost all of the film, and songs grow out of dramatic situations. In fact, a performance number that was to have opened the film, "It's Not in the Cards," was cut so that there are no songs for nearly thirty minutes. When we do get a song, it is presented in pretty much the same manner as "Isn't This a Lovely Day?" in *Top Hat*. Astaire meets Rogers in a dance studio where she works as a teacher. As he takes a free tryout lesson, he deliberately stumbles and falls, much to her exasperation. Seated on the floor, he sings the verse of "Pick Yourself Up," and Ginger joins him on the chorus of a song that resonated not only with their dramatic situation but with the spirits of all Americans in the midst of the Great Depression. Their next attempt to dance winds up with them both on the floor, and she tells him he is hopeless, a remark overheard by Eric Blore, manager of the studio, who promptly fires her. Astaire redeems the situation with a reprise of "Pick Yourself Up," asking Rogers to dance with him again to show her boss how much she has taught him. They then do a spectacular tap duet that persuades Blore to reinstate Rogers.

While "Pick Yourself Up" follows the pattern of "Isn't This a Lovely Day?"—a dramatic scene of conflict between Astaire and Rogers merging into an integral song that is followed by a dance that resolves their conflict—the next song in *Swing Time* is the first song in an Astaire-Rogers film to be presented without a dance following it. Seated at a piano in her hotel suite (no explanation is given as to how a woman who works as a dancing teacher has a luxurious apartment including a white piano) he sings "The Way You Look Tonight" while she washes her hair in the bathroom. The fact that Astaire plays it at the piano makes "The Way You Look Tonight" a performance song, yet it expresses his feelings for her at that moment. Musically and lyrically, it is as simple and casual as a film song can be. Kern's melody stays comfortably within Astaire's vocal range, with intervals ranging over only a few notes. Although there is a change of key, it is nowhere as dramatic and demanding as in songs Kern wrote for Broadway singers. Fields's lyric is a series of casually idiomatic catchphrases—"when I'm awf'ly low," "laugh that wrinkles your nose," "Won't you please arrange it?" The longest word in the lyric has three syllables; there are only eighteen words of two syllables; more than a hundred words are monosyllabic.

"The Way You Look Tonight" established the convention that a song in an Astaire-Rogers movie need not be followed by a dance. We see Rogers, her hair in shampoo suds, in the bathroom, so charmed that she wanders into the living room to stand beside him. Originally, the script called for Rogers to be in "a contrasting state of disarray" but, as screenwriter Howard Lindsay recalled, "The producers lacked the courage to do this....She entered with her hair covered with white foam, but so beautifully sculptured that it looked like a white wig." As she puts her hand on his shoulder, Astaire turns to gaze into her eyes, expressing shock at her shampooed hair, then she sees herself in a mirror and runs from the room.

While "The Way You Look Tonight" is not followed by a dance because of this sight gag, the next song in *Swing Time*, "A Fine Romance," does not flow into dance because the song keeps Astaire and Rogers apart, romantically, where a dance would have brought them together. Although Fred is falling in love with Ginger in New York, he is still engaged to the girl back home, played by Betty Furness. That complication forces Astaire to keep his distance from Rogers at a snowy country retreat. As she cuddles up to him to keep warm, he remains impervious. When she says she is cold, he suggests she flap her arms to restore circulation. She says that their relationship has blossomed

into a "romance," but he continues to keep her at bay by countering, "As we say in French, 'La belle romance.'" She shoots back, in forthright American slang, "A swell romance" and tries to embrace him. When he withdraws, she storms off and, for the first time in one of their films, Rogers sings to Astaire.

Dorothy Fields gave her a deft lyrical twist to express her frustration; instead of pronouncing "romance" properly, with the accent on its second syllable—"ro-**mance**"—Fields reverses the accent to place it on the first syllable—"**ro**-mance." That reversal of accent sets up a series of feminine rhymes as Rogers complains that they should be "like a couple of hot to*matoes*/" but that he is as "cold as yesterday's mashed po*tatoes*." Then, in a reference to their previous arm-flapping, she bemoans the fact that he is "calmer than the seals in the Arctic

Ocean" who, at least, "flap their fins to express e*motion*." "A Fine Romance" is a charming list song, a genre Cole Porter had made popular in the 1930s with such lyrics as "You're the Top," in which one clever image, metaphor, or allusion follows another in a catalogue of romantic compliments. Fields provides Rogers with a litany of images to describe Astaire's seeming frigidity—he's "harder to land than the 'Ile de France,'" she never musses the crease in his "blue serge pants," and while he can "take romance," she'll settle for "Jello." The fact that they do not follow the song with a dance underscores her romantic frustration.

To vary the formula yet again, the big finale in *Swing Time*, "Never Gonna Dance," *is* done as a dance—but a dance that separates rather than unites Astaire and Rogers. The complications of the plot have Astaire going off to marry Furness and Rogers engaged to marry smarmy bandleader Georges Metaxa. Before they part, Astaire confesses to Rogers that he is in love with her and vows, "I've danced with you—I'm never going to dance again." That vow launches him into "Never Gonna Dance," integrating the song thoroughly into the dramatic situation. In a further instance of such integration, Fields rhymes "la belle" with "la perfectly swell" from the earlier dialogue exchange between Rogers and Astaire before "A Fine Romance." Musically, the initial strain of their dance to "Never Gonna Dance" echoes "The Way You Look Tonight," and lyrically the parallel is reflected in the word "Never"—"in the repeated title phrase of one and in the beautiful phrase, 'never, never change' in the other."

"Never Gonna Dance" is plaintive yet avoids bathos with wryly comic allusions to the Marx Brothers, Major Bowes's radio amateur show, and, in reference to the *Three Little Pigs* cartoon of 1933, a "discreet" wolf who has taken everything from Astaire except his dancing feet. "Kern's haunting music for the song is extremely unusual in form and in effect. It is a kind of rondo, ABACA, with the strident B and C sections contrasting sharply with the gently rocking rhythms of the main strain." Unlike the performance presentation of "Let's Face the Music and Dance" in *Follow the Fleet*, "Never Gonna Dance" enacts a genuinely moving dramatic moment of romantic separation that quotes from several of their earlier songs and dances. The dance culminates in a dramatic flight up a twin staircase that is filmed in a crane shot in one long continuous take. Only when Astaire and Rogers reach the landing at the top of the staircase, do we get another shot. "This dance on the landing was shot forty-seven times during a ten-hour shooting day, and Rogers' feet were bleeding before it was over." No other song in their films so integrates and ties together all of their previous songs and dances.

RKO stuck to the same kind of integral song for *Shall We Dance* (1937) and brought another Broadway songwriting team, George and Ira Gershwin, out to Hollywood. The brothers Gershwin had written together successfully on Broadway since their first hit show, *Lady, Be Good!* in 1924, which had starred Fred and Adele Astaire. Along with musical comedies, such as *Oh, Kay!* (1926), *Funny Face* (1927), which also starred the Astaires, and *Girl Crazy* (1930), which introduced not only Ginger Rogers but also Ethel Merman to Broadway, the Gershwins had written political satires in the vein of Gilbert and Sullivan (one of which, *Of Thee I Sing*, was the first Broadway musical to win a Pulitzer Prize) and, with Dubose and Dorothy Heyward, the opera *Porgy and Bess* in 1935. Those latter accomplishments, along with George Gershwin's concert works such as *Rhapsody in Blue* (1924) and *Concerto in F* (1925), raised concerns in Hollywood that the Gershwins had become too highbrow, but George telegrammed his agent to tell studios "RUMORS ABOUT HIGH-BROW MUSIC RIDICULOUS STOP AM OUT TO WRITE HITS." And write hits they did. During their year in Hollywood, they wrote so many superb songs that Irving Berlin observed that no other songwriters had crafted so many great songs in a single year.

Two of the best of these are presented practically back-to-back in *Shall We Dance*, where they advance the narrative of the film. After a series of plot complications that involve rumors that they are married, Astaire and Rogers try to escape reporters by going roller-skating in Central Park. Dialogue leads fluidly into song as Rogers corrects Astaire's upper-class pronunciation of "eyether" to her proletarian "eether," then his "nyether" to her "neether." That exchange sends Astaire into the verse, lamenting "Things have come to a pretty pass/ Our romance is going flat/ 'Cause you like 'this and the other'/ While I go for 'this and that.'" The presentation of the song, however, confuses their pronunciations, for "this and the other" should be the upper-crust phrase of Astaire, while Rogers should use the more commonplace "this and that." The confusion continues into the chorus when Rogers claims for herself the more arch "lawfter" and "awfter" while giving Astaire the lower-class "laafter" and "aafter," even affecting a monocled hauteur as she intones "Havahna" and "banahna" to his "Havana" and "banana." In a Broadway musical, where lyricist and composer would have been more closely involved in rehearsals, Ira Gershwin would surely have corrected the discrepancy between their characters and their pronunciations, but in Hollywood the songwriters probably were not even present on the set during filming.

"Let's Call the Whole Thing Off" is followed by a rollicking dance on roller skates, after which Astaire and Rogers decide that the only way to deal with the rumors of their marriage is to actually *get* married—then get divorced. The scene cuts to the home of a justice-of-the-peace in New Jersey who pronounces them man and wife. As Astaire and Rogers take the ferry back to Manhattan, they discuss plans for starting divorce proceedings the next morning. Once again, dialogue drifts smoothly into the chatty verse of "They Can't Take That Away from Me," a song that deftly sidesteps sentimentality by having Astaire catalogue the memorable qualities he will always treasure about Rogers—from the understatedly simple "The way you hold your knife" to the wryly comic "The way you sing off key." A lover who cherishes such qualities, however, is much more ardent than one who celebrates only the beloved's more conventionally beautiful attributes. In this AABA song, Ira Gershwin cleverly leaves the lyric of the B-section dangling,

> *We may never, never meet again*
> *On the bumpy road to love.*
> *Still I'll always, always keep*
> *The mem'ry of*

so that its sense and syntax spill over into the final A-section:

> *The way you hold your knife,*
> *The way we danced till three . . .*

The song thus expresses Astaire's deepening love for Rogers in a way that he cannot articulate in dialogue.

George Gershwin's music, according to composer Alec Wilder, expresses the same understated affection: "The arresting nature of the *b* flat over "No!" in the thirty-second measure is a masterpiece, as are the quarter and half notes of the ending, achieving a calm, pastoral resolution in the face of the lyric's refusal to be separated from all those loving qualities." George Gershwin, however, was upset that no dance followed the song. On Broadway, particularly in their satiric operettas and in *Porgy and Bess*, he thought of song in integral and expressive terms. But in Hollywood he wanted some element of "performance" to make a song stand out. Presented as it is, however, "They Can't Take That Away from Me" is as poignant as any song could be.

Despite the excellence of such songs as "Let's Call the Whole Thing Off" and "They Can't Take That Away from Me," *Shall We Dance* earned only $400,000—considerably less than Astaire and Rogers's other films. Actually, according to Astaire himself, the two had "wondered how long it would be safe to carry on this cycle of team pictures. We didn't want to run it into the ground and we discussed the situation with each other frequently." As early as 1935, Astaire began "to wait for some small clue from the public as to whether or not they had had enough." Finally, amid the usual rave reviews for *Swing Time*, it came. One critic wrote:

THE SINGING AND DANCING LIMIT

Ginger and Fred are at it again in "Swing Time," singing and dancing like anything. One begins to wonder how many more of that type of film the public is prepared to enjoy. I know of at least one member of it who has reached the limit.

"Well, there it was," Astaire said to himself.

Astaire had planned for this inevitable surfeit. His 1936 five-film contract with RKO specified that at least one of the films team him with someone other than Rogers. Ruby Keeler and British musical star Jessie Matthews were considered, but RKO finally decided on a nineteen-year-old American actress, Joan Fontaine, sister of Olivia deHavilland. Fontaine could neither sing nor dance, and this would forestall comparisons to Ginger. To put further distance between this new film and Astaire's previous ones, the cast did not include such performers as Eric Blore, Edward Everett Horton, and Erik Rhodes. Blore and Horton were older, plain-faced comics who made Astaire seem young and handsome by contrast, while Rhodes played an effeminate fop who made Astaire seem virile. They were replaced by the comedy team of George Burns and Gracie Allen, who play Astaire's press agent and secretary. Excellent songs again were provided by the Gershwins, and the story of a rebellious British aristocrat who is romantically pursued by an American performer on tour in England was based on a novel by P. G. Wodehouse, who helped with the screenplay. Since Wodehouse was also a lyricist, who had worked with the Gershwins on Broadway, there was excellent integration between story and songs. Despite these sterling elements, *A Damsel in Distress* (1937) was one of the few Astaire films that lost money.

The major problem was the absence of a singing and dancing co-star for Astaire. He sings "I Can't Be Bothered Now" on his own when he meets and, of course, falls in love with Fontaine as she takes refuge from pursuing family members in his cab. He, Burns, and Allen sing "Stiff Upper Lip," as they cavort through an amusement park, stumbling down moving stairs, mugging in the house of mirrors, and dancing on treadmills, turntables, and inside a rolling barrel. The lyric bubbles with its own playfulness as it tosses around

British catchphrases such as "stout fellow," "in a stew," and "Carry on, old bean." Many of the phrases—"sober or blotto," "Pip-pip to Old Man Trouble," and "Chin up! Keep muddling through"—indicate that Ira Gershwin was another lyricist who realized that the prerecording and playback system freed him to use the harsh plosive and guttural consonants so native to the English language.

When Astaire sings the romantic ballad "Things Are Looking Up" to Fontaine, however, the actress's singing and dancing limitations mar the presentation of a superb song. In the verse, Astaire chattily "apologizes" to Fontaine for breaking into song when he realizes she loves him:

> *If I should suddenly start to sing,*
> *Or stand on my head—or anything,*
> *Don't think that I've lost my senses;*
> *It's just that my happiness finally commences.*

Ira Gershwin admired the way Astaire sang the last two lines of the verse with their subtle end-rhyme:

> *And it seems that suddenly I've*
> *Become the happiest man alive.*

Most singers, Gershwin lamented, sustained the last syllable of "suddenly" because it gave them a long vowel to display their vocal tones; Astaire, however, perfectly enunciated the lines.

In the chorus, Gershwin again takes advantage of the prerecording and playback system, ending most lines with an abrupt consonant:

> *Things are looking up,*
> *I've been looking the landscape over,*
> *And it's covered with four-leaf clover,*
> *Oh, things are looking up*
> *Since love looked up at me.*

Even when she didn't sing with Astaire, Ginger Rogers could react wonderfully to his singing. Fontaine, however, barely seems to take note of Astaire as he sings. Reportedly, she was greatly apprehensive of performing with Astaire, and, as he sings and dances, she, except for a few hesitant turns with him, walks along a woodland path on her castle grounds, much of her movement discreetly hidden by trees.

It may have been Fontaine's inability to perform with Astaire as he sang and danced that led to the transposition of the film's other romantic ballad "A Foggy Day (in London Town)." Originally it was to be sung when Astaire first meets and falls in love with Fontaine in London. When the Gershwins were working on the song, they were clearly thinking in terms of a London setting. George played what Ira described as a "wistful" air, and Ira offered to match it with either "A foggy day in  London" or "A foggy day in London town." George preferred the latter because it made the song seem more quaint and added an extra note to accommodate "town." Ira had more "British" touches, such as the adverb "decidedly" in the verse—"The outlook was decidedly blue"—and a specific allusion to a London institution: "The British Museum had lost its charm." The song would thus perfectly suit the moment when Astaire meets Fontaine in London:

For, suddenly, I saw you there—
And through foggy London Town
The sun was shining ev'rywhere.

In the course of filming, however, the song Astaire sings when he meets Fontaine became "I Can't Be Bothered Now," which isn't even a romantic song but one about the joys of dancing ("I'm dancing and I can't be bothered now").

"A Foggy Day" was moved closer to the end of the movie, and Astaire sings it when he is completely alone, walking to a party at Fontaine's castle. He traverses the same path he had strolled with her during "Things Are Looking Up," but now it is bathed in misty moonlight, giving the song a haunting, brooding quality. When Astaire finishes the song with the line "through foggy London town the sun was shining ev'rywhere," the moonlight pours through the mist around him. Despite the fact that the setting is utterly at odds with the lyric— down to moonlight rather than sunlight—the visual presentation is stunning.

A Damsel in Distress closes with a song, "Nice Work If You Can Get It," which Astaire sings at Fontaine's party with a group of madrigal singers who are trying to do "swing" songs. As Astaire joins in, he jazzes the number to the delight of the madrigal singers. The song, musically and lyrically, oscillates between romance and swing: in the first half of each A-section, George's melody is a smooth and straightforward progression of quarter, half, and whole notes, and Ira sets it with equally simple romantic phrases:

> *Holding hands at midnight 'neath a starry sky...*
> *Strolling with the one girl, sighing sigh after sigh...*

But in the next four bars the music turns sharply syncopated as dotted eighth- and sixteenth-notes leap up and down the scale, and Ira gives an equally bumptious turnaround to his colloquial title phrase:

> *Nice work if you can get it,*
> *And you can get it—if you try.*

In the film, the madrigal singers warble the traditionally romantic phrases while Astaire joins them on the upbeat, vernacular ones. Although the title of the song sounds like an American catchphrase, its origin, according to Ira Gershwin, lay in a cartoon published in *Punch*, the British humor magazine. In the cartoon, two charwomen are scrubbing steps and discussing the daughter of a third charwoman. "The first says she's heard that the discussee 'as become an 'ore. Whereat the second observes it's nice work if you can get it." After the song is sung, Fred reprises it with a dazzling drum solo that also becomes a tap dance, and the film closes on him alone rather than in a romantic shot with his co-star.

In *A Damsel in Distress*, as in Astaire's previous films, he plays a performer who sings and dances. While he occasionally presents a song as a performance before an audience, as he does "Nice Work If You Can Get It," he usually renders songs that are integral to character and story. By portraying performers, however, his breaking into song always carried with it a realistic excuse for song. In his next film for RKO, *Carefree* (1938), which reunited him with Rogers, Astaire plays a psychoanalyst, albeit one who in his youth wanted to "escape reality" by becoming a dancer (but, as he explains, "psychoanalysis showed me I was wrong"). Rogers is his patient, and he tries to cure her of her marriage phobia. As part of the treatment, Astaire has her eat dream-inducing foods in the hope that she will dream of her fiancé, played by Ralph Bellamy. Instead, she dreams of Astaire, as her groom, singing "I Used to Be Color Blind." The Irving Berlin song is presented in slow motion to suggest movement in a dream. As originally planned, it was also to be shot in color, and Berlin's lyric pointedly refers to someone who was once color-blind but, after finding love, can see green grass, a golden moon, and blue skies. As Berlin explained to a newspaper reporter, "They were going to do it in Technicolor, and I wanted to write a Technicolor song that would be good in and out of the picture." After the box-office losses of *A Damsel in Distress*, however, RKO cut back on production costs for the musical numbers in *Carefree*, though the film was still the costliest of the Astaire-Rogers films to date.

When Rogers tells Astaire of her dream, he uses hypnosis to exorcise her affection for him and focus it on Bellamy instead. Naturally, however, Astaire falls in love with Rogers, and, through another song, "Change Partners," undoes his hypnotic spell so that she is free to love him again. He starts "Change Partners" as he dances with Luella Gear (Ginger's "Aunt Cora") but tries to cut in on Rogers as she dances with Bellamy. As the lyric indicates, Astaire's strategy for getting to Rogers is to have a waiter tell Bellamy "he's wanted on the telephone." As Astaire gets Rogers alone, he hypnotizes her again to undo the hypnotic trance, giving the song a function in the story. Before Astaire can complete the hypnosis, however, Bellamy returns and accidentally punches Rogers, undoing Astaire's original hypnotic spell. Having "changed partners" twice, Rogers now, as the lyric promises, "will never want to change partners again."

The last film Astaire and Rogers did together at RKO, *The Story of Vernon and Irene Castle* (1939) is their most disappointing. Perhaps because the studio was leery of putting too much money into another Astaire picture, RKO did not commission an original set of songs for the film but used older songs to create what would come to be called a musical "biopic" about the married couple who tamed the wild dances of the World War I era—the fox trot, tango, and others—and made them socially acceptable. The film is filled with song and dance, but every number is done as a performance, even "Only When You're in My Arms," the one new song written for the film (by Bert Kalmar, Harry Ruby, and Con Conrad). Such a reversion to the backstager formula of songs done as performances is a sad finale to a series of musical films that had done so much to further the convention of expressive, integral song. Yet the legacy of the Astaire-Rogers films at RKO was that now ordinary, American characters could move from dialogue into integral expressive song without the realistic excuse that they were rehearsing or performing. That convention would enliven musical films for another thirty years.

6

Thanks for the Memory

No decade saw more film production than the 1930s. In 1937 alone there were more than 500 feature films. Although the movies could not undercut the free entertainment offered by radio, one could see a feature film in a neighborhood theater for twenty-five or thirty cents. As further inducement, theaters offered "Dish Nights," "Bingo Nights," and "Bank Nights" (where one could win as much as $1,000 in a drawing). They also introduced the "double feature," where thrifty consumers could see two pictures for the price of one. With such incentives, Americans flocked to the movies. "In 1938, there were some 80 million movie admissions every week, a figure representing 65 percent of the population of the United States."

With such a virtually captive audience, Hollywood could afford to experiment with the presentation of song. While most musical films of the decade were some form of "backstager," several films followed the lead of RKO, where Fred Astaire and Ginger Rogers had established the convention that ordinary characters could break into song—song that was integrally related to their dramatic situation. MGM's *Born to Dance* (1936), for example, tested this convention by presenting an integral song by a performer who could barely sing. Jimmy Stewart, playing a sailor on leave in New York, sings Cole Porter's "Easy to Love" to Eleanor Powell as they walk through Central Park. Porter originally wrote "Easy to Love" as a theater song for William Gaxton, who, with his resounding Broadway voice, was to have sung it in *Anything Goes* (1934). Despite his vocal abilities, however, Gaxton complained that "Easy to Love" was not easy to sing. The melody, as Alec Wilder notes, has a "fairly wide range, an octave and a fifth, but this is not asking too much of a musical theater singer. Unfortunately, even the best of pop singers seldom have a wide range, which results, in the case of this song, in their either not attempting it or else destroying it by trying to sing the dotted quarter note *a* of the second measure an octave higher."

Rather than rewrite the song for Gaxton—"Rewriting ruins songs," Porter always said—the composer created a different song for him, "All through the Night," and put "Easy to Love" into his proverbial trunk. When he played "Easy to Love" for producers in Hollywood, Porter recalled, "The response was instantaneous. They all grabbed the lyric and began singing it, and even called the stenographers to hear it." When Porter suggested that Jimmy Stewart sing it, however, the producers were concerned that the actor's voice could not do justice to such a difficult song.

At Porter's request, Stewart sang "Easy to Love" for him the next day. The song betrays its theatrical origins in its many long vowels that help a singer project the lyric from the stage—"You'd be so easy to love"—and its dramatic upward leap on, appropriately, the second syllable of "above"—"so easy to idolize all others *above*"— yet Stewart transformed it into a casually cinematic song by his amateurish rendition. "He sings far from well," Porter reported back to the studio but thought him "perfectly suited for the role of a clean-cut sailor." Had Stewart boomed out "Easy to Love" in stentorian, theatrical tones, it would have ruined the illusion that this song is sung by an ordinary sailor to a girl he has just met. Just in case, MGM had Jack Oness, a professional baritone, prerecord "Easy to Love" so that it could be dubbed for Stewart's voice, but the studio dropped all dubbing plans in favor of what one critic called Stewart's "pipsqueak though earnest tenor." That Porter was willing to offer up one of his most challenging theater songs to an actor who could barely sing indicates that he recognized it was more important for the song to grow out of character and dramatic situation rather than receive a professional performance. Stewart's struggles with a difficult theater song, in fact, make his rendition even more charming—much as his stuttering, stammering delivery of lines gave him a winning vulnerability as an actor.

The sheer abundance of films in the 1930s made it possible for an innovatively presented song to shine in an otherwise lackluster movie. RKO's *Down to Their Last Yacht* (1934), for example, is the inane story of a wealthy family who loses everything in the Depression but clings to its yacht, which it charters to the *nouveau riche* of the era. The formerly wealthy family members and their friends must now work as servants on their own yacht, and a song, modeled on the presentation of "Isn't It Romantic?" in *Love Me Tonight*, depicts their comic plight. As the daughter, in a maid's outfit, dusts furniture, including a globe that she sets spinning, she sings Ann Ronell and Max Steiner's "This Funny World"—"You've got to take it or else.... You've got to like it or else.... It's the 'or else' age." The song is picked up by her mother as she empties ashtrays, then it is passed among other family members and their friends as they work, binding them together as they confront their lot with stoic cheer.

Some of the best integral songs of the 1930s emerged from the decade's creakiest performance formula—the radio backstager. Radio had begun broadcasting in the early 1920s but did not attract a large audience until it began playing popular songs. "There is radio music in the air, every night, everywhere" newspapers reported, "Anybody can hear it at home on a receiving set, which any boy can put up in an hour." Radio sales rocketed: $60 million in 1922; double that in 1923; a half-billion dollars in 1925. In 1935, more than two-thirds of American homes had radio. By providing "free" entertainment, radio competed with Hollywood, particularly in the early years of the decade when movie attendance dropped off more than 30 percent.

Paramount fought back with a series of "Big Broadcast" movies that were, in effect, backstagers about putting on a radio program. People in large cities had seen Bing Crosby and other radio stars in theaters and nightclubs, but those in small towns only knew these performers by their voices. Paramount reasoned that they would pay to see what radio stars looked like. What made such backstagers even duller than movies about performers putting on a Broadway show was that while the latter at least showed singers and dancers moving on stage, in a radio backstager singers usually stood stock still before a microphone.

The first of these films, *The Big Broadcast* (1932), presents a series of radio performers, including the Mills Brothers, the Boswell Sisters, Cab Calloway, Kate Smith, and, of course, Bing Crosby, who are gathered together for radio's biggest live broadcast. The backstage story has Crosby and Stu Erwin, the station owner, involved with the same girl. Crosby knows she and Erwin are made for each other, but to get them to realize it he feigns drunkenness when Erwin arrives to escort him to the broadcast. From that point, Erwin frantically tries to reach the station in time to play a record of Crosby singing Leo Robin and Ralph Rainger's "Please," thinking that listeners won't be able to tell the difference between the recording and a live performance. The film cuts between Irwin rushing through the streets—dropping records, losing records—with shots back at the studio as the other stars perform, building up to Crosby's appearance. Erwin arrives in the nick of time—but with a warped record—so he tries to sing the song himself in imitation of Crosby. "Please" proves too difficult, however, partly because its first note, which takes the monosyllabic title, is the highest in the melody and thus must be struck perfectly at the outset of the song. The ruse fails to fool listeners but wins the heart of the girl, and, as she and Erwin embrace, Crosby appears in the studio to sing "Please" himself.

For all of its lame contrivance and wooden presentation of song, *The Big Broadcast* was enormously successful, and Paramount made an annual series of *Big Broadcast* musicals. The formula wore out in just a few years, but the last of the series, *The Big Broadcast of 1938*, presented one of the wittiest and most moving integral songs ever written for a Hollywood film. It was Bob Hope's first feature movie, and the song, "Thanks for the Memory," became forever associated with him. He plays a radio emcee giving daily broadcasts from *The Gigantic*, an ocean liner in a transatlantic race from New York to Cherbourg with another liner, *The Colossal.* Also on board is Shirley Ross, playing the only one of his several ex-wives who still loves him. The director, Mitchell Leisen, asked Leo Robin and Ralph Rainger to write a song for the couple, an unusual request at a time when divorce was still considered shameful. "I want them to show that they are still in love, but they dare not say it," Leisen explained to the songwriters, but then added that Hope was a comedian so "while it's a serious song, a guy like that has got to get laughs."

Faced with the task of writing a song—a funny song—for a divorced couple, Robin and Rainger created a catalogue song, then at the height of popularity after such successful list songs as Porter's "You're the Top (1934)," Ira Gershwin and Vernon Duke's "I Can't Get Started" (1936), and Rodgers and Hart's "The Lady Is a Tramp" (1937). The lyric of "Thanks for the Memory" is a back-and-forth duet in which Ross and Hope reminisce about their marriage's good times and bad. The first A-section rises through a series of repeated musical phrases, while the lyric mixes elegant images of "candlelight and wine," "castles on the Rhine," and the Parthenon with such prosaic American allusions as the Hudson River Line and "nights in Baltimore." Similarly, the second A-section builds from "swingy Harlem tunes" through "motor trips" to "burning lips" but drops off to the mundane "burning toast and prunes."

The characters delineated by such a lyric are urbane sophisticates who feel compelled to deprecate the sentimentality they secretly wish they could indulge. They come close to expressing their feelings for each other in the release but still keep up their mordant guard:

> We said good-bye with a highball;
> Then I got as high as a steeple.
> But we were intelligent people,
> No tears, no fuss.
> Hooray for us.

In the final A-section, the lyric moves these desperately insouciant lovers as close as they can come to emotional honesty:

> So thanks for the memory,
> And strictly entre nous,
> Darling, how are you?

And how are all the little dreams
That never did come true?

From the artificial intimacy of "entre nous," nonchalantly framed by "strictly," the lyric suddenly shifts to "darling," at once the most openly affectionate yet affectedly sophisticated of addresses. The simple "How are you" that follows thus is transformed from the utterly banal to the guardedly tender, hardly the thing that needs to be whispered "entre nous" in its normal context of everyday greeting but here, so framed, the tip of their emotional iceberg.

"Thanks for the Memory" is presented not as a performance but as a casually integral conversation. Hope is sitting at the ship's bar glumly drinking martinis, Ross slides into the stool beside him to try to cheer him up, and as they begin to recall such moments as his singing in the bathtub, they ease into "Thanks for the Memory." They both talk-sing their way through the song, frequently pausing to exchange dialogue. But as they down drink after drink, their sophisticated facades slowly crumble, and Ross, after a convulsive laugh, breaks down in tears. Hope comforts her with an "I know, I know, dear" that understates the love they still feel for each other.

In addition to the *Big Broadcast* series, Paramount made other radio backstagers, some featuring Kate Smith, one of the biggest—in every sense—stars of the airwaves. In most of her films, she presented songs as on-air performances, but in *Hello, Everybody!* (1933), she sang an integral song, Sam Coslow and Arthur Johnston's "Moon Song," that gave expression to her character's feelings. Playing a farm girl whose magnificent voice makes her a radio star, Smith falls in love with Randolph Scott. But when she sees Scott kiss her pretty, petite sister (played by Sally Blane), Smith ruefully sings "sweet moon song—that wasn't meant for me" in acceptance of the fact that romance, at least in a Hollywood movie, was not possible for the outsized and unattractive.

Many musical films of the 1930s centered on comic stars for whom breaking into integral song was no less zany than their other antics. Some of these comics, such as Bert Wheeler and Robert Woolsey, have faded, along with films such as *Half Shot at Sunrise* (1930). Others, most notably Eddie Cantor, have endured as period figures whose songs are heightened expressions of his manic character. His first major film was Samuel Goldwyn's adaptation of *Whoopee!*, Cantor's hit

Broadway musical, in 1930. Although technically a "book" show, most of the songs in the stage production bore little relation to plot or character. Goldwyn threw out all of the original songs by Gus Kahn and Walter Donaldson except for "Makin' Whoopee," which is presented as if it were a stage production. When Kahn and Donaldson arrived in Hollywood, Goldwyn insisted on "the key word 'motivation.' Every song or dance sequence…had to grow organically from the show's plot and characters." As a result, the songs in the film adaptation of *Whoopee* were more integral than those in the stage original. In one of them, "A Girlfriend of a Boyfriend of Mine," Cantor refrains from his usual cavorting about the set and instead sits—*sits*!—on the running board of an automobile and sings expressively about his romantic failures, his hypochondria, and other aspects of his character: "Why am I pale and nervous?/ Why do I weep and pine?/ Because she turned out to be the real friend/ Of a heel friend of mine."

Whoopee is also notable as the film where Busby Berkeley—at Cantor's insistence despite Goldwyn's concern that Berkeley had a drinking problem—made his choreographic film debut. Already present are hallmarks of Berkeley's camerawork—the crotch shot, the overhead kaleidoscopic shot, and the close-up of individual chorines. Yet *Whoopee* also manifests what would become staples of Cantor's other films—overblown gags, frenetically delivered songs, and the obligatory blackface number. In *Palmy Days* (1931), for example, he plays an efficiency expert in a bakery (one of his efficiencies is to cut the corners off his boss's desk so people won't waste time by sitting on them). When he mistakenly thinks the boss has chosen him to marry his daughter, Cantor sings "My Baby Said 'Yes'" to his fellow workers in a near-hysterical frenzy. In *The Kid from Spain*, the most popular and successful musical of 1932, he impersonates a matador and does an equally frenzied "What a Perfect Combination" in blackface. *Roman Scandals* (1933) had Cantor, transported from Depression-era America to ancient Rome, exhorting girls to "Keep Young and Beautiful" in blackface (thanks to the gimmick of a mud bath). One of the most lavish musicals to date, *Roman Scandals* featured extravagant production numbers staged by Busby Berkeley, including "No More Love," sung by Ruth Etting as a spurned Roman concubine, to a bevy of nude slave girls (their nudity discreetly covered by long blonde tresses).

While these musicals were hugely successful, Cantor's contract with Goldwyn limited him to only one film a year so that he could continue to perform on Broadway. Soon he found another outlet for his talent in radio as the long-running star of *The Chase and Sanborn Hour*. As biographer Herbert G. Goldman observes, Cantor was "essentially a visual comedian with a strong talent for pantomime" that was "not naturally suited to radio." Yet the very constraints of radio enabled him to connect with listeners by talking directly and informally to them about his wife, his daughters, and his career in a way no previous radio performer had done. Instinctively, Cantor had seized the opportunity radio gave him to enter America's homes, and listeners consistently chose him as their favorite on-air personality in numbers that eclipsed his fame on stage or screen.

Unlike the frenetic Cantor, when Groucho Marx sang in films, his delivery was deadpan and understated, spoken as much as sung, in a style that reflects his fondness for Gilbert and Sullivan patter. Early in his career, he heard a fellow actor singing in the wings. "That's a goddamned good lyric," Groucho remarked. "Did you write that?" The actor explained that it was by William Schwenck Gilbert, and Groucho was forever afterward a devotee of Gilbert and Sullivan operetta. Friends who came to his home would spend the evening, not always happily, listening to and singing along with *H.M.S. Pinafore*, *The Pirates of Penzance*, and other Savoyard fare. In Bert Kalmar and Harry Ruby, Groucho found songwriters who could write patter songs in the style of Gilbert and Sullivan, replete with puns, double and triple rhymes, and allusive catalogues of images. For the 1928 stage production of *Animal Crackers* the songwriters created "Hello, I Must Be Going" and "Hooray for Captain Spaulding," which Groucho sang in droll Gilbert and Sullivan fashion.

In adapting *Animal Crackers* for film in 1930, however, Paramount faced the same problem they had encountered in their 1929 adaptation of *The Cocoanuts*. Victor Heerman, the director assigned to film *Animal Crackers*, had seen the stage version of the show and felt that the songs interrupted the comic flow. He wanted, therefore, to cut songs from the film. "'I already have ten reels of film with these funny scenes,' he told the Marxes. 'We don't need the music.'" The brothers protested that their success in vaudeville and on Broadway was based on a combination of comedy and music, but still most of the songs were cut. In their next film at Paramount, *Monkey Business* (1931), the only featured song was a hilarious version of "You Brought a New Kind of Love to Me," which Zeppo, Chico, and Groucho sing as they impersonate Maurice Chevalier (and Harpo lip-synchs to a recording on a phonograph strapped to his back).

Only in *Horse Feathers* (1932) and *Duck Soup* (1933) does Groucho return to the kind of Gilbert and Sullivan patter song he had performed in the brothers' stage productions. *Horse Feathers* opens with his installation as the new president of Huxley College. After the outgoing president urges him to follow the suggestions of the board of trustees, a row of hoary, bearded men in caps and gowns seated behind him, Groucho breaks into "I'm Against It" to express his resistance to advice of any kind. Kalmar's lyric rhymes "against it," "commenced it," and "condensed it" with the kind of comically feminine rhymes Gilbert frequently used. Groucho's performance of the song finally wins over the trustees who join him in a rousing chorus.

Duck Soup presents song even more fully in the Gilbert and Sullivan manner. When Margaret Dumont asks him, in song, to describe his policies as the new ruler of Freedonia, Groucho lists prohibitions against smoking, whistling, telling dirty jokes, and chewing gum, tossing in such Gilbert-like triple rhymes as "prohibited" and "exhibited." As in Gilbert and Sullivan, the chorus responds by echoing his phrases and the pastiche of song defines character and advances plot. Just as Gilbert and Sullivan operettas were send-ups of grand opera, delivering songs with cool British reserve rather than flaming Italian passion, the Marx Brothers' movies spoofed musical films where characters burst into romantic effusions of song. Groucho rattles off his songs with clinical detachment, seemingly oblivious to their absurdities, which, of course, makes them seem even funnier.

In the mid-1930s, the Marx Brothers joined Jeanette MacDonald, Maurice Chevalier, and other stars who left Paramount for MGM. There, beginning with *A Night at the Opera* (1935), Irving Thalberg insisted the Brothers tone down their anarchic comedy and adhere to a story line. The result, some critics have found, was that the films the Marx Brothers made at MGM lacked the satirical punch of their Paramount films: "Instead of making sport of romance, they now facilitated it. Instead of whacking away at the powerful institutions of government or the military or education, they battled the toothless enemy of grand opera.... They were not outrageous anymore, they were only frivolous."

The presentation of songs, too, was different at MGM, where they were done as performances rather than as integral exchanges between characters. Yet it was in one such performance number in *At the Circus* (1939) that Groucho got his best song in film, one he renders in a train car carrying a circus troupe. It was written by a young songwriting team, E. Y. "Yip" Harburg and Harold Arlen. Harburg, like Groucho, was an admirer of Gilbert and Sullivan. In high school he found a classmate, Ira Gershwin, who shared his love of light verse. When "Yip" confessed to "Gersh" that his favorite poet was William Schwenck Gilbert, Ira asked him if he knew that Gilbert's "poems" were actually song lyrics. "There's music to them?" asked an incredulous Harburg, who lived in the wretched poverty of the Lower East Side. Ira then took him back to his relatively comfortable middle-class apartment and played *H.M.S. Pinafore* on the Gershwin family Victrola. "There were all the lines I knew by heart," Harburg recalled. "I was dumbfounded, staggered."

What Harburg did not realize until he began writing lyrics himself was that while Gilbert wrote his light verse and then gave it to Sullivan to be set to music, in American songwriting, the process was reversed: it was the music that came first, and the lyricist had to fit syllable to note, verbal phrase to musical phrase. That made writing clever, literate lyrics much more difficult, but it also made for more colloquial, conversational lyrics. Gilbert's light verse follows a metrically regular rhythm of alternating accented and unaccented syllables:

> *When I mere/ ly from him par/ ted*
> *We were near/ ly broken hear/ ted.*
> *When in se/ quel reuni/ ted*
> *We were eq/ ually deligh/ ted.*

Harburg, however, had to match his syllables to Arlen's music. By fitting syllables to that irregular sequence of notes—rather than to a poetic meter that has the same number of syllables in each line—Harburg created lyrics that have the uneven rhythm of conversation rather than the metrical regularity of poetry:

> *Lydia,/ oh, Lydia,*
> *That "en-/cyclo/-pidia"*
> *Oh, Lydia,/ the queen/ of tattoo.*
> *On her back/ is the Bat-/tle of Waterloo,*
> *Beside it/ the Wreck of/ the Hesperus too*
> *And proudly/ above waves/ the red, white and blue*
> *You can learn/ a lot/ from Lydia.*

Such a conversational, colloquial lyric lent itself perfectly to Groucho's off-handed delivery.

The song was almost cut, however, when the Breen Office raised its eyebrows at risqué images that went far beyond anything in Gilbert and Sullivan:

> *When her muscles start relaxin'*
> *Up the hill comes Andrew Jackson…*
> *For two bits she will do a mazurka in jazz*
> *With a view of Niag'ra that nobody has*
> *And on a clear day you can see Alcatraz…*
> *Here's Nijinsky doin' the rhumba,*
> *Here's her social security numba…*

Harburg and Arlen saved the song by adding a chorus at the end that describes how an admiral was so taken by "the ships on her hips" that "he went and married Lydia." Nothing, however, could get these lines past the censors:

When she stands, the world grows littler.
When she sits, she sits on Hitler.

Enough of the lyric passed muster, however, to give Groucho a thoroughly Americanized version, informal and colloquial, of his beloved Gilbert and Sullivan patter.

The passing of Irving Thalberg in 1936 deeply affected Groucho Marx. "After Thalberg's death," he said, "my interest in the movies waned. I appeared in them, but my heart was in the Highlands. The fun had gone out of filmmaking. I was like an old pug, still going through the motions, but now doing it solely for the money." MGM dispensed with the services of songwriters Bert Kalmar and Harry Ruby for *Go West* (1940). "They had been favorites of Irving Thalberg's, but Thalberg was long dead, and the studio seemed hell-bent on removing traces of his influence." Kalmar and Ruby had written the script as well as the songs for Marx Brothers films, so that their songs were integral to the story. But with *Go West*, their songs were all cut, including a delightful title song, "Go West, Young Man." With its flippant sentiments—"A cowboy and his missus went to court for a divorce/ The cowboy got the children and the missus got the horse"—the song became part of Groucho's party repertory. Along with dispensing with Kalmar and Ruby, MGM dropped Margaret Dumont, who had played opposite Groucho in nearly all the brothers' films. Most damaging of all, Groucho was given no songs to sing in *Go West*.

With one more film left to do under their contract with MGM, Groucho grew increasingly despondent. "The amount of work, politics, intrigue and chicanery involved in assembling even as important a triviality as a Marx Brothers comedy is appalling," he wrote to a friend. "It's really unbelievable—all the meetings, conversation and arguments that have to be gone through with before one of these turkeys is completed!" His depression was exacerbated by the escalating war in Europe and, closer to home, by his crumbling marriage to an alcoholic wife. When he compared himself to a fellow-comic, Jack Benny, who had fashioned a wonderfully miserly persona that could get laughs merely by pausing as he counted his money, Groucho was envious and self-disparaging: "I had no character as a Marx Brother," he ruefully reflected, "I wasn't real. I just talked fast."

Still, for his last film with his brothers for MGM, *The Big Store* (1941), Groucho mustered one last burst of enthusiasm. He lobbied to get Margaret Dumont back, and she took pride in her reinstatement. "I'm not a stooge," she said, "I'm the best straight woman in Hollywood." Producer Louis K. Sidney told the Marx Brothers at the outset, "Your last two pictures lost money.... I have never had a loser. *We* are not going to lose money. And we are going to have a good picture." Yet one of the problems with the film was that it gave most of the songs over to Tony Martin rather than to Groucho. Martin sings several songs as performances, the most lugubrious and pretentious of them "Tenement Symphony," a kind of tone poem about life in a Lower East Side slum where nationalities and music mix—"The Cohn's pianola/ The Kellys and their Victrola.... The songs of the ghetto/ Inspire the allegretto." Groucho has only one song, "You've Got to Sing While You Sell," a big production number that he sings to salespeople in the department store as he moves from one area to another, using merchandise as props to drive home his musical point. Although the number is integral to character and story, it lacks the energy and anarchy of his patter songs at Paramount.

During the filming of *The Big Store*, Grouch told a reporter, "When I say we are sick of movies, I mean the people are about to get sick of us. By getting out now, we're just anticipating public demand, and by a very short margin. Our stuff is simply growing stale. So are we.... What happened to us is that we were defeated by our own specialty. The fake moustache, the dumb harp player, and the little guy who chased the ladies, all were funny at first. But it became successively harder with each picture to top the one before. We couldn't get out of the groove, without getting out of the movies. So we decided to get all the way out."

Integral song, having flourished in films featuring comic figures such as Eddie Cantor and Groucho Marx, found another home in cartoons. Since cartoon characters are unrealistic to begin with, it is no strain on credulity to have them burst into song. One of the biggest hits of the decade was "Who's Afraid of the Big Bad Wolf?" (by composer Frank Churchill, with some additional lyrics, first by Ted Sears, then by Ann Ronell) from the 1933 Disney cartoon, *Three Little Pigs*. It caught the country's imagination as people struggled with the ravages of the Great Depression that, in 1932, had thrown 18,000,000 Americans out of work. "It came out in the depths of the Depression," Ronell recalled, "and I think people liked it because it was the song of the little guy laughing at the big, bad guy. I like to write music for the little guy." As Walt Disney wrote to his brother Roy, "At last we have achieved true personality in a whole picture."

Yet Disney chafed at what he felt was the short-changing cartoons received at the box office. Where a feature film could rent for $3,000 a week in a first-run theater, his cartoons received only $150 a week. In neighborhood and small-town theaters, cartoons could rent for as little as $3 a week, and they were sometimes "bicycled"—taken by bike riders from one theater to another on a single rental—thus further reducing Disney's income. As double features became more prevalent, some theaters were eliminating cartoons altogether to squeeze in more feature showings in the course of a day. Even though Disney charged more for his cartoons than did his competitors, he found that even *Three Little Pigs* was not making significant profits. He justified his higher rentals by saying that his films cost more to make, and he believed that audiences would pay more for higher quality. That belief was strengthened when Disney took a trip to Europe and noticed that his cartoons were frequently given top billing above feature films. Even more important, some theaters showed no feature film at all—just a series of cartoons. These revelations confirmed a hunch he had been nursing about making a full-length feature cartoon with songs. "We will use a full symphony orchestra and fine singers," he vowed. "We've got to be sure of it before we start, because if it isn't good we will destroy it."

The project he selected was based on the Grimm Brothers' fairy tale, and from conception to completion, *Snow White and the Seven Dwarfs* (1938) took five years. Although Disney estimated that the film would cost $250,000, it quickly doubled, then reached $1.7 million. Still he faced opposition from inside and outside his studio, voices urging him to not make a movie based on a fairy tale but to turn it into a love story between a princess and a prince. Even his wife, who had earned his lifelong professional respect by advising him to change the name of his first major cartoon character from "Mortimer Mouse" to "Mickey Mouse," said she thought a story involving dwarves was sordid: "There's something so nasty about them."

Yet Disney managed to do what he would do again and again in his films—tell a story through integral songs—songs, in this instance, by Larry Morey and Frank Churchill. When we first see Snow White, she is scrubbing steps, and when she goes to a well to get water, accompanied by doves, she sings "I'm Wishing" to express her romantic longing. Then the film moves immediately to another song as a prince, who happens to be riding by, hears her and, enchanted by her voice, leaps over the wall to join her. As he sings "One Love," Snow White demurely flees to her room and listens to him from her balcony, responding only by kissing one of the doves, who flies down and, with even more maidenly shyness, passes on the kiss to the prince.

The presentation of these songs is marred only by Disney's use of operatic voices for the animated characters, so that rather than sounding like two young lovers, the prince and Snow White sound like Nelson Eddy and Jeanette MacDonald. As a result, the songs that advance the love story, even the wonderful "Some Day My Prince Will Come," are rendered theatrically rather than in the kind of simple, conversational style that had become characteristic of film songs. The comic songs for the dwarfs, on the other hand, "Heigh-Ho" and "Whistle While You

Work," animate the film with their easy, colloquial style:

> *We dig up diamonds by the score,*
> *A thousand rubies—sometimes more,*
> *But we don't know what we dig 'em for.*

Snow White and the Seven Dwarfs repaid Disney's $1.7 investment with a first-run gross of $8.5 million and launched a whole new venue for the presentation of integral song in feature-length cartoons, one that is still alive and kicking today with films such as *Aladdin* (1992), *The Lion King* (1994), and *Pocahontas* (1995).

Although many films of the 1930s featured integral songs, far more continued to present songs as performances. The performance formula, however, was greatly expanded beyond the backstager model. Instead of films that had characters rehearsing or singing songs as part of a Broadway musical, there were films set in other locales conducive to singing. One setting that figured prominently in films of the 1930s was Hawaii, a place at once familiar to Americans yet exotic enough to make singing seem more "natural." In such films as *Waikiki Wedding* (1937), *Hawaii Calls* (1938), and *Honolulu* (1939), song seems to flow spontaneously from the natives much as it did from blacks in such earlier films as *Hallelujah!* In *Waikiki Wedding*, for example, Bing Crosby plays a public relations agent who creates a "Miss Pineapple" contest to promote tourism in the islands. When Shirley Ross wins the contest, she finds Hawaii far less romantic than promised, and Crosby's publicity stunt is in jeopardy. He takes her sailing in the moonlight where she hears natives singing. When she asks him what the words mean, Crosby "translates" "Blue Hawaii" as they glide across the moonlit waters, and the song changes Ross's feelings about the islands—and, of course, about Crosby.

Another setting conducive to singing was the college campus, where students, armed with ukuleles, banjos, and guitars, broke into song in such films as *College Rhythm* (1934), *College Holiday* (1936), and *College Swing* (1938). For the most part, songs were presented as performances at dances, student shows, and fraternity initiations. A more interesting presentation occurs in *College Humor* (1933), where fraternity boys and sorority girls talk and sing their way casually through Arthur Johnston and Sam Coslow's "Down the Old

Ox Road"—a nickname for any secluded necking spot, from lover's lane to the last row in a movie theater. The presentation of the song begins with dialogue between two couples, shifts into rhymed dialogue among coeds getting dressed, then to a trio of homely girls lamenting, in song, that they'll never find the Old Ox Road. The song bounces from one group of singers to another, including older married couples and even a pair of affectionate puppies. At the finale, Bing Crosby, playing a professor, sings it from his balcony to a student couple (Jack Oakie and Mary Kornman) who have hitherto held back from lovemaking. Crosby's singing of the song entices the couple to join in the amours of their fellow students so that the song propels the narrative much as "Isn't It Romantic?" did in *Love Me Tonight*.

An even more congenial setting for the presentation of song was the nightclub, an institution revived by the repeal of Prohibition in 1933. A Paramount film of that year, *Torch Singer*, combined the nightclub setting with a radio backstager that featured Claudette Colbert, who sang in her own unprofessional voice in an informal style that was wonderfully suited to the film. She plays an unwed mother who gives birth to a baby girl in a charity hospital and tells her newborn daughter, "Why couldn't you have been a boy? This world's a tough place for a girl." At first, she tries to raise the child on her own, singing her such tough-nosed lullabies as "Don't be a cry baby or the bogey man will get you/ If you let him catch you starting to sing the blues." Soon, however, she has to give the child up to the nuns at the hospital, and, in signing the papers, asks only that she carry her father's last name and the first name "Sally." "Don't let any man make a sucker out of you," she tells her daughter as she leaves.

She becomes a nightclub singer whose big hit is the torch song, "Give Me Liberty or Give Me Love," which portrays her as a prisoner of love—"I'm only a slave to you/ Now you can have me if you really want me"—but in reality she has become cold and callous. One of her admirers is a socialite who owns a radio station, and when he takes Colbert for a visit to the studio, she steps in for a child psychologist who freezes on a radio show for kids. Colbert ad libs to the kids, then, with a drink in her hand, sings the same lullaby she had sung to her own baby. In true Hollywood fashion, she becomes a radio star and uses her program to find her little girl, who has been adopted by the father. He, in turn, has been searching for Colbert for years, but when he finds her he accuses her of being selfish and hard." "Sure I am," she retorts, "Just like glass—so hard nothing will cut it but diamonds. Come around someday with a fistful—maybe we can get together." After that obligatory quarrel, however, mother, father, and child are reunited at the end.

Nightclubs proved to be a more erotic setting for song than the Broadway backstager. A woman performing a song in a nightclub could present herself as an object of sexual attraction—even as a woman who desires sex as much as she is desired—since she is, after all, just singing a song. When Marlene Dietrich sings "Falling in Love Again" (in German, "Ich bin von Kopf bis Fuss auf Liebe

eingestellt"—the much more sensuous "I am from head to feet designed for love") in *The Blue Angel* (1930), or Mae West sings "I Like a Guy What Takes His Time" in *She Done Him Wrong* (1933), the performance convention allows them to give voice to their sexuality in ways that would have been unthinkable if they were singing integral songs about their feelings in a particular dramatic situation.

In *Morocco* (1930), Dietrich makes her musical entrance in a cabaret wearing male evening attire—top hat, white tie, and tails. "I planned to have her dress like a man," said director Josef von Sternberg; "I wanted to touch on a lesbian accent." At her appearance, the audience is at first appalled at the cross-dressing, but Gary Cooper, as a French legionnaire, bullies his comrades into warmly welcoming her. As she sings her first song, Dietrich passes among the tables, and the audience gradually finds her beguiling. At the end of the song, one gallant offers her a glass of champagne, which she downs, then she asks a woman at the

table if she can have the flower in her hair. When the woman says, "Of course," Dietrich plants a mildly impassioned kiss on her lips, then tosses the flower to Gary Cooper, who tucks it behind his ear. In the course of the song, she has transformed an initially hostile audience, flirted with another woman, and reduced Cooper to girlish submission—all as part of her sexually charged performance.

The success of Dietrich's erotic presentation of song may have prompted Paramount to bring Mae West to the screen. Long a risqué stage performer, West presented songs in the style of such black blues singers as Ma Rainey and Bessie Smith, whose performances she had studied in Harlem nightclubs. Her dialogue, too, was laced with double-entendres. However, she insulated her films by setting most of them in the 1890s, where she wore tight-fitting but nonrevealing outfits. Although she usually sang as a nightclub performance, one song from *Belle of the Nineties* (1934), "My Old Flame," resonates with her character. After her nightclub appearance, West goes to the bar where she is regaled by the assembled gentlemen. There is a series of her classic one-liners: in answer to what kind of men she likes best, West retorts, "Two kinds—foreign and domestic"; in response to their ogling of her figure, she snaps, "It's better to be looked over than overlooked." The men press her to sing one more song, and ask her to choose her own favorite. After a brief reflection, she agrees, nods to Duke Ellington's orchestra, and does a subdued version of "My Old Flame," written for the movie by Sam Coslow and Arthur Johnston. Although the lyric gives her characteristically flippant lines—"My old flame/ I can't even remember his name"— it suggests that her brazen sexuality is the carapace for a lost youthful love:

> *I've met so many who had fascinatin' ways,*
> *A fascinatin' gaze in their eyes;*
> *Some who took me up to the skies,*
> *But their attempts at love*
> *Were only imitations of*
> *My old flame.*

For one of the rare times in one of Mae West's movies, a song comes close to presenting genuine romantic feeling.

Closer still to romantic expression was "I Want You—I Need You" (by Harvey Brooks, Gladys DuBois, and Ben Ellison) from *I'm No Angel* (1933), which she sings as a "private" performance to her fiancé (played by Cary Grant). They sit together at the piano, and as he declares his love for her, she eases into the song that expresses her feelings for him. Grant continues to talk while she sings, and she shifts between singing and banter with him. At one point, for example, he says, "I could be your slave," and she pauses from singing to quip, "That could be arranged," then resumes singing. At the end of the song, West engages in one of her few passionate kisses, though we see only Cary Grant's back as he takes her in his arms. Like Dietrich, West sang in a style that fused talking with singing. "I preferred to half-speak most of my songs," she said, "it gave them a more suggestive effect." For all of her sexual allure, West, like Dietrich, rarely engaged in physical love scenes. Her sexuality subsists in her on-screen image, her wisecracks, and her songs. Song, for both Mae West and Marlene Dietrich, became a vehicle for the expression of sexual desire and desirability that was contained by the performance convention.

What precipitated the sudden demise of Dietrich's and West's nightclub backstagers was the growing strength of the Production Code. The Code forced a title change from *It Ain't No Sin* to *The Belle of the Nineties* (1934), and Mae West's script had to be revised to culminate in her character's marriage to the leading man. By *Klondike Annie* (1936) she was impersonating—with considerable conviction—a Salvation Army worker.

Twentieth Century-Fox, however, figured out how to keep making night-club musicals even in the new era of the Code by featuring Alice Faye, whose

looks resembled those of blonde bombshell Jean Harlow but whose persona was pristine. She had started out as a vocalist with Rudy Vallee's orchestra, then made her first film, *George White's Scandals*, a typical backstager, in 1934. In her next film, *She Learned about Sailors* (1934), she played a waterfront singer in Shanghai, and her nightclub singer role followed her in *Sing, Baby, Sing* (1936), *In Old Chicago* (1938), and *Alexander's Ragtime Band* (1938).

In the last of these, the title song is presented with considerable dramatic resonance for a performance number. Faye walks into a San Francisco Barbary Coast saloon with the sheet music of this "new" song in her hand, greets the owner and bartender, then absent-mindedly leaves the music on the bar to sit with some old friends. In the meantime, a small orchestra led by violinist Tyrone Power is trying to get a job playing in the saloon. When they're finally given the chance to audition, they find they've forgotten their music. The bartender hands them the sheet music for "Alexander's Ragtime Band" that Faye has left on the bar. At first, the musicians struggle with the unusual style of ragtime, but then Power, playing a classically trained musician whose teacher and family are chagrined at his longing to play poplar songs, figures out the swinging lilt of the song's rhythm. As the band gets into the number, Faye realizes they have taken her sheet music and runs over to protest. When she sees how the customers are enjoying the song, however, she decides to join in with them.

Alexander's Ragtime Band established another convention for the presenta-tion of performance song in film. Although all of its songs were by Irving Ber-

lin, few were written specifically for this movie. Instead, studio head Darryl F. Zanuck thought a movie narrative could be written around a group of preexisting songs. Berlin realized that such an "anthology" film could preserve his older songs whose popularity had faded. He was particularly concerned about the accelerated turnover of popular songs in the 1930s, when radio's inces-sant playing of the "top hits" of the day wore out songs much more quickly than ever before.

Zanuck initially wanted to make the film as what later would be called a "biopic"—the story of the songwriter's life told through his songs. When Berlin rejected the idea, Zanuck "'schemed with a way of getting a portion of Irving

Berlin's life on the screen, particularly his musical life' and approached Berlin with the idea of inventing a story that would...include certain incidents from his life 'without violating his private life.'" Berlin responded to that suggestion enthusiastically: "We can make this man a combination of Paul Whiteman, George Gershwin, Irving Berlin, anything that we want." It was Berlin's idea to open the film on San Francisco's Barbary Coast rather than New York's East Side where he had grown up. Berlin worked on the script, using twenty-two of his own songs to weave a story about the evolution of American popular song from ragtime through patriotic songs of World War I, to sob ballads of the 1920s and crooner songs of the 1930s.

In one of his classic memos, Zanuck insisted upon revisions that would make the script a "character story" rather than a "situation story" about the history of American song. "Maybe our trouble is that we are trying to tell a phase of American musical evolution...instead of a story about two boys and a girl." Still, Zanuck balanced his call for a story about the love triangle of Faye, Power, and Don Ameche with his recognition that the movie's songs represented the history of American popular music during the first thirty years of the twentieth century:

> Give Alexander credit for every innovation that has been given to bands in the last couple of decades. He is the first one who uses someone to get up and sing in a megaphone, the first one to introduce specialties. But Alexander can't be a prophet—his innovations are casual inspirations—must be shown and let audience draw its own conclusions. We want to put over songs in sock-o fashion. Each time lapse should introduce something new.

This formula of writing a screenplay around a group of existing songs would later produce such wonderful films as *An American in Paris, Singin' in the Rain*, and *The Band Wagon*.

If the nightclub setting for the presentation of song was more informal than the Broadway backstager, opera provided a more formal dramatic context for song. The first "opera backstager" was made by Columbia, one of the last studios to create musical films. Svelte opera star Grace Moore starred in *One Night of Love* (1934), which was surprisingly successful, given Hollywood concerns that audiences would find opera too highbrow. The film presents songs in compelling ways, beginning with the title song, written by director Victor Schertzinger and lyricist Gus Kahn, which Moore sings at the opening of the film as part of a radio contest (linking it to radio backstagers) whose prize is the chance to become a student of a famed Italian singing teacher. Although Moore does not win the contest, she decides to take what money she has and go to Italy to study opera on her own. Working as a nightclub singer to support her opera studies (linking the film with nightclub backstagers), she sings such popular operatic songs as "Ciribiribin" to the audience and is, lo and behold, discovered by the very singing teacher who judged the radio contest.

The Cinderella plot and the Italian setting, where people of all classes embrace opera, appealed so much to American audiences that several other opera "backstagers" were mounted. One of the ways such films could incorporate pop songs as well as arias was to make the central conflict a clash between classical music and pop. *I Dream Too Much* (1935), RKO's response to Columbia's *One Night of Love*, featured petite French Lily Pons in her film debut as an opera singer who at first devotes herself to the career of her husband, a composer played by Henry Fonda. But once Fonda hears her sing, he declares, "My wife has a voice like an angel." He then sets his own ambition aside and takes a job as a tour guide to earn money for her singing lessons. When he leads a party of tourists to what he promises will be a dangerous nightclub, however, he finds Pons singing the lowdown "I Got Love." He warns her that she will ruin her voice by singing such songs and whisks her off, insisting that she must let him work to support her career. Not to be outdone in altruism, Pons takes the score of Fonda's opera to an impresario and insists he listen to at least one song. When she sings Dorothy Fields and Jerome Kern's "I'm the Echo, You're the Song," the impresario is so taken by the beauty of her voice that he vows to make her a star. When she pleads, echoing the song's lyric, that what is important is not her voice but her husband's music, the impresario dismisses Fonda's work as "a nice tune but it's not opera."

She then implores him to produce Fonda's opera as a musical comedy, and Pons herself oversees rehearsals—at one point interrupting a dance routine with "Faster. It must go faster. This is not opera! This is musical comedy!" When Fonda arrives at the theater, he is startled to see a poster advertising *I Dream Too Much* with his name as composer. He then hears Pons sing the title song rapturously—but, to his chagrin, in a musical comedy. After the performance, he is congratulated by the impresario, but Fonda is still angry at what he thinks has been a cruel joke. The impresario tells him not to be a fool, that his career is made, and that twenty million people will be singing his songs. Just then, a woman asks if he is the composer of the show and tells him his songs are like those of Schubert. Fonda, finding the adulation he has so long sought, undergoes a change of heart and accepts the compliment by saying, "It's nothing, nothing at all. You see, I just write the kind of music people want—tunes they can whistle," adding that Pons "sings my songs just the way I write them."

MGM hopped on the classical versus pop bandwagon with *San Francisco* (1936), a film that made the opera-pop conflict part of a personal clash between

saloon owner Clark Gable and boyhood-friend-turned-priest Spencer Tracy. Caught in the middle is opera singer Jeanette MacDonald, who asks Gable for a job in his Barbary Coast nightclub. When she sings "San Francisco" in rehearsal, however, he tells her to "jazz it up" and plays (obviously dubbed) the tune in ragtime style on
the piano. She develops a performance style that balances jazz and opera but is still virtuosic enough to prompt San Francisco's leading impresario to beseech Gable to let MacDonald out of her contract so she can sing in his opera house.

Abetted by Spencer Tracy, MacDonald becomes the toast of San Francisco's opera world, but Gable pursues her, intent on stopping the performance and enforcing his contract with her. As he listens to her sing—his first taste of opera—he is so entranced that he allows the performance to continue. She, in turn, tries to help him out with a song. His hopes for keeping ownership of his nightclub—and winning political office—hinge on winning a local talent contest, and MacDonald leaves her society friends to sing "San Francisco" as the contestant representing Gable's club. Just as he refuses her help and rejects the winning trophy, the San Francisco earthquake erupts and during the ensuing destruction, Gable and MacDonald are reconciled when he finds her singing in a hospital camp. MGM did
not have the chutzpah to have her reprise "San Francisco" but took the safer route of giving her "Nearer My God to Thee" and then "The Battle Hymn of the Republic." Nevertheless, the movie is driven by a combination of opera and popular song.

MacDonald, who sparkled in this film as she had in original film operettas at Paramount with Maurice Chevalier, also made a series of film adaptations of stage operettas at MGM with Nelson Eddy such as *Naughty Marietta* (1935), *Rose Marie* (1936), and *Maytime* (1937). In these films, the style of performance was operatic, so that songs sung by Eddy and MacDonald are the polar opposite of pure film songs such as those of Astaire and Rogers—orotund, bombastic, theatrical. Occasionally, however, there were moments in their films when a song, while originally written for the Broadway stage, was presented in more casually conversational Hollywood terms. After Eddy booms out "Rose-Marie" in his best operatic baritone while rowing MacDonald in a

canoe, he reprises the song and errantly substitutes "Caroline" for "Rose-Marie." She interrupts him saying, "Uh-uh-uh-uh-uh-uh. It was 'Rose-Marie' a minute ago." When he admits his mistake, she realizes his ploy. "What do you do?" she asks, "Change the name to suit the girl?" "If it fits the rhythm," he admits. She then parodies him, singing, "Oh Genevieve, I love you…Oh, Annabelle, I…That must come in very handy." "It doesn't work with some names," he admits. "It didn't work with Maude, but then nothing worked with Maude." The joke was based on a legendary trick of George Gershwin, who kept a secret song to seduce women. He would sit down at the piano, pretend the girl had just inspired him to compose a song, then play the secret tune and incorporate her name into the lyric. Supposedly, it never failed.

The classical versus pop musical formula prompted Universal to capture a dynamic young singing star, Edna Mae Durbin, who had initially been signed by MGM. Her signing alarmed Judy Garland, who had given up her vaudeville career, as part of the Gumm Sisters, for a contract with MGM. Despite their potential rivalry, Durbin and Garland sparkled together in a screen test, where Garland, playing a rough-and-tumble American girl, sang in a jazz idiom, while Durbin, playing a European princess, sang in classical style. The test was followed with a one-reel short called *Every Sunday*, where "Edna" and "Judy," "classical" and "hot," play two friends who try to drum up interest in concerts at their local park. The studio had already decided, however, that it could not carry two young female singers, and when Louis B. Mayer saw the screen test, he supposedly said, "Drop the fat one," meaning Garland.

But it was the pretty, willowy Durbin who left when plans were scuttled for a film where she was to be featured. Joe Pasternak, a producer at Universal, wanted to do a film called *Three Smart Girls* (1936), about three sisters who save their parents' marriage from divorce. He had seen the MGM screen test of Durbin and Garland and wanted both girls, respectively, for the oldest and youngest sister roles, but MGM would release only Durbin. Pasternak grabbed her, and *Three Smart Girls* made Durbin, her first name changed from "Edna Mae" to "Deanna," an overnight star. When Garland saw the film and realized that Universal had put their complete faith behind Durbin while MGM had yet to feature Garland despite her long experience in vaudeville, she spent the entire night crying.

In *Three Smart Girls* (1936) and the other films Durbin made at Universal she presented songs purely as performance numbers. "Someone to Care for Me," for example, is first sung by Binnie Barnes, playing a scheming gold digger intent on marrying Charles Winninger, father of three girls determined to reunite their father with their mother. When youngest daughter Deanna is sent off to bed after dinner in her father's luxurious New York apartment, Barnes entertains everyone by sitting at the piano and singing "Someone to Care for Me." Deanna hears her in her bedroom overhead and causes a racket by moving furniture around. Winninger goes up to scold her, but father and daughter wind up laughing together. Later, as Winninger sits with his three daughters, his heart begins to soften, then Durbin melts it completely by criticizing Barnes's singing—pointing out her "poor tremolo"—and offering to sing the song as it should be sung. The result, ironically, points up the difference between cinematic and theatrical song: Barnes gave a movie song rendition which, in its way, is charming; Durbin's reprise, however, is utterly operatic. Still, the song functions as the start of the conversion of the father, weaning Winninger away from Barnes and back toward their mother. Deanna Durbin followed her success in *Three Smart Girls* with *One Hundred Men and a Girl* (1937), *Mad about Music* (1938), *That Certain Age* (1938), *Three Smart Girls Grow Up* (1939), and *First Love* (1939), but no matter what she sang or in what dramatic context, Deanna Durbin would always be performing.

So too, in a very different series of movies made at Twentieth Century-Fox in the 1930s, would Shirley Temple, whose films helped Fox move from near-bankruptcy to million-dollar profits between 1934 and 1936. She could have been given integral songs, since children, like clowns, blacks, and cartoon characters, can sing without having to have a realistic motivation. Temple, furthermore, had a charmingly child-like voice—not the operatic delivery of Deanna Durbin, Bobby Breen, and other youthful stars. Yet Twentieth Century-Fox presented her songs as performances. In her first feature film, *Baby Take a Bow* (1934), she sings only one song, "On Accounta I Love You," with her ex-con father to celebrate her birthday. She entertains aviators by singing "On the Good Ship Lollipop" in *Bright Eyes* (1934), and in *Curly Top* (1935), she regales her fellow inmates in an orphanage with "Animal Crackers in My Soup." While her singing outrages the headmistress, it enchants John Boles, playing a multimillionaire who has just joined the board of trustees. He asks to talk alone with Shirley, puts her on his knee, and charmed by her song, offers to adopt her. At his mansion, Boles, an amateur composer, writes a new song, "It's All So New to Me," as he imagines Shirley winking at him from the frames of paintings, such as *The Blue Boy*, which hang in his living room. In another performance number, which Shirley renders as part of a benefit show she has planned to raise money for her old orphanage, she sings "When I Grow Up," where she changes costumes offstage to become, first, a girl of "sweet sixteen," then a bride of "twenty-one," and finally, a grandmother. Teamed with Alice Faye and Ray Bolger in *Poor Little Rich Girl* (1936), one of the performance numbers, "You've Got to Eat Your Spinach, Baby," at least grows out of Shirley's aversion to spinach.

One of the few times Shirley Temple was given an integral song was in *Captain January* (1936), where she sings "The Right Somebody to Love" to her gruff old guardian, played by Guy Kibbee, as he reads a bedtime story to her. Then Shirley fantasizes that Kibbee is a baby, sitting in a high chair sucking his thumb, and she is the nurse who gives him his medicine and bottle. As in so many of Shirley Temple's films, her affection is for an older man, which probably was an important factor in her popularity during the Depression when so many men were out of work.

By the end of the decade, Shirley Temple's success began to wane, and in 1940 Fox released her from her contract—at the age of twelve. In more than forty films, Temple sang and danced but almost always within the performance convention. It would take Judy Garland to show how a young girl could give voice to her feelings of longing, wistfulness, and confusion in integral song.

7

OVER THE RAINBOW

Beginning with *The Wizard of Oz* (1939), no studio created and presented songs more imaginatively, lavishly, and integrally than MGM. That achievement was the result of a coordinated effort among several people who shared the belief that songs, even when presented as performances, must be expressive of character and advance the dramatic narrative. At the center of this group was Arthur Freed, a lyricist, who, when he became a producer, brought a songwriter's understanding to how song should be presented in film. The son of Max Freed, a Hungarian art dealer, Freed traveled all over the world as a child, acquiring a taste for art, particularly modern art, antiques, and music. He went to the prestigious Phillips Exeter Academy in New Hampshire where he wrote poetry and songs, then in 1914 returned to his family, which after his father's retirement, lived in a large house filled with art and antiques, overlooking Lake Washington in Seattle. Although Max Freed was an amateur musician who saw that his children took music lessons, he did not consider music an acceptable profession and urged his oldest son to attend the University of Washington and go on to become a lawyer.

One night, however, Freed went to the Orpheum Theatre in Seattle to see vaudevillian Gus Edwards, who was also a songwriter who had written "In My Merry Oldsmobile" (1905) and "By the Light of the Silvery Moon" (1909). Freed showed him some of his songs, and Edwards offered his encouragement as well as a job in one of his shows. Along with touring with Edwards's company, Freed worked in the Chicago branch of the Waterson, Berlin and Snyder music-publishing company, where he played his company's songs for vaudeville acts in search of new material. This experience at "plugging" gave Freed a sense of how song formulas could be refreshed and enhanced. Freed also wrote his own songs with composer Louis Silvers, some of which were used in the 1917 revue, *Over the Top*, featuring Fred and Adele Astaire in their Broadway debut.

Freed served in the army in World War I. Stationed at Camp Lewis in Washington, he was in charge of musical entertainment, giving him experience in producing shows. After the war, he wrote songs and "special material"—comic sketches—for Manhattan cabaret acts, adding yet another dimension to his theatrical apprenticeship. Returning to Los Angeles, Freed had his first songwriting success in 1923 with bandleaders Abe Lyman and Gus Arnheim on "I Cried for You." As Michael Lasser notes, the lyric "was an early example of Freed's search for different approaches to familiar material. 'A lot of people were writing torch songs,' he explained in later years. 'I felt, well, I will write one that takes revenge.'" Freed twisted the torch song cliché by having the singer exult, "Now I found two eyes just a little bit bluer,/ I found a heart just a little bit truer."

Gravitating to Hollywood, Freed found a position as an assistant director at Paramount, where he also played mood music on the sets of silent movies to help actors find their motivation. Together with composer Nacio Herb Brown, Freed wrote songs for annual revues at the Los Angeles Music Box Theatre. They also collaborated on revues at the Orange Grove Theatre, which Freed managed for four years. During his tenure, Freed hired a young singer from Spokane named Bing Crosby for his stage debut in one of the Orange Grove revues. Freed had already developed a shrewd eye—and ear—for musical talent.

For the 1927 edition of the annual *Hollywood Music Box Revue*, which featured Fanny Brice, Freed and Brown wrote "Singin' in the Rain," their first big hit. Two years later, Irving Thalberg selected the two West Coast songwriters to write the score for MGM's *Broadway Melody*. They went on to write such classic film songs as "Should I?" (*Lord Byron of Broadway*, 1930), "Temptation" (*Going Hollywood*, 1933), "All I Do Is Dream of You" (*Sadie McKee*, 1934), "You Are My Lucky Star" (*Broadway Melody of 1936*), and "Would You?" (*San Francisco*, 1936). During this period, Freed immersed himself in all aspects of film production. As fellow-lyricist Ned Washington recalled, "There were a lot of us songwriters working at Metro in those days. We'd all get to the studio at about 11:30 or so, and start working on our songs. All except Arthur Freed, that is. He would get to the studio by 8 or 9 o'clock, and he'd be on the set, learning camera angles and director's set ups, and things like that. To us, it seemed strange for a songwriter to be interested in those things."

In 1934, while he was still a staff lyricist at MGM, Freed hired a young piano player and vocal arranger named Roger Edens. Edens had come to Hollywood from Broadway, where he had played in the legendary pit orchestra for *Girl Crazy*, an ensemble that included Red Nichols, Jimmy Dorsey, Gene Krupa, Jack Teagarden, Benny Goodman, and Glenn Miller. When Ethel Merman's accompanist and vocal arranger suffered a heart attack after the show's opening night, Edens took over the on-stage role and later went with Merman to Hollywood. Edens and Freed shared the conviction that song must be integral, expressive, and dramatic. Given the relatively brief length of a film, compared to that of a Broadway musical, song had to be integral to character and story, growing out of dramatic situations and advancing the narrative. "I brought in a whole new crowd of people," Freed later reflected. "I wanted a fresh start from what had been done before, a combination of the new ideas that had been happening on the stage and what could be done with film. The early musicals were novelties, but few of them were *real* musicals."

Fortunately for both men, a performer came along who would be the perfect exponent for the way they wanted to present songs. Composer Burton Lane was impressed by Frances Gumm, one of "The Gumm Sisters," a vaudeville act from Grand Rapids, Minnesota. She had changed her last name to "Garland" when, "on a bill with George Jessel, he told her she was as pretty as a 'garland of flowers'... Hoagy Carmichael's song 'Judy' inspired the rest of the name. Frances Gumm became Judy Garland." Lane brought the thirteen-year-old to Jack Robbins, who ran MGM's sheet-music publishing company. After hearing her sing, Robbins set up an audition the next day for Freed and Edens. "Garland and her sister came to audition for me," Freed recalled. "Her mother played the worst piano I ever heard. So I said to the little girl, 'You just sing by yourself!' She sang 'Zing! Went the Strings of My Heart.' That was it! You just couldn't mistake that talent. There was so much of it." Both Freed and Edens flipped. "The biggest thing to happen to the MGM musical," Edens later said, "was the discovery of Judy Garland."

Freed rushed across the Metro lot, barged into Louis B. Mayer's office, and insisted the studio head hear her. Mayer loved her singing but he worried about her looks (he would, according to Hollywood legend, refer to her, with sarcastic affection, as "my little hunchback"). Playing it safe, he planned to use her in a feature with another young performer, the operatic—and beautiful—Deanna Durbin, but Durbin's contract at MGM had lapsed, and Garland was left idle. She was sent to New York with Edens to work in vaudeville, and then both came back to Hollywood where she did the weekly radio program *The Camel Caravan*. Edens taught Garland that singing into a microphone required her to tone down her dynamic vaudeville delivery, "to sing softly and from the heart."

Garland's break came when MGM threw a birthday party for Clark Gable, who was turning thirty-six. Freed organized the event, and he asked Edens to handle the music. Edens put Judy on the program and arranged a song and dialogue number for her to sing as a fan of Clark Gable. Taking a 1913 song by Joseph McCarthy and James Monaco, "You Made Me Love You," which Al Jolson had made into a standard, Edens bowdlerized the lyrics by changing such lines as "Gimme, Gimme, what I cry for/ You know you got the brand of kisses that I'd die for" to something less impassioned for a teenage girl: "I must tell you how I'm feeling/ The very mention of your name sets my heart reeling." He also composed a new verse for the song that portrayed her as a fan writing a letter to the star: "Dear Mr. Gable, I am writing this to you." After she sang one chorus of the song, Edens had her break into a monlogue—the same combination of singing and talking and singing again that had electrified audiences when Al Jolson did "Blue Skies" in *The Jazz Singer*. "Ah, gee, Mr. Gable, I don't want to bother you," Judy begins, then, after gushing out her affection for him and his movies, she reprises the chorus in a dramatic expression of adolescent adulation.

Her performance led to a role in *Broadway Melody of 1938*, where she sang the song—and spoke the monologue—to a photograph of Gable. In the scene, her mother, played by Sophie Tucker, scolds Judy after she finds an autographed photo of Gable in her bed. Warning the child not to dream about movie stars, Tucker leaves and Judy props open her scrapbook on her desk and writes a letter to Gable while singing—and speaking—to his photograph. Her performance was precisely the kind of intimate, expressive, dramatic rendition of song that Freed and Edens wanted to create in film.

Broadway Melody of 1938 was also Nacio Herb Brown's final film under his contract with MGM, and he left the studio to devote himself to classical composition. Freed now was at a turning point in his career. Drawing on his standing invitation for breakfast at Louis B. Mayer's house, he turned back from his journey to the studio one morning and called upon Mayer. Pointing out that *Broadway Melody of 1938* was getting critical acclaim and doing superbly at the box office, he raved about Garland. "They love the kid!" Freed exulted. "I'd put my bet on her if I were a producer." "Well, Arthur, now is the time," Mayer replied. "Find a property and make a picture."

Freed then chose a decidedly ambitious property for his first production. *The Wizard of Oz* by Lyman Frank Baum was an exotic fantasy (though, beneath the surface, it was also a political allegory about the way farmers, symbolized by the Scarecrow, and factory workers, symbolized by the Tin Man, had united in the Populist movement against the forces of Wall Street, symbolized by the Wicked Witch of the East, only to see their cause go down with the defeat of William Jennings Bryan, symbolized by the Cowardly Lion, in the election of 1896). *The Wizard of Oz* had been the basis of a Broadway musical in 1903 and two silent movies (in 1910 and 1925). As a movie musical, it would involve complex sets, costumes, and special effects—a challenge for a first-time producer. With one of the biggest budgets an MGM film had seen in years, more than $2 million, the studio, following in the tradition of Irving Thalberg, did not plan to make a large profit on the film. "Once a year," explained lyricist Yip Harburg, "they did a loser for prestige." *The Wizard of Oz* would be MGM's prestige "loser" for 1939—the studio's way of occasionally living up to the motto that surrounded the roaring head of its roaring lion logo: "Ars Gratia Artis"—"Art for the Sake of Art." The final cost for the film was $2,777,000, and in its initial release it took in $3,017,000—not a "loser" but compared to *Babes in Arms*, released the same year, costing $748,000 and grossing $3,335,000, hardly a profitable undertaking.

Mayer was aware of the problems posed by *The Wizard of Oz* as the basis for a musical film, particularly one by a neophyte producer, so he brought in the more experienced Mervyn LeRoy, who had directed such films as *Gold Diggers of 1933* at Warner Bros. Mayer made LeRoy executive producer and Freed the associate producer. Mayer hoped LeRoy would step into the shoes of Irving Thalberg, who had died of pneumonia in 1936 after a typically cavalier gesture: when his wife, Norma Shearer, had shivered at an outdoor evening social event, the frail Thalberg had gallantly removed his jacket and placed it around her shoulders.

LeRoy, who would not be happy as a producer and would soon go back to his role as a film director, sensed that *The Wizard of Oz* would need an established star and asked Mayer to approach Darryl F. Zanuck at Twentieth Century-Fox for the services of Shirley Temple. Zanuck agreed only if his studio got Clark Gable and Jean Harlow on loan for a picture. Freed, who had chosen *The Wizard of Oz* expressly as a vehicle for Judy Garland, fought against Shirley Temple as star and enlisted the support of Roger Edens. After Edens auditioned Temple, he reported back to Freed. "What can I say, Arthur? Her vocal limitations are insurmountable." The fact that Temple had presented virtually all of her songs as performances ill-suited her for the kind of expressive and integral songs Freed and Edens wanted and knew they could get from Judy Garland. When the deal between Twentieth Century-Fox and MGM fell through because of Harlow's sudden death, LeRoy approached Universal for the loan of Deanna Durbin, but was again rebuffed. Finally, Freed persuaded Mayer to give the role to Judy Garland.

Since LeRoy was still shooting another film, much of the preproduction work on *The Wizard of Oz* was left to Freed. He started working with screenwriters Noel Langley, Florence Ryerson, and Edgar Allan Woolf, the first three of ultimately eleven screenwriters for the film. They resisted the temptation to base the script on the 1903 Broadway musical and instead, with copious suggestions from Freed, went back to Baum's book. In one of Freed's memos to the writers, he clearly is thinking of song as a vehicle that would carry the story: "I believe that we should go through the whole script with the thought in mind of using the minimum of dialogue," he observes and urges the writers to get "a rhythm through the whole script."

To write songs that expressed character, developed dramatic conflict, and advanced the narrative, Freed initially considered his friend Jerome Kern, with lyrics by Ira Gershwin or Dorothy Fields. But ultimately Freed was making a thoroughly new kind of musical film, and he decided to go with a younger team, Yip Harburg and Harold Arlen. Although Freed and Harburg had never met, Harburg realized that "Arthur had sensed my love of whimsy, and he was right. He told me to read *The Wizard of Oz*. I read the book and loved it. It was my sort of thing." "Harburg had a great sense of fantasy in his lyrics," Freed later recalled, and Harburg responded to Freed's idea of using song to replace dialogue as a way to express character and advance the narrative. "One function of song," Harburg said, "is to simplify, to take the clutter out of too much plot and too many characters, to telescope everything into one emotional idea."

In Yip Harburg, Freed gained more than a lyricist, for, like Freed himself, Harburg threw himself into all aspects of a production. When the screenwriters decided to include the character of the Cowardly Lion along with the Scarecrow and Tin Man, Harburg suggested to Freed and LeRoy that they cast Bert Lahr, who had starred in one of Harburg's stage revues, *Life Begins at 8:40*, in 1934. "Put up your dukes! Put up your paws!" Harburg said, quoting from the script. "Can you imagine Bert doing that?" Arlen and Harburg had only two months to turn out songs that would be more closely integrated with characters and story than in any previous MGM musical. That integration initially was limited to the sections of the film that take place in the Land of Oz. The old shibboleth that actors needed a realistic excuse to break into song would be honored by having the opening scenes in Kansas shot in sepia tones—without song—then move to Oz where the fantasy setting and Technicolor would make anything believable—including characters bursting into song and dance.

Song takes up nearly half of the movie, 45 minutes of the film's 101-minute running time, introducing characters, developing conflict, advancing the narrative. The project brought out Harburg's love of Gilbert and Sullivan patter, and some of the lyrics stretched, as he told Max Wilk, into "not just songs but *scenes*," such as those that introduce the Munchkins, the Lullaby Girls, and the Lollipop Guild. The greatest patter sequence, however, comes with Dorothy's meeting the Scarecrow, Tin Man, and Cowardly Lion. Harburg and Arlen had written "I'm Hanging on to You" for their 1937 stage revue *Hooray for What!* but the song was cut from the show. Taking the melody, Harburg indulged his love of puns and other wordplay to introduce the Scarecrow as a character who is a lot more clever than he appears:

I'd unravel ev'ry riddle
For any individle

In trouble or in pain. . . .
And perhaps I'd deserve you
And be even worthy erv you
If I only had a brain.

Then the Tin Man, whose lyric is less verbally playful, more emotionally earnest, befitting his longing for a heart:

Just to register emotion
"Jealousy," "Devotion,"
And really feel the part.
I would stay young and chipper
And I'd lock it with a zipper
If I only had a heart.

And finally the Cowardly Lion, whose lyric bristles with slangy tough talk that belies his timidity:

Life is sad, believe me, Missy,
When you're born to be a sissy
Without the vim and verve . . .
But I could show my prow-ess
Be a lion, not a mow-ess
If I only had the nerve.

Harburg's wordplay carried over into a special number for Lahr, "If I Were King of the Forest," where he butchers words in a fantasy of power, rhyming "respect to me" with "genuflect to me," "my tail would lash" with "I would show compash," "rhinocerous" with "Imposserous," "hippopotamous" with "top to bottomamus" and "elephant" with "wrap him up in cellophant."

After a marvelously song-driven first half, however, in the latter part of *The Wizard of Oz* songs tell the story only sporadically. As Harburg later reflected, "I am always disappointed when I see the picture . . . because they deleted several songs at the end of the picture and they made it a chase and I feel the loss of music there; they should not have done that. Several songs were taken out at the end of the picture which should have been in—it would have been a much better picture." The major cut was "The Jitterbug," in which Dorothy, the Scarecrow, the Tin Man, and the Cowardly Lion are attacked by insects on the way to the castle of the Wicked Witch. Although it took five weeks to film and cost $80,000, "The Jitterbug" is a slow number that doesn't advance the story or develop the characters. Viewed today in restored footage, it is difficult to imagine that it would have enhanced the second half of *The Wizard of Oz*.

The film's most famous song expresses character and provides an important narrative transition. From the very first, Arthur Freed had been concerned about the abrupt shift from Kansas to Oz: "There is no tie-over from Kansas to Oz," he complained to the screenwriters. Finally, he decided to resolve the problem with a song. The songwriters, however, were too caught up in their patter sequences to create a song set in Kansas. "Harburg and Arlen didn't want to do a ballad for the picture," Freed recalled, "I talked them into writing 'Over the Rainbow.'"

Faced with the demand for a ballad, Arlen encountered writer's block. "I can't tell you the misery that a composer goes through when the whole score is written but he hasn't got that big theme song that Louis B. Mayer is waiting for," Harburg recalled of his collaborator's dilemma. "He surely sweated it out, but he couldn't get a tune." One evening Arlen and his wife decided to go to a movie at Grauman's Chinese Theatre, and as they drove past Schwab's drugstore on Sunset Boulevard, where so many stars had been discovered, a "broad, long-lined melody" popped into the composer's mind and he jotted it down. "It was as if the Lord said, 'Well, here it is, now stop worrying about it!'" When Arlen played the song for Harburg at midnight, however, the lyricist balked at setting a lyric to a melody that began with two notes that leapt up an entire octave interval and was filled with "symphonic sweep and bravura." "'Oh, no, not for little Dorothy!' Harburg. exploded 'That's for Nelson Eddy.'" The two men took the melody to their friend Ira Gershwin, even though it was now two o'clock in the morning. When Ira listened to Arlen play the music with resounding chords and flourishes, he stopped the composer and asked him to just pick out the notes of the melody with one finger. When Harburg heard the melody in its bone-simple purity, he realized it would work as a song for Dorothy.

Proudly noting that Frank Baum's book never mentions a rainbow, Harburg explained that the image came to him as the one truly colorful thing a Kansas farm girl could use to brighten up her daydreams. The image also prepared for the transition from the sepia tones in which the Kansas scenes were filmed to the Technicolor splendor of Oz. As Harburg later recalled, however, fitting words to Arlen's soaring melodic line was painstaking work for a lyricist:

"Over the Rainbow Is Where I Want to Be" was my title, the title I gave Harold. A title has to ring a bell, has to blow a couple of Roman candles off. But he gave me a tune with those first two notes. I tried *I'll go over the rainbow, Someday over the rainbow or the other side of the rainbow.*

I had difficulty coming to the idea of *Somewhere*. For a while I thought I would just leave those first two notes out. It was a long time before I came to *Somewhere over the rainbow*....I was given a tune which, for the most part, I couldn't use consonants. I couldn't write, "Say bud." It wouldn't sing. You have to use open vowels. "Somewhere o-ver the rainbow…" The "o" comes right in—that is an important part of the writing. So, on top of that playfulness of words, on top of the meaning and the poetry, the sound has an importance.

Harburg fitted Arlen's leaping notes with long vowels in the three A-sections—"lullaby," "skies are blue," "why can't I?" and, most deftly, the arch from the "o" in "Over" to the "o" at the end of "rainbow." In the release, however, Arlen shifts to short, repeated notes, and Harburg's lyric follows with short vowels and crisp consonants:

Where troubles melt like lemon drops
Away above the chimney tops

The real magic of the song comes when Harburg and Arlen decided to extend it beyond the AABA standard formula by adding a repetition of the B melody but drawing upon the lyric of the final A-section:

If happy little bluebirds fly
Beyond the rainbow
Why oh why can't I?

This final section fuses the A and B melodies and lyrics to give the song an ending at once hesitant yet hopeful. Garland's delivery reflects the tutoring she had received from Roger Edens, for rather than singing the song in theatrical fashion, she renders it in the intimate, informal style that was better suited for movies. It was the last song Harburg and Arlen wrote for the score and the last to be filmed.

The fate of the song was precarious. Almost every time the film was previewed, plans called for cutting "Over the Rainbow." As Harburg recalled, Victor Fleming, one of several directors assigned to the film, said,

"I'm sorry to say that the whole first part of that show is awful slow because of that number, 'Over the Rainbow.' We gotta take it out." Now, when a man like that comes in, who doesn't talk but makes pronunciamentos, you've got to listen. Mervyn LeRoy, who was the producer of the picture, suddenly regressed to the little Mervyn Levine again, and the song was out of the picture.

Harold and I just went crazy; we knew that this was the ballad of the show; this is the number we were depending on. We decided to take action. We went to the front office; we went to the back office; we pleaded; we cried; we tore our hair. . . . Finally, Arthur Freed went to Louis B. Mayer and pleaded with him.

Freed must have known, with his instincts as a songwriter, that "Over the Rainbow" was one of the great presentations of song in film, one in which music, lyric, character, and setting coalesce as a child expresses a universal emotion that fits a particular dramatic moment. Sam Katz, executive producer of MGM's musical division, complained, "This score is above the heads of children." Jack Robbins, head of music publishing, chimed in that it was like "a child's piano exercise. Nobody will sing it—who'll buy the sheet music?" Freed, in perhaps his finest moment, laid his job on the line: "The song stays—or I go! It's as simple as that." Louis B. Mayer tried to make light of the controversy by saying, "Let the boys have the damned song. Get it back in the picture; it can't hurt." At the Academy Awards, where nearly every Oscar went to *Gone with the Wind, The Wizard of Oz* won for Best Original Musical Score and "Over the Rainbow" was named Best Song. Arthur Freed's stature as a producer of musical films rose immensely at MGM, as did that of Judy Garland, who was given a special Oscar for her performance.

The Wizard of Oz was a tremendous advance in the integral presentation of song in film, but its base in a fantasy world made it difficult to carry over to films in more realistic settings. The next movies produced by Arthur Freed were either adaptations of Broadway shows, such as *Strike Up the Band* (1940), *Lady Be Good* (1941), and *Cabin in the Sky* (1943), or conventional backstagers such as *Babes on Broadway* (1942) and *For Me and My Gal* (1942). Still, songs were integral to the story and characters. In *Babes in Arms* (1939), for example, "Where or When" was one of the few songs Freed retained from Rodgers and Hart's superb original score, but it was presented in a way that defined the difference between a stage song and a film song. It is first sung as a rehearsal number by Douglas McPhail and Betty Jaynes in an operatic fashion reminiscent of Nelson Eddy and Jeanette MacDonald (in fact, they are sitting in a canoe, evoking the setting of "Rose-Marie"). Mickey Rooney criticizes their rendition to Judy as too overblown and lacking in "feeling." When he asks if she knows what he means, she says she does, then demonstrates it by singing a chorus with utter informality and understated passion. Like "Thanks for the Memory" and

"Easy to Love," "Where or When" is part of the conversation between her and Mickey, a demonstration of how a song should be sung in a movie.

When Arthur Freed produced *Strike Up the Band*, he threw out the satirical script about war profiteering and most of the songs by the Gershwins, substituting new ones, mostly by himself and Roger Edens. The film became a vehicle for Mickey Rooney and Judy Garland as high school kids entering a band contest. One of the new songs added to the film was "Our Love Affair," first sung at the piano by Mickey Rooney to demonstrate his newest song to Judy Garland. Garland then sits beside him and reprises it in a fuller rendition complete with verse and second chorus, once again drifting from singing into talking and back again. Staging a production number for the song, however, posed a problem for director Busby Berkeley. Freed turned to the newest member of his MGM team, Vincente Minnelli, who also had come from Broadway with experience as a costume designer, art director, and director. "I asked him to come out," Freed said, "and he came for the price of his hotel bill." At first, Minnelli was given no assignment so that he "had the opportunity to absorb the atmosphere and study the work then going on in the various departments of the Freed unit." "When I arrived in Hollywood," Minnelli recalled, "I didn't look down on musicals as so many people who were doing them there did, treating them as a romp, a slapstick, nothing to be taken seriously. Busby Berkeley's large-scale numbers never moved me. I'm only interested in musical stories in which one can achieve a complete integration of dancing, singing, sound and vision. I would often look at Mamoulian's *Love Me Tonight*, as it was such a perfect example of how to make a musical."

Freed told Minnelli that Berkeley was having trouble thinking up a production number for "Our Love Affair" and asked him if he had any ideas. Minnelli remembered an article in *Life* magazine about Henri Rox, a German sculptor who transformed pieces of fruit into musical instruments. Minnelli suggested the number portray an orchestra made up of a pear as a violinist, a long-haired leek who plays an organ with asparagus pipes, and bassists with oranges for heads who play pineapple halves—all led by a conductor with a head of grapes reminiscent of Leopold Stokowski. In the movie, Mickey fantasizes to Judy about leading an orchestra, then arranges fruit on her dining room table to simulate members of the orchestra, who come to life to play "Our Love Affair."

The best of Garland and Rooney's songs was "How About You?" by Ralph Freed (Arthur's brother) and Burton Lane for *Babes on Broadway*. The pair play two New York kids trying to make it in show business, and after meeting Garland and walking her back to her apartment, Mickey tells her he can tell she has talent—"lighting everything around you"—and asks her to sing a song. "How do you know I can?" she asks. "Because you sing when you talk," he replies.

Encouraged, she launches into "How About You?" a simple catalogue song that juxtaposes urbane images—"I like New York in June…I like a Gershwin tune"—with prosaic and romantic ones—"I like potato chips/Moonlight and motor trips." Mickey joins her on a second chorus with similar juxtapositions— "I like banana splits, late suppers at the Ritz"—and exchanges of dialogue. When she sings, "I like Jack Benny's jokes," he can only muster a faint, "To a degree." Musically, Burton Lane provides a jaunty framework for Freed's witty lyric that bristles with surprising intervals, unusual cadences, and effectively repeated phrases. Yet, as Alec Wilder observes, "It does present in thirty-two measures a perfectly fashioned melodic line…It comes off so naturally that one forgets how unusual it is." Equally simple but striking is the way Garland and Rooney shift from the second chorus into a patter sequence of rhymed dialogue—"I'm so delighted I've ignited a spark in you"—that combines talking and singing. Finally, they dance around the tiny apartment, Mickey leaping over the piano bench, couch, and chairs then out the door and down the street in a wonderfully choreographed sequence by Busby Berkeley that has none of the opulence of his more characteristic productions but is a minimalistically "rationed" number appropriate to its wartime setting.

With *Meet Me in St. Louis* (1944), Freed, Edens, and Minnelli undertook another film, like *The Wizard of Oz*, where songs were integrally woven into story and character. The basis for the movie seemed an unlikely property. Sally Benson had written a series of sketches for the *New Yorker* about growing up in St. Louis at the time of the St. Louis World's Fair, which celebrated the centenary of the Louisiana Purchase. Even Benson herself, whom Freed brought to MGM to work on a screen treatment, did not consider her work suitable for dramatization. "Nothing much happens," she observed, "just little incidents." MGM executives criticized the project, one asking, "What the hell is Arthur trying to do? After all the glamour he has given us! What is in this dull family moving to New York?" What Freed sensed intuitively was that unlike all of the backstagers, operettas, and most other musical films that preceded it, *Meet Me in St. Louis* would present songs as part of the texture of everyday family life. As he explained to a skeptical Mayer, "The boys are all harping on 'there's no plot! Well, I'll make a plot with song and dance and music. That's the way my characters will come to life—that'll be my plot!" Freed then added, "I want to make this into the most delightful piece of Americana ever. Sets, costumes…it'll cost a bit, but it will be great!" Mayer reluctantly gave his go ahead but added, "Either you'll learn or we'll learn."

Freed found a sympathetic collaborator in Vincente Minnelli, who saw the wonderful visual possibilities for the presentation of song in the most ordinary domestic American contexts. Together, they insisted that a whole new house and street set be erected on the MGM back lot rather than use the Andy Hardy set, as Mayer had urged. They then saw that every detail was authentic—down to a copy of the 1904 Sears and Roebuck catalog.

Judy Garland, however, was reluctant to accept the role of Esther, another teenage part when she longed for an adult role. She'd been warned that the main character in the story was not Esther but her younger sister Tootie (who played Sally Benson as a child). She was also wary of working with Minnelli, who had directed only one previous film. "Judy came to see me," Minnelli recalled. "She thought—a director from New York. 'This is awful!' she said, 'isn't it?' I said, 'No, I think it's marvelous.'"

Freed had initially considered using only period songs in the film, such as the title song, which is sung by one family member after another, from the youngest child to the grandfather, as they move about the house. As a popular song of 1904, it naturally is on everyone's lips, and in the scene the song knits the family together. Such a "'passed-along song,'" as Jane Feuer observes, "appears to be a specifically cinematic technique," because the camera can follow the course of the song in a way that would be impossible in a stage production.

Freed changed his mind about using only period songs after he heard the work of Ralph Blane and Hugh Martin. The young team had started out as vocal arrangers for such Broadway shows as *Du Barry Was a Lady* (1939), *Cabin in the Sky* (1940), and *Pal Joey* (1940), then had success with their own show, *Best Foot Forward* (1941). Freed asked them to write several new songs for *Meet Me in St. Louis* that worked integrally with character and story. Their first song was an introspective number for Garland, reminiscent of "Over the Rainbow," that expresses her longing for her handsome next-door neighbor. After an unsuccessful attempt to catch his eye as she sits on her porch, Judy goes inside and sings to herself as she gazes out her window at his house. The verse of the song is chattily prosaic, ending with their street addresses:

> *So it's clear to see*
> *There's no hope for me,*
> *Though I live at fifty-one thirty-five*
> *Kensington Avenue*
> *And he lives at fifty-one thirty-three.*

Blane and Martin worked so closely from Benson's *New Yorker* stories that they only altered the address (it was Benson herself who lived at 5133 Kensington Avenue) to make it rhyme.

The chorus is winsome, capturing an adolescent's first crush in casually conversational terms,

How can I ignore the boy next door?
I love him more than I can say.

then in childish petulance:

Doesn't try to please me,
Doesn't even tease me,
And he never even sees me glance his way.

The chorus ends in plangent feminine rhymes:

I just adore him,
Though I can't ignore him,
The boy next door.

To underscore the unresolved longing of the lyric, Martin's melody in the chorus, as Alec Wilder points out, relies on a "device…a series of suspended dominant  ninth chords." Throughout the song Garland stands or sits at her window, but after singing she twirls around the room, primps before a full-length mirror, and dances a few hesitant steps. When she returns to the window, she sings the last two lines of the chorus again as the camera moves in for a close-up. As the song concludes, she lets the curtain she has been holding back slowly sweep across the window, as if we had been watching a stage performance.

In a very different vein, Blane and Martin wrote a rousing number for Garland and her friends to sing as they take the trolley to the site of the fair grounds. "Hugh and I thought it was too corny to be on the nose in writing a song about a trolley," Blane recalled. "Instead we went home and wrote a marvelous song that would be great to sing *on* the trolley—not *about* it.…Arthur said, 'I love it! It's great! But,' he said, 'you know what, I'll use it in *The Follies*. I know exactly where it should go. Now, about the spot where Judy sings *about* the trolley here.'…We knew he was not happy with the number for that spot, so we went home and tried again. We wrote four numbers. Each time we'd feel we had a smash. They'd love it, but Arthur would say, 'I'll put it in *The Follies*.' He wanted a song *about* the trolley. He was right, but we didn't think so. Anyway, in desperation, and a bit of anger too, we went home and just said, 'Oh hell! Let's just write something about the trolley, and to hell with it!'" Looking through some books about St. Louis in the Beverly Hills Public Library, Blane found a photograph of a trolley from 1903. "Believe it or not, under the picture was written 'Clang, Clang, Clang Went the Trolley.' Well, I dashed back—told Hugh the title and we wrote it in about ten minutes." They cast the melody in the strophic form of nineteenth-century song, where a refrain alternates with a series of verses that narrate a story. When they demonstrated the song in Roger Edens's office, Freed, his songwriter instincts justified yet again, exclaimed, "That's the song for Judy!"

The song is presented as a performance number but one that resonates integrally with the scene. Judy has finally met Tom Drake as the boy next door, and they have agreed to meet to take the special trolley to the fairgrounds. When she boards, however, he has not yet arrived, and the car takes off without him. All the other teenagers are singing the song exultantly, but Judy wanders to the rear, silent and forlorn. As the first chorus finishes, however, she spots Drake running to catch up with the trolley, and she sings the verse. With its detailed description of a woman in a "high starched collar," "high-topped shoes," and "my hair piled high upon my head," the lyric clearly does not portray her, nor when she sings of meeting a young man on the trolley in a "light brown derby" and "bright green tie" does that description match what Drake is wearing. Instead, the song's description of a love-at-first-sight meeting on the trolley is a joyous parallel to the previous scene at the end of the party at her house where she and Drake put out the gas lights in the chandeliers, smitten with each other in quiet chiaroscuro. Now the song gives her the opportunity to sing about falling in love with him, indirectly, as she recounts an imaginary meeting with a stranger on the trolley:

He tipped his hat
And took a seat.
He said he hoped he hadn't stepped
    upon my feet.

The genteel meeting suits the Victorian costumes and manners of the group, but as the chorus develops, Judy expresses a more than genteel passion:

As he started to go
Then I started to know

How it feels
When the universe reels.

When she sings the second chorus, her feelings make her even bolder;

> *As he started to leave,*
> *I took hold of his sleeve with my hand,*
> *And as if it were planned,*

He stayed on with me
And it was grand,
Just to stand with his hand
Holding mine,
To the end of the line.

By this point, Drake has boarded the car and made his way through the crowd to the seat beside her, and she quickly reverts to a demure Victorian maiden. Yet as the rest of the crowd joins her in singing about the "Clang, clang, clang of the trolley," "Ding, ding, ding" of the bell, and "Chug, chug, chug" of the motor, mechanical energy that resounds with the "Zing, zing, zing" and "Thump, thump, thump" of her heartstrings so that the trolley ride manifests a passionate power that she only expresses in song.

Blane and Martin's last song for the film was fully integrated with plot and character. The father has told the family that his law firm is transferring him to New York and that they will move after the Christmas holidays. Everyone else is upset at the thought of leaving their beloved St. Louis just before the great fair, but no one is more distraught than the youngest daughter, "Tootie," played by Margaret O'Brien. Older sister Judy Garland tries to reconcile her to the move with a song, but the lyric reveals her own unhappiness. Pointing out that O'Brien can take all of her toys and dolls with her to New York, Garland jokes that it would be impossible to take the snowmen they had built in the front yard. The song Garland sings, "Have Yourself a Merry Little Christmas," has a bittersweet character that emerges from

the catchphrase that forms the title, the sour grapes tone of "Have yourself a merry little party without me." Originally, the lyric was even grimmer:

Have yourself a merry little Christmas
It may be your last.
Next year we will all be living in the past.

But Garland, who had been entertaining troops stationed in California thought the time was not right for such despair. "The mood of the song was negative," Blane recalled. "Roger didn't say anything nor did Arthur; but they brought Judy in to hear it. 'I love the song,' Judy said, 'but it's too sad. If that lyric is sad and I'm sad on top of it, the audience is going to say, 'Oh my God,' and they're going to be leaving the theatre.'" Blane revised the lyric to:

> *Have yourself a merry little Christmas,*
> *Let your heart be light.*
> *Next year all our troubles will be out of sight.*

Still, the melancholy undertone remains:

> *Some day soon we all will be together.*
> *If the Fates allow.*
> *Until then we'll have to muddle through somehow*
> *So have yourself a merry little Christmas now.*

(When the song was published in sheet music, Blane again tried to lighten its tone by changing the penultimate line to "Hang a shining star upon the highest bough.")

At its conclusion a tearful Margaret O'Brien rushes out of Garland's room and smashes the snowmen in the yard with a club—a violent gesture that persuades her father to cancel their planned move to New York. (In real life, alas, Sally Benson's father moved his family to New York, and Benson, upon whom O'Brien's character is based, missed the Fair.)

The next great achievement in the presentation of integral song in film by the Freed unit was inspired by Roger Edens's seeing *Oklahoma!* on Broadway, which ran for a record-breaking 2,212 performances. More important, with this show Rodgers and Hammerstein established the principle, advanced by such earlier musicals as *Show Boat* (1927), *Pal Joey* (1940), and *Lady in the Dark* (1941), that songs should be integral to the characters and story of a musical rather than free-standing "numbers" that stopped the narrative—the same principle that Freed, Edens, and others had been nurturing at MGM. When Edens proposed that MGM create its own western musical, Freed considered the story of the young women who had come west to work in Fred Harvey's chain of restaurants that stood along the railroad line that followed the Santa Fe Trail. These establishments introduced a refinement that, as much as anything else, helped tame the West.

Seeing another chance to produce a musical film steeped in Americana, Freed set a bevy of screenwriters to work and brought in Johnny Mercer and Harry Warren to write the score. Even before the script was complete, Edens, as associate producer, met with Mercer and Warren, who had worked together at Warner Bros. on typical backstagers, to let them know that the songs in *The Harvey Girls* (1946) had to be fully integrated into the story. The song that Mercer and Warren wrote to open the picture is sung by Judy Garland as she stands on the back platform of a train car. With the scenery of the west rolling past, she sings of roaming to a valley "where the evening sun goes down," building a home, and sitting in a rocking chair beside her husband "as the evening sun goes down."

In the train car, she meets a group of "Harvey Girls" going to the same town where they will work in a Fred Harvey restaurant. Judy confesses that she is a mail-order bride who has never seen her fiancé, but she reads from  one of his letters that has a lyrical description of open country, with mountain sunlight and clean wind, that needs to be settled. Her reading of the letter alters, retrospectively, the opening song, for we realize that she was singing a lyric based upon his letters about the West. When she arrives and meets her groom, the self-described "mangy old buzzard" Chill Wills, he recognizes the disparity between them and confesses that the letters he sent her were really written by John Hodiak, the proprietor of the town saloon. While Garland forgives Wills, she tears into Hodiak for his deceptive ploy by quoting a line from one of his letters, "When the setting sun lowers its mantle of purest gold over the little valley that shall soon be our home…" What she does not realize is that Hodiak really does cherish a secluded valley outside of town where he goes for aesthetic and spiritual solace. While he cannot reveal this dimension of himself to anyone in town, he pours it into the letters he wrote to Garland. The opening song thus gains another integral dimension in that it expresses Hodiak's secret lyricism about the West.

The big production number in *The Harvey Girls* was "On the Atchison, Topeka and the Santa Fe," which celebrates the arrival of Garland and the Harvey girls on the train. Mercer had mentioned to Warren that he once noticed a phrase on a railroad boxcar, "The Atchison, Topeka & Santa Fe." "I thought it had a nice, lyrical quality to it," he said. "Like Stephen Vincent Benét says, 'I've fallen in love with American place names.'" When he suggested the phrase as a song title, Warren said, "Fine, I've just the right tune for it." "It was an easy one to write," Mercer said, "As I recall, it took me about an hour."

Mercer may have been exhibiting his usual patrician pose of never having to work hard on his lyrics. In truth, he was a painstakingly slow worker, a perfectionist who sometimes took up to a year to complete a lyric. Perhaps aware of Mercer's slow work habits, Roger Edens did not even assign him to write the elaborate set of verses that introduced each of the Harvey girls. Instead, Edens himself, with vocal coach Katie Thompson, wrote verses such as "Oh, I'm from Chillicothe—my middle name's Hiawathy/ I'm going to get the gold in them thar hills/ So I said good-by-o Ohio." The com-

bination of chatty verses and rousing chorus, culminating in Garland, Ray Bolger, and the rest of the cast "chugging" alongside the train as it pulls out of the station makes for a great production number, the song literally driving the on-screen narrative. When Mercer saw the scene, however, he was furious that he had had no role in crafting the extra verses. "They're going to make me look like an idiot," he fumed. "Everybody's going to think I wrote that junk." Mercer took his protest to Freed, hoping for sympathy from a fellow lyricist, but Freed simply said, "It's done, it's too late. What are you talking about? It's wonderful." Mercer was intractable, however. Although the song earned him his first Oscar, he refused to attend the Academy Awards ceremony.

Not every original film musical produced by Arthur Freed turned to gold. Freed had read a fairy-tale story by Tyrolean writer Ludwig Bemelmans and thought it would be a wonderful vehicle to showcase lovely Lucille Bremer—despite the fact that her voice would have to be dubbed—opposite Fred Astaire in *Yolanda and the Thief* (1945). Freed decided to write lyrics himself and collaborated with Harry Warren on a score that took only three weeks to complete. Despite the direction of Minnelli, not one of the song presentations was enduring. For all of his dedication to integral song, Freed created most of the numbers as performances that highlighted Bremer's dancing talent. The failure of

the film reflected how crucial it was to have not only producers, directors, songwriters, and choreographers think in terms of integral song but to have performers, such as Garland and Astaire, who could render such songs as expressions of character and dramatic situation.

Even when all the requisite talent was assembled, however, the results could still be disappointing, as in *The Pirate* (1948), which had Garland, Gene Kelly, Minnelli as director, and a score by Cole Porter. Porter, after his successful Broadway shows of the 1930s, had been crippled in a horseback-riding accident in 1937. While he continued to write both stage shows and films, his success diminished until it was rumored that he was "written out." It took a suggestion from Gene Kelly that he write a clown number for *The Pirate* to stir Porter into action. As a boy growing up in Peru, Indiana, headquarters for the Hagenback and Wallace Circus, Porter loved seeing elephants barge into the local drugstore, watching the bareback riders train, and talking to the Wild Man of Borneo, who spent winters shining shoes in the town barbershop. "The lure and love of the circus filled our thoughts," a boyhood friend recalled, adding that "Porter aspired to be a circus performer and treasured his own clown suit." Drawing on those boyhood roots, Porter wrote a set of lyrics overnight that displayed his flair for combining literate diction with everyday slang:

> *Be a clown, be a clown,*
> *All the world loves a clown.*
> *Act the fool, play the calf,*
> *And you'll always have the last laugh.*
> *Wear the cap and the bells*
> *And you'll rate with all the great swells.*

"Tears came to my eyes," Kelly recalled, "that's wonderful—so great! But, of course, we'll need more verses; we'll have to reprise."

Sparked by Kelly's enthusiasm, Porter came back the next day with several more lyrics that included such lines as

> *Be a crack jackanapes*
> *And they'll imitate you like apes.*
> *Why be a great composer with your rent in arrears,*
> *Why be a major poet and you'll owe it for years,*
> *When crowds'll pay to giggle if you wiggle your ears?*
> *Be a clown, be a clown, be a clown.*

"It's the best number Cole has ever written," pronounced Freed. While his other songs for *The Pirate* lacked the musical and lyrical sparkle of "Be a Clown," Porter would go on to prove that reports of his artistic death were greatly exaggerated later in that same year with his finest stage musical, *Kiss Me, Kate.* Although "Be a Clown" was originally planned as a duet for Kelly and Garland, Garland's decline into addiction forced her to miss 99 of the 135 days of the shooting schedule for *The Pirate*. Instead, Kelly danced to it with the spectacular Nicholas Brothers, one of the first times blacks and whites had danced together, as equals, on the screen. One number, however, could not save the film, which lost $2 million.

With *Easter Parade* (1948), Arthur Freed had another resounding success that melded the backstager formula with the integrated film musical, combining classic Irving Berlin songs done as performances with new ones written specifically for the characters and story of the film. *Easter Parade* was set in 1912, an era Berlin knew well from his early days on Tin Pan Alley, and he wanted it to be a historically accurate, grittily realistic portrayal of show business at the time. Director Charles Walters, however, "privately complained to Freed that the script was, if anything, too authentic and harsh. It was important for all concerned to recognize that they were not setting out to make the next *42nd Street*; *Easter Parade* was to be pure light, escapist fare, whose darkest emotion was nostalgia."

Some of the dark impulse behind the film seems to have been fueled by plans to pair Judy Garland with Gene Kelly. After growing up dancing for coins in Pittsburgh bars, Kelly had established himself on Broadway in Rodgers and Hart's *Pal Joey* (1940), where he played John O'Hara's title character—a sleazy, ruthless gigolo. In *For Me and My Gal* (1942), his first film for MGM, Kelly played a hard-nosed hoofer who breaks his own fingers in order to escape the draft in World War I. Paired opposite Garland, the combination of his edgy, aggressive persona with her open vulnerability was a dynamic 1940s counterpart to the coupling of Astaire-Rogers in the previous decade. Kelly replaced Astaire's urbane grace with boyish athleticism, but it was that athleticism that cost him his role in the film when he broke his ankle playing touch football. "What are we going to do, Arthur?" Berlin asked. "Don't worry," Freed replied, "I'll handle it."

In a movie musical, the accident would have resulted in the chance of a lifetime for a young unknown; in real-life Hollywood, Arthur Freed brought an old-timer out of retirement. Fred Astaire's career had faltered since his separation from Ginger Rogers, and he had decided to call it quits after *Blue Skies* in 1946. After filming one of his most spectacular numbers, where he danced with seven images of himself in top hat, white tie, and tails to Berlin's "Puttin' on the Ritz," Astaire tore off his toupee, stomped on it, and exulted, "Never, never. Never will I have to wear this blasted rug again!" After Freed visited Astaire at his ranch, however, the dancer considered coming out of his brief retirement. Always the consummate gentleman, on-screen and off, he told Freed, "Let me go and talk to Gene before I say yes." When it was clear that Kelly could not work for six to eight months, Astaire began a second career that he never regretted. "My experiences with Arthur have been professional bonanzas," Astaire later reflected on his trust in a songwriter to produce musical films. "It was exciting—and most of all it was top stuff. Arthur was a very good guiding light because he was a music man. He was a songwriter of note and he couldn't be fooled."

What enticed Astaire, however, threw the screenwriters for a loop. "You can't put Judy Garland opposite a grandfather," Sidney Sheldon told Freed. "The audience will be rooting for them *not* to get together." "Write the script," was Freed's curt reply. Irving Berlin, on the other hand, responded to the replacement of Kelly by Astaire with the relish with which he always accepted a challenge. "If Kelly had played it, the picture would have been heavier," he said. "In fact, we planned it as a heavier story. Kelly can do that sort of thing. With Astaire it was all lighter." Berlin's old songs fit even more comfortably into the story of the veteran Astaire tutoring neophyte Garland in the art of vaudeville song and dance. As they run through such classic Berlin hits as "I Love a Piano" and "When the Midnight Choo-Choo Leaves for Alabam,'" the master-apprentice relationship between the two stars paves the way to romance. Their relationship culminates in the title song, which Garland, now the seasoned trouper, sings *to* Astaire as she places his classic top hat upon his head. Not only did Berlin's songs negotiate their developing romance, it gave Astaire a new persona that he evinced in many more musical films—that of the debonair older man who, without lifting a finger, proves irresistibly attractive to younger women such as Cyd Charisse in *The Band Wagon* (1953), Leslie Caron in *Daddy Long Legs* (1955), and Audrey Hepburn in *Funny Face* (1957).

In writing seven new songs for the film, Berlin thought in the new "integrated" terms he had already proven he could master with his hit stage musi-

cal *Annie Get Your Gun* (1946). When Garland meets Peter Lawford in a downpour, Berlin gave them "A Feller with an Umbreller" for a duet, then "Better Luck Next Time" as a torch song for Garland to sing to a sympathetic bartender. But Berlin's most extraordinary achievement in *Easter Parade* was to create two songs that performed the seemingly impossible task of exorcising the ghost of Ginger Rogers, which had haunted Astaire for nearly ten years. *Easter Parade* begins when Ann Miller drops Astaire as her dancing partner—a clear allusion to his split with Ginger Rogers. As Miller and Astaire dance gracefully and sensuously to "It Only Happens When I Dance with You," the song asserts that the couple's magic can never be recaptured. Without Miller, Astaire seems a has-been who will never find another partner with the same chemistry.

The breakup prompts him to make a drunken bet that he can teach any woman to dance as well as Miller. The woman he chooses to demonstrate his Svengali powers is, of course, Garland, but she proves utterly recalcitrant material when he tries to replicate the kind of elegant, romantic dances he performed with Miller. Only when Astaire realizes that Garland's genius lies in comedy rather than romance does their act succeed. That success, in turn, requires Astaire to change from his debonair  persona to a knockabout hoofer (a role that had long been part of his act with his sister Adele in vaudeville). The song Berlin wrote to crystallize Astaire and Garland's new comic partnership was to have been "Let's Take an Old-Fashioned Walk"—with "walk" rather than "dance" being the critical term in the lyric. Freed, however, counting on his songwriter instincts yet again, asked for a different kind of song.

"Let's have a 'tramps' number," Berlin suggested in response, and in an hour wrote "A Couple of Swells." Casting it in the musical style of the turn of the century, with lengthy verses alternating with refrains, Berlin developed a "walking" melody that advances upward like the determined pair of Garland and Astaire.

> *We're a couple of swells;*
> *We stop at the best hotels.*
> *But we prefer the country,*
> *Far away from the city smells.*

In a parody of his elegant top hat, white tie, and tails, Astaire and Garland play hoboes in tattered evening clothes, their top hats crushed and their teeth blackened. Instead of competing with the image of Astaire and Rogers, Fred and Judy burlesque that romantic icon, and the lyric frees  Garland from having to perform a romantic ballroom dance. In their rough-and-ready penury, Astaire and Garland complain that because there is no way to ride or sail "up the Avenue," they will "walk" (rather than "dance"):

> *We would sail up the Avenue,*
> *But we haven't got a yacht.*

We would drive up the avenue,
But the horse we had was shot.
We would ride in a trolley car,
But we haven't got the fare.
So we'll walk up the Avenue,
Yes, we'll walk up the Avenue,
Yes, we'll walk up the Avenue till we're there.

Their comic walking turns out to be as entertaining as Astaire's dancing with Miller to "It Only Happens When I Dance with You," one song brilliantly triumphing over another in a film where performance numbers function as integrally as expressive ones. With a gross of $4,200,000 (and, even more impressive, $5.8 million worldwide), *Easter Parade* was the second biggest moneymaker of 1948.

The enormous success of *Easter Parade* may have started a subtle shift away from integral song at MGM. While Arthur Freed would continue to produce integrated musicals such as *An American in Paris*, he would increasingly return to the backstager formula in *Royal Wedding, Singin' in the Rain*, and *The Band Wagon*, where songs are primarily presented as performances. One wonders if the age difference between Astaire and Garland subtly ruled out integral song, since audiences may not have accepted an older man singing openly of his feelings for a considerably younger woman. Containing such romantic expression in the context of songs done as performances may have seemed a safer strategy.

The next film MGM planned for Astaire and Garland was another backstager. Originally it was entitled *You Made Me Love You*, which had become one of Garland's signature songs, and portrayed Astaire and Garland as a bickering vaudeville couple in something of a sequel to *Easter Parade*. The script was by Betty Comden and Adolph Green, newly arrived at MGM from New York where they also wrote and performed their own songs in cabaret. Songs for the film were written by Ira Gershwin and Harry Warren, both seasoned songwriters who had not worked together before. They created several comic songs for Garland—"Natchez on the Mississip," a parody of songs about the South, and a hillbilly parody, "The Courtin' of Elmer and Ella." Once into rehearsals, however, Garland's emotional problems, exacerbated by her addiction to the drugs prescribed by studio doctors, forced Freed to replace her. He chartered a plane to carry the script to Ginger Rogers at her Oregon ranch, and his offer to pay her $12,500 a week—more than double what Garland had been getting—brought Rogers out of retirement. The script and the songs were changed to suit Astaire and Rogers, and even the title of the picture was changed, when it was completed in 1949, to *The Barkleys of Broadway* to remove any association with Garland.

In the course of the filming of *The Barkleys of Broadway* (1949), Judy Garland made a visit to the set, much to the consternation of Ginger Rogers, who retreated to her dressing room and refused to go before the camera while Garland was present. It took director Charles Walters to forcibly remove her, just as Fred Astaire was arriving, who, seeing her upset face, asked "What are they doing to that poor kid?" Astaire's question could reverberate over Garland's whole career at MGM, which was  rapidly approaching its end as she slid further and further into addiction and depression. She would be removed from the starring role in *Annie Get Your Gun* (1950) and replaced by Betty Hutton. She struggled through Joe Pasternak's backstager, *Summer Stock* (1950), where her weight fluctuated noticeably from number to number. Most of the songs, done with Gene Kelly, were integral to character and story. But the highlight of the film was a solo performance number of an interpolated song from 1930 that was added at the last minute. Garland, slim and sexy, managed to pull off a dynamic rendition of "Get Happy," her last song in an MGM film. Attired in a man's dinner jacket, leotards that showed off her shapely legs, and a black hat tipped rakishly over her eye, she brilliantly rendered her swan song at MGM. Still, it was ironic that a singer who had helped Arthur Freed, Vincente Minnelli, and others at MGM present song integrally in film, should bow out in a backstager with a song presented as a performance.

8

Blues in the Night

The films produced by Arthur Freed at MGM in the 1940s are all the more impressive when one looks at movies from other studios during the decade. World War II closed the profitable European and Far East markets for Hollywood films, and as studios cut back on production, the first to suffer were musicals—the most expensive kind of movie to make. The most dramatic contrast to MGM's integral musicals were the films of Warner Bros, which rigidly adhered to the backstager formula but still managed to produce some superb songs. One of the studio's first films of the decade, originally entitled *Hot Nocturne*, told the story of a band struggling to make it to the big time. With a narrative that involved addictive gambling, alcoholism, and suicide, the film was even grittier than Warner Bros. musicals of the 1930s. The songs—"This Time the Dream's on Me," "Hang on to Your Lids, Kids," "Says Who? Says You, Says I!"—by Johnny Mercer and Harold Arlen, were suitably jazzy and swinging, but the best was an intricate blues lament. "I went home and thought about it for two days," Harold Arlen recalled. "After all, anybody can write a blues song. The hard thing to do is to write one that doesn't sound like every other blues song."

Arlen developed the melody in the twelve-bar phrases of classic blues as well as the eight-bar phrases of popular song formulas, and when he finished, the music stretched to fifty-two bars—much longer and more complex than a blues or pop song refrain. Mercer found the unusual structure difficult to set, and his original lyric began with the sentimental line, "I'm heavy in my heart." When Arlen saw that "weak tea" opening, he said nothing but kept reading. "On the third or fourth page of his work sheets I saw some lines—one of them was 'My momma done tol' me, when I was in knee pants.' Now he had that as one of his choices, probably forgot about it, and I said why don't you try that. It was one of the few times I've ever suggested anything like that to John." When Mercer moved that section to the beginning of the song, "Blues in the Night" took off in a vernacular wail:

My mama done tol' me
When I was in knee pants,
My mama done tol' me—"Son!
A woman'll sweet talk
And give ya the big eye,
But when that sweet talkin's done,
A woman's a two-face,
A worrisome thing who'll leave ya t'sing
The blues in the night."

Arlen liked the phrase "My mama done tol' me" so much that he thought it should be the title of the song, but Mercer insisted that "blues in the night"—a phrase repeated several times in the lyric—should remain the title. So they took their song to Irving Berlin, who listened to them play it, then, with his practiced ear at placing a title phrase so that it figured prominently in a lyric (underscoring it in the listeners' mind so they would remember what song to ask for in the sheet-music and record store), sided with Mercer. Once the studio heard it, they promptly changed the title of the movie from *Hot Nocturne* to *Blues in the Night*.

The song is first sung by a black man in a jail, where it is overheard by white band members in another cell. Their leader, played by Richard Whorf, proclaims it "the real lowdown New Orleans blues" and appropriates "Blues in the Night" for his band. As Whorf slides into drunkenness and depression, however, he finds that he cannot recall the song: "I keep reaching out to grab it, but it won't stand still," he tells band members. They then whistle the tune to jog his memory (Arlen and Mercer had written a section of the song to be whistled so their efforts incorporate that segment dramatically into the film). As we watch a montage of Whorf's breakdown, hospitalization, and eventual recovery, "Blues in the Night" plays over and over on the soundtrack as a kind of interior monologue.

Blues in the Night (1941) could have set a new standard for harsh realism in backstager musicals as *42nd Street* had in the 1930s, but Warner Bros. made few other musical films over the rest of the decade. "Jack Warner imposed a moratorium on musicals," Clive Hirschhorn notes, "the public having grown weary of the genre by the end of the thirties." Harry Warner took a more patriotic view of the shift away from musicals: "I don't want us to be known as the studio that made the best musical comedies during the war."

One kind of musical film Warner Bros. did produce was the "biopic"—a film that traced the career of a performer or songwriter. Such films incorporated tried and tested songs, frequently ones that Warner Bros. owned as a result of its acquisition of the Tin Pan Alley firm of T. B. Harms. Under the guidance of Max Dreyfus, Harms specialized in songs written for Broadway musicals and prided itself that its "theater" songs were a distinct cut above the usual fare cranked out by Tin Pan Alley tunesmiths. With the Harms catalogue, Warner Bros. owned the entire output of songs by such composers as George Gershwin and Cole Porter, and what better use of such material than biopics such as *Rhapsody in Blue* (1945) and *Night and Day* (1946) that portrayed, usually loosely, the way the composer's songs were inspired, created, and performed.

The arc between the initial creation of a song and its on-stage performance allowed for several reprises that made for a dramatic narrative propelled by song. In *Yankee Doodle Dandy* (1942), for example, James Cagney, as George M.

 Cohan, is just putting the finishing touches to "Mary," a song he has written for his wife "Mary" (played by Joan Leslie), to sing in his next show. As she plays the melody at the piano, Cagney dictates the lyric in a tight-lipped, business-like manner, yet his affection for the song—and its namesake—percolates under his crusty veneer:

For it is Mary, Mary,
Plain as any name can be.
But with propriety,
Society will say Marie.
But it was Mary, Mary,
Long before the fashions came.
And there is something there
That sounds so square.
It's a grand old name.

Then Leslie sings the lyric, and Cagney quietly prompts her with his spoken lines—another instance of the combination of song and dialogue. Cagney's "spoken" song articulates his feelings more expressively than his own stage performance of the song would have done.

In the next scene, Cagney and Richard Whorf, as his co-producer Sam Harris, approach the great Fay Templeton (played by Irene Manning) to ask her to star in their next show. Templeton knows Cohan only by reputation as a flag-waving, pushy, crowd-pleaser and refuses his offer to write a show for her. She arrogantly tells him that after her performance, "I'm going home to New Rochelle. It's only forty-five minutes from here." Then, looking disdainfully at Cagney, adds, "But thank heavens it's like a thousand miles from all the noisy, neurotic people one has to associate with in our profession!" As she storms out to make her entrance on stage, Cagney remains in her dressing room, and goes to her piano. We then cut to the end of the first act when Templeton returns to her dressing room only to find Cagney and Whorf still there—with a song, "Forty-five Minutes from Broadway," inspired by her parting shot and written, start-to-finish, during her first act. Impressed by his brash energy, she agrees to listen to Cagney demonstrate the song, which she finds fresh and "different." When Whorf pushes the advantage by showing her Cohan's other recent composition, "Mary," Cagney protests, but Templeton takes the music, sits at the piano, and finds the song equally charming. As she sings the lyric, the scene cuts to Joan Leslie

back at their apartment, rehearsing "Mary." Cagney winces as he opens the door with flowers and candy in hand. When he confesses that he's given her song to Templeton, Leslie nonchalantly replies that she knew he'd done so when he came home with candy and flowers. After yet another reprise of "Mary" by Manning on stage, Leslie, sitting in the audience with Cagney, whispers that while Fay Templeton may have the song, she has its composer. Thus "Mary" propels the narrative of *Yankee Doodle Dandy* in a way that expresses Cohan's affection for his wife almost as if he had sung the song to her himself.

In addition to biopics, Warner Bros. found another way to incorporate its valuable catalogue of Tin Pan Alley songs by inserting older songs into dramatic films. While the songs were still done as "performances," they became expressive of characters' feelings. One of the most poignant presentations of song in a dramatic film was Claire Trevor's rendition of "Moanin' Low" in *Key Largo* (1948). The song, by Howard Dietz and Ralph Rainger, was originally written for the 1929 Broadway revue *The Little Show*, but Trevor's rendition of it in *Key Largo*, for which she won an Oscar, helped make the song a standard. Trevor plays the boozy moll of gangster Edward G. Robinson, who holds Humphrey Bogart, Lauren Bacall, and other hostages at gunpoint in a Florida hotel. Trevor begs Robinson to give her a drink from the bar, and when he refuses, lambasting her drunkenness, she says "You're as mean as can be." One of his henchmen reminds Robinson that the line came from a song she used to sing when she was a Broadway star. With a sadistic gleam in his eye, Robinson tells her he'll give her a drink if she sings the song. "With no accompaniment?" she asks and begs to have the drink first. When Robinson insists she sing in front of the hostages, she gamely launches into "Moanin' Low," but midway through the song she realizes that the lyric, about a woman helplessly in thrall to a cruel man, is truly expressive of her miserable situation. What had once been her performance song has now become integrally expressive. That realization makes her falter as she finishes the song, and Robinson, grimly shaking his head at her poor showing, refuses to give her the drink. "But you promised," Trevor sobs; "You were rotten," Robinson snaps. Throughout the humiliating performance, Bogart, Bacall, and the other hostages watch helplessly, but then Bogart, defying the guns of Robinson and his henchmen, walks behind the bar, pours a hefty drink, and takes it to Trevor.

Songs performed in dramatic films could be integral and expressive even when the characters themselves did not sing them. One of the first songs to be presented in this way, and one of the most enduring presentations of any song in film, was "As Time Goes By" in the 1942 Warner Bros. film *Casablanca*. The song, by Herman Hupfeld, had flopped when it was first written in 1931, despite a recording by Rudy Vallee. Murray Burnett, a Cornell undergraduate at the time, was one person who loved "As Time Goes By." When Burnett collaborated with Joan Alison on a play, *Everybody Comes to Rick's*, they made "As Time Goes By" the song Rick and Ilsa loved when they met in Paris before

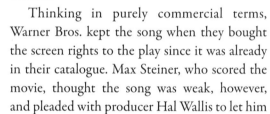

the war.

Thinking in purely commercial terms, Warner Bros. kept the song when they bought the screen rights to the play since it was already in their catalogue. Max Steiner, who scored the movie, thought the song was weak, however, and pleaded with producer Hal Wallis to let him write a replacement. Wallis finally agreed, since he had thought Dooley Wilson would be a better singer—and could play the piano. He was disappointed when Wilson talk-sang his way through "As Time Goes By" in his raspy voice and his piano playing had to be dubbed. Before they could substitute a different song, however, shooting was completed, and when Wallis tried to bring back the cast for a reshoot with a new song, he found Ingrid Bergman had already cut her hair short to play Maria in *For Whom the Bell Tolls*.

In retrospect, "As Time Goes By" seems to be quintessentially suited to *Casablanca*'s story and characters. Wryly sophisticated and casually world-weary, it captures the persona projected by Humphrey Bogart. The melody of each A-section of this typical AABA song ascends for three phrases,

You must remember this,
A kiss is still a kiss,
A sigh is just a sigh.

Then just before musical and lyrical sentiments can soar, the melody descends, and the lyric becomes offhandedly romantic and philosophical:

The fundamental things apply
As time goes by.

The polysyllabic "fundamental" stands out in a lyric composed almost entirely of monosyllables, as does the practical "apply," giving the song the same kind of stoical, understated passion that Bogart himself projects. While it is unthinkable that Bogart would sing in a movie, if he did, this is the kind of song he would do, and his performance would be as rough and unsentimental as Wilson's, spoken more than sung.

Casablanca won the Academy Award for Best Picture, but "As Time Goes By" could not be considered for the Oscar because it had not been specifically written for the film. Nevertheless, the song stayed on *Your Hit Parade* for twenty-one weeks, proving the wisdom of incorporating songs the studio already owned into films to give them renewed popularity. Such recycling of songs in films was a major factor in transforming an otherwise ephemeral popular song into an enduring "standard."

While not as draconian in its cutback on musical films, Paramount significantly reduced its production of musical movies in the 1940s. After making more than ninety musical films in the 1930s, Paramount made fewer than forty in the next decade, and nearly half of those were built around its biggest star, Bing Crosby. In most of these, Crosby presented songs as performances, but in his "Road" pictures with Bob Hope and Dorothy Lamour he frequently got to sing more integral songs. Dixie Crosby and Dolores Hope had been friends since their chorus girl days on Broadway in the 1920s; the couples socialized regularly, so Crosby and Hope had an informal, easy rapport. Each star had gag writers who fed them lines to throw in as ad libs, and the pair took it from there. When they land a swordfish in *Road to Singapore* (1940), the creature keeps flopping, and Crosby observes "It won't give up." "Must be a Republican," quips Hope in an allusion to Roosevelt's unprecedented election to a third term over his Republican opponent. Directors simply let their banter unfold, and co-star Dorothy Lamour quickly learned to forget the script and keep up with the boys.

As the series of "Road" pictures progressed, Hope and Crosby increasingly broke with cinematic realism to speak directly to the camera and even allude to their own movies. In *Road to Morocco* (1942), for example, they sing the title song whose lyric promises "We're sure to meet Dorothy Lamour." As Hope and Crosby ride a dogsled across Alaska in *Road to Utopia* (1946), among the mountains in the distance appears the Paramount logo, and Hope says, "It may look like a mountain to you, but it's bread-and-butter to me." In each of the "Road" films, Hope and Crosby fight their way out of trouble by playing patty-cake with one another then suddenly slugging their enemies. When they dupe two heavies in *Road to Rio* (1947) into playing patty-cake and punching

themselves out, Hope observes, "That's what they get for not seeing our pictures."

Such self-conscious intrusions eased the presentation of integral songs, most of which were supplied by Johnny Burke and Jimmy Van Heusen, whom Crosby dubbed the "Gold Dust Twins" because of their string of hits. Burke, whom fellow-lyricist Sammy Cahn called "the Irish poet," had a whimsical strain that was always informally conversational and thus perfectly suited to Crosby's style of delivery. In presenting the songs, the films balanced romance with humor in a way that fit the overall tone of the series where nothing was ever taken too seriously. The pattern was set in their very first film, *Road to Singapore*, where Crosby and Hope both court Dorothy Lamour. Crosby sends Hope off in a canoe, and sings the self-deprecating "I'm Too Romantic" on the balcony of their hut. Lamour then sings a chorus back to him—"How can you say to me that you're too romantic?'—and he counters her sung lines with bits of spoken dialogue—"Well, I mean it—I'm really sincere about it," thus establishing that interweaving of song and speech so characteristic of Hollywood films. As Lamour reaches the end of her chorus with "Well then if you fall...," Crosby literally falls off the balcony railing as Hope pulls him down with a hook.

In *Road to Morocco*, Crosby serenades Lamour with "Moonlight Becomes You," a wonderfully insouciant ballad that sounds barely a notch above casual conversation:

> *Moonlight becomes you,*
> *It goes with your hair.*
> *You certainly know the right thing to wear.*

Lamour has wandered onto her balcony in her nightgown, and Burke's lyric takes gentle cognizance of the fact as Crosby gazes up at her from the garden below:

> *You're all dressed up to go dreaming.*
> *Now, don't tell me I'm wrong.*
> *And what a night to go dreaming!*
> *Mind if I tag along?*

The conversational ease of the lyric perfectly suits the understated romanticism of Crosby and the "Road" pictures.

One of their most innovative presentations of a song occurs in *Road to
Rio* with "But Beautiful." After saving a depressed and confused Lamour from
throwing herself overboard on a cruise ship bound for Brazil, Crosby tries to
comfort her as they sit behind the movie screen while passengers watch a film
on deck. Nodding to the performers on screen, who dance like Fred Astaire and
Ginger Rogers, Crosby tells Lamour that they manage to project a romantic
gaiety even though the actress is suffering economic hardship and the actor is
hung over. When Lamour asks him how he knows such things, he points to the
orchestra where he and Hope are musicians, explaining they'd done a stint in
films. He then sings "But Beautiful" to her against the on-screen image of the
dancers, an effect both romantic and comic. The song also combines lightness
and passion in its lyrical and musical shifts:

> *Love is funny or it's sad,*
> *Or it's quiet or it's mad.*
> *It's a good thing or it's bad,*
> *But beautiful!*

As the song concludes, so does the film, and Crosby kisses Lamour just as "THE
END" comes up in reverse mirror image. The ship's lights come on and, much
to the amusement of the other passengers, Crosby and Lamour appear in silhou-
ette on the screen.

In addition to the "Road" pictures, Crosby did more than a dozen other
films for Paramount in the 1940s. He played a songwriter in *Rhythm on the
River* (1940), a Dixieland clarinetist in *Birth of the Blues* (1941), lullabied
grumpy fellow-priest Barry Fitzgerald with "Too-Ra-Loo-Ra-Loo-Ral (That's
an Irish Lullaby)" and taught parish kids "Swinging on a Star" in *Going My Way*
(1944), sang and danced with Fred Astaire in *Blue Skies* (1946), and portrayed
a phonograph salesman in Franz Joseph's Tyrol in *The Emperor Waltz* (1948).
In most of these films, songs were presented as performances but in the best
of them, Irving Berlin's *Holiday Inn* (1942), that backstage convention was
handled with innovative verve. Berlin had originally planned a Broadway show,
Holiday Revue, that would be based on American holidays, just as his successful
stage revue, *As Thousands Cheer* (1933), had been built around the sections of
a newspaper. Initially, he intended to tell the story solely through songs—with
no intervening dialogue or narration, just the annual rotation of holidays to
give the revue structure. While such revues had been popular in the 1930s, by
the 1940s they were replaced by more thoroughly narrative "book shows," such
as *Pal Joey* (1940) and *Lady in the Dark* (1941). So Berlin took his idea to Hollywood, where Mark Sandrich, who had directed several Astaire-Rogers films

at RKO, was now a producer-director at Paramount. "I told him about my idea of a musical revue based on holidays and he thought it would make a perfect movie for Bing Crosby," Berlin recalled. "But first there would have to be a story line since the revue format was considered unsuitable for the screen." As a dramatic showcase for his holiday numbers, Berlin imagined Crosby as an entertainer who leaves the bustle of show business to refurbish a Connecticut farm. When his farming venture fails, Crosby decides to turn the huge farmhouse into a country inn that would feature elaborate floor shows. While Crosby plays the entertainer who longs for the simple life, Astaire portrays his big-city rival—in show business as well as love. Since his split with Ginger Rogers, Astaire had been struggling to redefine himself, and in *Holiday Inn* he plays the dark underside of his 1930s persona of elegance and charm. Representing show business in its crasser incarnation, Astaire even dances drunk in one number and has to be carried from the floor.

Originally, Berlin had planned to write twenty new songs for the film, including numbers for St. Patrick's Day, Flag Day, Labor Day, Columbus Day, Hallow-

een, and Armistice Day. Although he ultimately wrote only fourteen new songs, that still was one of the most plentiful scores that had ever been created for a film. While most of these songs are done as performances, they resonate with character and dramatic situation. The film opens in a New York nightclub with Astaire and Crosby doing what Berlin would call a "challenge" song

to woo their co-star, Virginia Dale. Crosby warbles, "I'll Capture Your Heart Singing," and Astaire retorts, with his feet as well as his voice, "I'll Capture Your Heart Dancing." The song reflects the backstage romance in which Dale leaves Crosby and his dream of a country retreat for the promise of Hollywood stardom with Astaire. The "showbiz" aura of the number also contrasts with the rest of the holiday songs, which are staged in the rural world of Holiday Inn.

Those songs drive the film's narrative as they trace national and religious rites as well as the cycle of the seasons. The romance between Crosby and Marjorie Reynolds takes root with the Valentine's Day number, "Be Careful, It's My

Heart," and blossoms in "Easter Parade," one of the few songs not originally written for *Holiday Inn* yet one that emanates directly out of a dramatic moment. Despite the big-city references to Fifth Avenue and newspaper photographers (tied to its original placement in the Broadway revue *As Thousands Cheer*), the setting for

"Easter Parade" in the film is not an urbane stroll through Manhattan but a congregation's exodus from a country church after Easter morning services. At the end of the song, as Crosby and Reynolds climb into their carriage, the rural peace is broken when Fred Astaire ominously returns. By midsummer, when he tap-dances around exploding firecrackers in the Fourth of July number, "Say It with Firecrackers," Astaire has insinuated himself into Crosby's pastoral Eden. After he has lured Reynolds to Hollywood, winter sets in, and Crosby is unable to eat his lonely Thanksgiving dinner as he sings "Plenty to Be Thankful For" with rueful irony.

Holiday Inn is framed dramatically by "White Christmas," one of Berlin's greatest songs and one of the finest songs ever written for a Hollywood film. The song may have been inspired by a lonely Christmas Berlin spent in 1938 when he had to stay in Hollywood, while his family spent the holiday back in New York. In working on a Christmas song for his holiday revue, Berlin started with a verse about the palm trees and balmy weather of Beverly Hills in December. He initially envisioned "White Christmas" as a mournful carol sung by a group of sophisticates lounging around a Hollywood swimming pool. With cocktails and cigarette holders in hand, they would reminisce about the snowy Christmases of their youth. In contrast to the days, weeks, even years it took him to compose other songs, Irving Berlin said he wrote "White Christmas," "in two rather brief sessions and that's fast for a song."

> We working composers all too often, in the interests of expediency, sharpen our pencils, get out that square sheet of paper and become too slick. Those forced efforts are "square" songs. But sometimes a song is a natural. We may start it to order for a specific scene or show, but our subconscious beings go to work and the song is just there. This is what I call a "round" song.

The result was a song that subtly departs from the fundamental tenets of songwriting. Because "White Christmas" was prerecorded in a Hollywood sound studio, Berlin could take greater liberties with short vowels and crisp consonants than he could in a song that had to be sung from the stage. The innovations themselves, however, came from a lifetime of manipulating words against music.

Another songwriter, for example, would have made the first line emphasize such important words as "dreaming" and "Christmas," verbs and nouns, with long notes, but Berlin deftly underscores the seemingly less important "I'm" with a whole note, then races over the other syllables to another whole note on "white," accenting the long *i* in each word:

I'm dreaming of a white Christmas

Although written in the basic key of C, the melody wanders chromatically. While it generally stays within the octave, it climbs above it at the beginning— "just like the *ones* I used to know"—then again in the phrase "with ev'ry *Christ-mas* card I write." Despite these upward strains, the melody's progress is steadily and almost despondently downward. After one last upward climb to "bright," it drops one note below middle C on "may all your Christ-*mases be* white" to give the ending a wandering, unresolved quality. The lyric too hesitates, particularly on the almost unsingable word "Christmases" that only a performer with Crosby's talent could enunciate with apparent ease.

The rhymes drift as elusively as the melody, which is structured not in the usual ABAB or AABA patterns but in the more asymmetrical ABAC pattern. The initial "know" does not find its true rhyme until we traverse the clipped feminine rhymes of

Where the treetops glisten
And children listen
To hear ... sleigh bells in the snow

The song ends on the tonic note of middle C, but that musical return to the home key is offset by the drifting off of the lyric on the adjective "white," which for the first time in the song is not followed by its noun—"Christmas"—but instead hangs alone to resonate ambiguously. The wandering melody and lyric reflect a singer who is remote from the memories he recalls so vividly. That alienation is more clearly expressed in the verse Berlin originally wrote for "White Christmas":

The sun is shining,
The grass is green,
The orange and palm trees sway.
There's never been such a day
In Beverly Hills, L.A.
But it's December the twenty-fourth,
And I am longing to be up north.

Like Berlin himself on his lonely Christmas in Hollywood, the singer cannot share but only recall the scene he describes. In a last-minute decision, Berlin cut the verse, giving the song a more universal but still hauntingly melancholy character.

When he handed the song to Bing Crosby, the singer looked at it, nonchalantly took his pipe out of his mouth, and with characteristic understatement, quipped, "You don't have to worry about this one, Irving."

Supposedly, however, Crosby had reservations about singing a song that might seem to commercialize a religious holiday, and the original script did not assign "White Christmas" to his character. In the film, however, he sings "White Christmas" twice, and both performances are beautifully integrated into the narrative. Early in the movie, Marjorie Reynolds sits in the deserted inn Crosby is trying to refurbish, and she notices a song he has written on the piano. Although he "performs" the song for her, it epitomizes the kind of pastoral joy he has come to the country to find.

When Crosby reprises "White Christmas" on a Hollywood soundstage at the end of the film, the song persuades Reynolds to leave the heady show business success she has finally attained and return with him to the New England countryside. Before she is aware that Crosby is in the studio, Reynolds prepares to sing "White Christmas" on a set that, her director tells her, is an exact replica of Crosby's country inn where she first heard him sing the song (in reality, of course, the set *is* the set used in the first presenta-

tion of the song in the film). For her "motivation," the director tells her, "Your Hollywood success was empty, you've lost the one man you love—the usual hoke." Reynolds of course, truly is unhappy with her success and misses Crosby. When he suddenly appears to sing "White Christmas," the camera pulls back from the reunited lovers to reveal that the scene is actually shot on the *Holiday Inn* set itself, with cameras and crew in clear view. Instead of being a replica of the real thing, there *is* no real thing—only, as John Mueller points out, "the set that has been used throughout the film, and there is something intriguingly disorienting in the way the film calmly shatters its own artful illusion by showing its beautiful central set to be merely that—a set." The combination of a great song, a dramatic setting, and a superb performance made "White Christmas" one of Hollywood's great achievements in song.

Although nowhere near the musical workhorse Crosby was, Bob Hope starred in Paramount's film adaptations of Irving Berlin's *Louisiana Purchase* (1941) and Cole Porter's *Let's Face It* (1943), but he introduced an original film song in *The Paleface* (1948). Ray Evans and Jay Livingston had gotten their big break by writing a title song for *To Each His Own* (1946), which became a huge hit and established the team in Hollywood. Assigned to write a song for *Paleface*, they created a witty, catalogue song for Hope, who plays a dentist from the East who is duped into marrying gun-toting Calamity Jane, played by Jane Russell. Russell bullies Hope, takes the reins of their wagon train, and does all the sharp-shooting that saves them from Indians. Evans and Livingston had Hope give voice to his emasculated plight in song:

> *East is east and west is west,*
> *And the wrong one I have chose.*
> *Let's go where they keep on wearin'*
> *Those frills and flowers and buttons and bows…*
> *Don't bury me in this prairie,*
> *Take me where the cement grows.*

Although Evans claimed he did not realize that he cleverly echoed "where" in "wearin'," the lyric bristles with other deft rhymes and climaxes in a list of eastern images of femininity:

> *And gimme eastern trimmin'*
> *Where women are women*
> *In high silk hose and peekaboo clothes*
> *And French perfume that rocks the room*

Musically, the melody is based on the pentatonic scale common to folk music, and the rhythm has the clip-clop feel of cowboy songs. The only blemish in the presentation of the song is that Hope sings it in a nasal, "hillbilly" style rather than in the "Easterner" persona that the song's lyric calls for. Nevertheless, "Buttons and Bows" went on to win the Oscar for Best Song.

While Warner Bros. and Paramount cut back on their presentations of songs in film, Twentieth Century-Fox held steady, producing between fifty and sixty musical films in both the 1930s and 1940s. Although the number of films Fox produced was substantial, it seldom created original songs for films or went beyond the backstager convention of presenting songs as performances. One reason was that studio head Darryl F. Zanuck loved nostalgic films set in the late nineteenth or early twentieth century. Thus films such as *My Gal Sal* (1942), *Coney Island* (1943), *The Dolly Sisters* (1945), *I Wonder Who's Kissing Her Now* (1947), and *Oh, You Beautiful Doll* (1949) were showcases for older songs presented as performances in vaudeville, burlesque, and other backstage venues. The major change was that while such films featured Alice Faye in the 1930s, in the 1940s she was replaced by Betty Grable.

For all of Zanuck's affection for the nostalgic backstager, however, he was aware that the Broadway musical had moved toward integrated song in such period shows as *Oklahoma!* (1943) and *Bloomer Girl* (1944). Zanuck may have hoped for a screen clone of *Oklahoma!* when he commissioned Rodgers and Hammerstein to write a musical film based on the 1933 movie *State Fair*, which had starred Will Rogers and Janet Gaynor, about an Iowa farm family going to its state's annual fair. After their bitter experiences in Hollywood in the previous decade, Rodgers and Hammerstein were reluctant to accept the invitation and did so only when Zanuck agreed to let them write the libretto and score in New York. Their *Oklahoma!*-based prestige also earned them another respectful nod from Hollywood—their score was accepted without any demands for revision.

One would think that with such deference, Rodgers and Hammerstein would have written a musical film filled with integral songs such as they had written for Broadway. *State Fair* (1945) begins promisingly in that direction, with an Iowa feed-truck driver singing a song about the state fair. His "pass-along" song is then picked up by a pig farmer, as he feeds the boar he hopes will win the blue ribbon, then by his wife as she prepares the pickles and pies she hopes will earn her prizes. The song functions, as did the title song at the opening of *Meet Me in St. Louis*, to bind family and community together. Even more promising is the next song, "It Might as Well Be Spring," which emerges when the mother chides her daughter, played by Jeanne Crain, for not having packed her bags for the fair, saying all the girl does is "sit around and mope." The film then cuts to Crain in her bedroom, acknowledging her mother's criticism and wondering "What has got into me anyway?" She looks at a photograph of her boyfriend "Harry" then slowly drifts into a verse that registers a young girl's confused emotional longings.

> *The things I used to like*
> *I don't like anymore.*
> *I want a lot of other things*
> *I've never had before.*
> *It's just like Mother says—*
> *I "sit around and mope"*
> *Pretending I am wonderful—*
> *And knowing I'm a dope!*

The song is interrupted when her mother calls up to her, and there is a brief exchange of dialogue, breaking up song and dialogue in the way that had become so effective in film.

Then Crain moves to her window to sing the chorus, which reveals Rodgers and Hammerstein at the top of their songwriting form. Ever since they had started their collaboration on *Oklahoma!* Rodgers and Hammerstein had approached songwriting in a way much different from the one Hammerstein had used with Jerome Kern or Rodgers with Lorenz Hart. In those earlier collaborations, as with most songwriting teams, the music was written first and the lyric was added afterward. When Rodgers teamed with Hammerstein, however, he recognized Hammerstein's talent as both a lyricist and a librettist, so he encouraged his partner to write lyrics first, lyrics that flowered out of the dramatic situations of his book. Rodgers would then take the completed lyric and set it to music, giving their songs a deeply integral character, musically as well as lyrically. "It Might as Well Be Spring" manifests that integral power better than any song Rodgers and Hammerstein wrote for film. Hammerstein had gotten the idea for the lyric when he puzzled over the fact that state fairs were held in the fall but so many love songs were set in the spring. Rodgers sensed that the liability could be turned into an asset with a song that portrayed a character so befuddled that she has "spring fever" in the fall:

> *I'm as restless as a willow in a windstorm,*
> *I'm as jumpy as a puppet on a string!*
> *I'd say that I had spring fever,*
> *But I know it isn't spring.*

Rodgers masterfully set the first phrase to a repetitive eighth-note sequence that traverses only four intervals; the second phrase, however, has uneasy dotted eighth-notes that jump up and down over a full octave before landing uneasily on a chromatic note for "string." Rodgers matches the lyric's eerie shift in the release as the girl imagines "walking down a strange new street" and "hearing words that I have never heard from a man I've yet to meet" by another haunting chromatic shift in the melody.

The only blemish in the song is that Crain is dubbed by Louanne Hogan, and, as so often happens with dubbing, a nonsinging actress does not move her hands and body as expressively as a professional singer. Still, "It Might as Well Be Spring" is beautifully woven into the narrative of *State Fair.* After a few more scenes, Crain's character reprises the song when she dreams that the man she seeks would be a combination of Ronald Coleman, Charles Boyer, and "Bing," all of whose voices speak or sing back to her in her reverie. In the next reprise, her lyric turns comically satirical as her boyfriend Harry comes to call and tells of his plan to build a home that will be thoroughly modern, right down to sanitary linoleum, rather than rugs or carpets, on the floor. Crain then chides his sterile efficiency.

In our air-conditioned, patent-leather farmhouse
On our ultra-modern, scientific farm,
We'll live in a streamlined heaven
And we'll waste no time on charm.

The song is reprised yet again when Crain arrives at the fair and meets a newspaper reporter played by Dana Andrews. As they stroll through the midway, "It Might as Well Be Spring" is heard on the soundtrack, voicing Crain's thoughts that at last she is "hearing words that I have never heard/ from a man I've yet to meet." Not surprisingly, such an integral song, wonderfully woven into the narrative, won the Academy Award.

After that integral song, however, *State Fair* follows the usual Hollywood convention of song as performance. Dick Haymes, as Jeanne Crain's brother, falls for Vivian Blaine, who plays a singer with the band that performs at the fair and sings "It's a Grand Night for Singing," "That's for Me," and other songs, sometimes joined by Haymes, who impresses her with his amateur but earnest voice. Rodgers and Hammerstein may have started out to make an integrated movie musical in the style of *Oklahoma!* but after twenty minutes the film reverts to the backstager formula. The shift may have been at the behest of Darryl F. Zanuck, who "noted that using the lyrics and music to advance the story had not really worked." Whoever was to blame, *State Fair* remains a disappointing attempt to adapt the integrated stage musical to the screen.

For all his love of period musicals, Zanuck extended Fox backstagers into more contemporary times. *Stormy Weather* (1943), for example, traced the history of black contributions to American entertainment. Perhaps inspired by the success of MGM's *Cabin in the Sky* (1943), a film adaptation of the all-black stage musical of 1940, *Stormy Weather* presented all of its songs as performances, but those performances drove the slender story of the film, which was primarily a vehicle for the presentation of song. One of its narrative lines traced the gradual "whitening" of black music as we move from a rustic "Dat, Dot, Dah," performed by rural blacks aboard a riverboat, replete with "gurning" (rhythmic facial distortions), through an authentic blues sung by Ada Brown, then into Fats Waller's black-inflected Tin Pan Alley song, "Ain't Misbehavin'," and finally to Lena Horne's mainstream rendition of Ted Koehler and Harold Arlen's mildly bluesy "Stormy Weather." The history traced by such a song sequence shows how black music increasingly accommodated itself to white audiences.

Another impetus that moved Zanuck to create movies that showcased more contemporary song was the signing of Harry Warren after the composer had left Warner Bros. Warren had intended to return to New York, which he had missed ever since coming to Hollywood, but Zanuck persuaded him to write music for Fox, teaming him with lyricist Mack Gordon. To showcase Warren's distinctively modern, jazzy music, Zanuck turned to more contemporary formulas, albeit still variations on the backstager. During the 1930s, "swing" bands led by Tommy Dorsey, Benny Goodman, Artie Shaw, and other musicians became a dominant force in American popular music, and Fox created a series of "Big Band" backstagers. The first of these, *Sun Valley Serenade* (1941), made Glenn Miller's band central to the story as it struggles to win an engagement at the Idaho ski resort. The big hit from the film, "Chattanooga Choo-Choo," is a driving Warren melody that Gordon set with crisply alliterative lyrics:

> *You leave the Pennsylvania station 'bout a quarter to four,*
> *Read a magazine and then you're in Baltimore.*
> *Dinner in the diner, nothing could be finer*
> *Than to have your ham 'n' eggs in Carolina.*

The song captures the rhythm of train travel where even the engine's whistle blows "eight to the bar."

The problem, however, was to present such songs in a cinematically interesting fashion, since Big Band musicians, as in radio backstagers, simply played their instruments and singers stood at a microphone. For the first chorus of "Chattanooga Choo-Choo," the camera enlivens the presentation of the song by cutting from one musician to another, looking down on the drummer then directly into Miller's trombone bell as the slide pushes forward. For the next chorus, singer-saxophonist Tex Beneke sits at a table with the singing group the Modernaires. While his homely, pockmarked face was not a problem on radio or recordings, Beneke donned a comic winter parka and cap to forestall any expectations of glamour. The song is presented as a rehearsal number climaxing in a dance routine by Dorothy Dandridge and the Nicholas Brothers in front of a railroad car. Their dance, featuring the brothers' patented splits, is so dynamic that no one questions the relevance of a song about a Tennessee-bound train in a movie set in the mountains of Idaho.

The presentation of songs in other Big Band backstagers, however, was far less imaginative. For *Orchestra Wives* (1942), which would be Glenn Miller's last film before he died in an airline crash while entertaining troops in England, Gordon and Warren wrote several superb songs, such as "At Last," "Serenade in Blue," and "I've Got a Gal in Kalamazoo." Each song, however, was presented as a straightforward performance by vocalists and the Miller orchestra. While "I've Got a Gal in Kalamazoo" is enlivened when the Nicholas brothers do a chorus followed by a dance, it still remains a wooden number by singers and orchestra. Like the "Big Broadcast" series at Paramount, such Big Band musicals did not even provide the production numbers of Broadway backstagers. Gordon and Warren's last great song at Fox was "The More I See You" for *Diamond Horseshoe* (1945), after which Warren left Fox to write for MGM, where he, at last, had the opportunity to write integral songs that expressed what characters felt at particular dramatic moments.

After RKO's extraordinary innovations in the presentation of song by Fred Astaire and Ginger Rogers in the 1930s, the studio's films of the next decade were largely uninspired adaptations of Broadway stage shows (*Irene; No, No, Nanette; Sunny*), radio backstagers such as *Radio Stars on Parade*, classical-versus-pop musicals (*Let's Make Music, Beat the Band*), and Big Band musicals (*You'll Find Out, Four Jacks and a Jill*). Even when an RKO film did feature Fred Astaire, such as *The Sky's the Limit* (1943), most of the songs were done as performances. The only integral song in the film is Johnny Mercer and Harold Arlen's "One for My Baby," but it is a gem. Astaire plays an ace pilot of the Flying Tigers who exchanges his uniform for civilian clothes to enjoy a ten-day leave. The exchange complicates his courting of Joan Leslie, who plays a magazine photographer totally dedicated to the war effort and who regards Astaire as a civilian slacker. Her disdain prompts Astaire to go on a binge just before he must return to his squadron, and as he goes from bar to bar, he sings this dramatic monologue:

> *It's quarter to three,*
> *There's no one in the place except you and me,*
> *So, set 'em up, Joe,*
> *I've got a little story you oughta know.*
> *We're drinking, my friend,*
> *To the end of a brief episode,*
> *Make it one for my baby*
> *And one more for the road.*

Astaire's heartache is made all the more painful by the way he never really tells the story of his lost love. Mercer had intuitively learned Hemingway's secret of the "iceberg" effect, leaving the bulk of a story's emotion "below the surface" so that the small portion that is articulated suggests enormous depths of unspoken feeling:

> *Could tell you a lot,*
> *But you've got to be true to your code,*
> *Make it one for my baby*
> *And one more for the road.*

By the end of the song, Astaire has broken glasses, smashed mirrors, and given a convincing performance of a distraught, bitter soldier about to return to the front.

RKO continued to serve as the distributor for Disney's films in the 1940s, but Disney himself grew more conservative in the way he presented songs in such cartoon musicals as *Pinocchio* (1940), *Dumbo* (1941), and *Bambi* (1942). Instead of using songs that were integral to character and story, as he had done in *Snow White*, Disney approached song almost as conservatively as Warner Bros. did. Even though they are cartoon characters who could burst into song without a realistic motivation, Dumbo never sings, Bambi never sings, and Pinocchio only sings "I've Got No Strings" as a "performance" number in a vaudeville show. Nor do any of the other characters sing with the spontaneity of Snow White or the Seven Dwarfs, even though the narratives are rife with opportunities to burst into song. One of the best of the Disney songs, "When You Wish upon a Star," which seemingly could portray Pinocchio's yearning to be a "real boy" is not given to him but to Jiminy Cricket, whose voice is dubbed by Gus "Ukulele Ike" Edwards. Edwards, moreover, sings it not dramatically and expressively but over the titles at the beginning of the film then reprises it at the conclusion after all the dramatic action has been completed. The only song he sings as an integral part of the narrative is "Give a Little Whistle," which defines his role as Pinocchio's conscience.

Why would Disney pass up the opportunity to use songs integrally in cartoons? Perhaps the answer involves his great commitment to realism, as described by biographer Richard Schickel: "When we do fantasy, we must not lose sight of reality," he quotes Disney intoning, adding that "the fantastic is always more acceptable to plain people—and sometimes to sophisticates—when it is rendered in the most realistic possible style." That commitment to realism put Disney increasingly in the same quandary as the earliest live-action "talkies." The more lifelike he made his cartoon characters, the more they needed a realistic "excuse" to sing. Thus in *Dumbo* neither the main character nor even his comic mouse side-

kick Timothy sings. We get some singing by the stork, dubbed by Sterling Holloway, as he delivers Dumbo to his mother. Roustabouts sing a work song as they raise the circus tents, drunken clowns sing "We're gonna hit the big boss for a raise," and an off-screen chorus sings "Pink Elephants on Parade" as Dumbo and Timothy share a tipsy fantasy. The most moving instance of song comes as Timothy takes Dumbo to visit his imprisoned mother, who sings "Baby Mine" as a lullaby, but all we see of her during the song is her trunk nuzzling Dumbo through the bars of her cage. It is a moving "performance" but no more integral a song than any lullaby a mother might sing to comfort her child.

If that "realistic" excuse for a mother to sing a lullaby to her baby seems a throwback to the earliest uses of song in film, one integral song in *Dumbo* recapitulates the early talkie principle that blacks can "spontaneously" burst into song in film. "When I See an Elephant Fly" relies upon that same racial stereotype as black crows sing and talk a jazzy, jivey catalogue song filled with witty puns such as "I saw a peanut stand, heard a rubber band.…I saw a front porch swing, heard a diamond ring." While racially insensitive, the song nevertheless defines character and advances the story.

Disney's self-imposed realistic constraints were even more rigid in *Bambi*, where his insistence on verisimilitude—even importing live deer for his animators to study—pushed integral song to the side. When Bambi courts Faline, neither animal sings; we only hear an off-screen chorus sing "I Bring You a Song." What had been an integral song, "I Like Falling," which raindrops sang as they fell over the forest, was cut and "Little April Shower," an off-screen choral song, was used in its place. Not even raindrops, given Disney's militant realism, could sing about their delight in falling over the forest. It is ironic that RKO, which had advanced the principle of integral song in the Astaire-Rogers films of the 1930s, should be the venue for Disney cartoons that eschewed songs that grew out of character and dramatic situation.

Columbia, which had made relatively few films that featured songs in the 1930s made more than seventy in the 1940s. Most of these presented songs as performances in some form of backstager, from *Reveille with Beverly* (1943), where Ann Miller plays a disk jockey on armed forces radio, to the phenomenally successful biopic, *The Jolson Story* in 1946 (and its sequel, *Jolson Sings Again*, in 1949), where Jolson himself dubbed his songs for young Larry Parks in an eerily aged voice. The best Columbia musicals featured Rita Hayworth, who danced wonderfully but whose singing (over her objections) was dubbed, usually by Martha Mears or Nan Wynn. The result was that Hayworth was more effective when rendering a song as a performance, where she merely had to act like a singer on stage. When she tried to sing expressively and integrally, some wonderful songs came off woodenly. In *You Were Never Lovelier* (1942), for example, Fred Astaire balks as he finds how much he and Hayworth have in common, saying she is much too elegant, cosmopolitan, and up-to-date for "an old duffer from Omaha" (Astaire's actual birthplace). To prove that she too loves simple things, such as moonlight and raindrops on a window pane, she sings "I'm Old-Fashioned," by Johnny Mercer and Jerome Kern, but Hayworth's rendition hardly portrays a woman who can wryly "classify" herself as "quaint." That Astaire does not join her in the song, whose lyric defines his character as well as it does hers, further weakens the presentation.

In *Cover Girl* (1944), Hayworth was paired with Gene Kelly, who plays the manager of a Brooklyn nightclub where Hayworth works as a dancer until she leaves him to find fame and glamour as a fashion model. When her success

proves hollow, she returns to Kelly as he is cleaning up his club after closing. As Hayworth enters, he rebuffs her with a crack about having known her for only "six months." She corrects him by spelling out—to the day, hour, and minute—how long ago they met. Hayworth then sings Ira Gershwin and Jerome Kern's "Long Ago and Far Away" as an expression of her love for Kelly. As she sings, he coldly continues putting up chairs on tables. After the song, she starts to leave, but he hums, then sings, some phrases of the lyric, his face framed by the legs of an upturned chair. Kelly truly renders the song as a dramatic expression of his character as he undergoes a change of heart that brings Hayworth rushing back to join him in a dance (around the now conveniently cleared tables).

Like Columbia, Universal, a studio that had been wary of musicals in the 1930s, turned out more than 150 films that featured songs in the following decade. In most of these, songs were presented as performances. Several films were built around Bud Abbott and Lou Costello, a radio comic duo who did not sing themselves but whose films usually included songs. *Buck Privates* (1941), for example, featuring The Andrews Sisters singing "Boogie Woogie Bugle Boy (of Company B)," was the top grosser of the year for Universal. The comedy team's other films featured excellent songs, such as Dorothy Fields and Jerome Kern's "Remind Me" ("Remind me, not to find you so attractive/ Remind me, that the world is full of men") from *One Night in the Tropics* (1940) and "You Don't Know What Love Is," by Don Raye and Gene De Paul, from *Keep 'Em Flying* (1941). Since Abbott and Costello were not singing, the numbers usually bore little relation to the story. In *Ride 'Em Cowboy* (1942), for example, Ella Fitzgerald suddenly appears in a railroad car singing "A-Tisket, A-Tasket" to entertain white passengers. Later, Dick Foran, playing a singing cowboy, serenades Anne Gwynne with Raye, Patricia Johnston, and De Paul's lovely "I'll Remember April," even though it's the kind of song one would more likely hear in a Manhattan nightclub than a western dude ranch.

Like all studios, Universal made backstagers about performers entertaining troops during World War II. One of the best of these was *Follow the Boys* (1944), where George Raft led a band of troupers into the South Pacific so that Sophie Tucker, Dinah Shore, The Andrews Sisters, and other stars could perform in war zones. One of the most moving presentations of song comes when Jeanette MacDonald sings for wounded soldiers in a field hospital. Asking the men to close their eyes and imagine she is their girl back home, she passes among their beds singing Gus Kahn and Isham Jones's "I'll See You in My Dreams" (1924) then comes upon a soldier whose eyes are bandaged, gently touching him as she concludes her number.

Universal made a few films in the 1940s in which songs were presented integrally, one of which emulated the kinds of musicals Arthur Freed created at MGM. *Can't Help Singing* (1944) was released the same year as *Meet Me in St. Louis* and featured a grown-up Deanna Durbin in a role that rivaled those portrayed by Judy Garland. *Can't Help Singing* had all the ingredients to be a superb, fully integrated musical film. The score was by Yip Harburg and Jerome Kern, the screenplay, about a girl who falls in love on a wagon trail westward was literate and lively, and the Technicolor cinematography, shot on location in Utah, was stunning. But compared to *Meet in St. Louis*, *Can't Help Singing* lacked the Freed magic that made songs flower out of dramatic moments. For example, we first see Deanna Durbin riding a horse and singing "Can't Help Singing" near the beginning of the film, but the song has no relation to the fact that she is galloping to Washington, D.C., to meet her army beau. When she follows her lieutenant westward, she meets a gambler, played by Robert Paige, as they take baths in a Missouri public bath house, separated by a wall, but open enough to allow for a duet. What they sing, however, is a reprise of "Can't Help Singing," which again bears no relation to their romantically comic situation and makes it seem like a preexisting song rather than one that expresses what characters feel at a particular dramatic moment. Both Durbin and Paige, moreover, have operatic voices that render a song more as a performance than an intimate soliloquy or conversation. Durbin "performed" "Any Moment Now," which registers her growing love for Paige, while Judy Garland quietly "acted" "The Boy Next Door" in *Meet Me in St. Louis*. These subtle but significant contrasts between *Can't Help Singing* and *Meet Me in St. Louis* underscore the difference between films produced by Arthur Freed at MGM and attempts to emulate those films by other studios. Clearly, creating films where songs grew out of character and dramatic situation was not easy: it required a producer like Freed and a director like Minnelli, who understood how song should emerge from the narrative, as well as performers such as Judy Garland, who, in turn, could render such songs with informal intimacy.

While it is understandable that other studios seldom tried to create the kind of musical films Freed produced at MGM in the 1940s, one wonders why other producers at MGM, notably Joe Pasternak and Jack Cummings, did not use the resources of the studio to create similar films. Pasternak, who came over

to MGM from Universal, where he made opera backstagers, usually featuring Deanna Durbin, continued with such musicals (in the 1950s he would build MGM movies around Mario Lanza). Cummings, who had produced *Born to Dance* in 1936, continued to grind out routine backstagers, but in 1949, he produced *Neptune's Daughter*, which featured swimming star Esther Williams—who could also sing, though she was given few opportunities to do so in films. While most of the film is a turgid comedy of mistaken identity, it featured one of the best integral songs to come out of the movies—even though the song was not written for the film. "Baby, It's

Cold Outside" was a number Frank Loesser had written for himself and his wife Lynne to perform at Hollywood parties as a contrapuntal duet between a wolf, who keeps insisting his girlfriend "mouse" stay at his apartment because of the cold weather. When Loesser, over Lynne's protests, offered the song to MGM, its witty repartee dictated how it must be presented. Esther Williams and co-star Ricardo Montalban talk-sing their way through the song. She protests "I really must go…," "My mother will start to worry…," "The neighbors might think…," while Montalban persists, "'I'll hold your hands, they're just like ice…," "Please don't hurry…," and "Baby, it's bad out there." The comic highpoints come as Williams wavers with such lines as "Well, maybe just a cigarette more." The song even survives a slapstick reprise by Betty Garrett, playing the feminine seductress of shy Red Skelton. Although an isolated moment in an MGM film *not* produced by Arthur Freed, "Baby, It's Cold Outside" demonstrated Freed's lesson of how a witty, integral song, informally and conversationally rendered, could enhance a movie (and win the Oscar for Best Song).

9

SINGIN' IN THE RAIN

MGM films of the 1950s continued to present songs in imaginative and integral fashion, particularly the musicals that were created by the "Freed Unit." Unlike their films of the 1940s, however, the best of the unit's musicals of the 1950s did not employ original songs. Instead, they took an existing body of songs by prominent songwriters and wove a new story around them. The first of these MGM "anthology" musicals, *An American in Paris* (1951), began when Gene Kelly suggested to Arthur Freed that they do a picture about an ex-GI who remains in Paris after the war to paint. That was, as Freed put it, an instance of "how pictures start in strange ways," for it made him recall George Gershwin's classical composition, *An American in Paris* (1928):

> Ira Gershwin is one of my closest friends, and I grew up with George Gershwin in New York when I was first writing songs. I used to spend a lot of time over at the Gershwins'. I still spend every Saturday night with Ira at his house, and we either play poker or pool. So one night I was with Ira Gershwin playing pool and afterwards it was about two in the morning, we sat talking about pictures and I said, "Ira, I've always wanted to make a picture about Paris. How about selling me the title *An American in Paris?*" He said, "Yes, if you use all Gershwin music."

Ira had intended to reach into his brother's "trunk" of unused melodies, as he had done for *The Shocking Miss Pilgrim* (1947), and create new lyrics for them, but Freed wanted to build a film around the Gershwins' existing songs. At most, Ira found, he was asked to write or rewrite "a line here and there in the old songs" to integrate them more fully into the film.

Freed then brought in Alan Jay Lerner to write the screenplay. Lerner, a brilliant lyricist himself, fresh from the Broadway triumphs of *Brigadoon* (1947) and *Paint Your Wagon* (1951), was also a librettist who, like Oscar

Hammerstein, could create moments in a story when characters' feelings flower into song. He forged a story around the Gershwin songs with the idea of dramatic integration uppermost in his mind:

> All I knew at this time was that I was going to write the story as if the Gershwin music had been written for it. I didn't want it to be just a cavalcade of songs. I wanted to write a story so the songs would appear because of the emotional and dramatic situation. I wanted them to seem like the original emotional expressions written for those particular moments in the film.

As a result of his dedication to musical and dramatic integration, *An American in Paris* is one of those rare films where the narrative is driven by song.

The rest of the Freed team shared Lerner's commitment to integration. As musical director Johnny Green put it:

> We were all "theater *Menschen*": we were all people from the theater, all of us, and, whether it's a tri-dimensional stage or a bi-dimensional screen, it's theater. So the *dramatic* values of the songs were most important to us. How do they apply to the story line? What can we make of it? Something that has both entertainment and good drama.

Under another theater person's direction, Vincente Minnelli, the wonderfully fused songs and story would be showcased in sets inspired by Impressionist and Post-Impressionist paintings—Renoir, Manet, Utrillo, Dufy, Rousseau, van Gogh, and Toulouse-Lautrec—that both he and Freed loved.

Drawing upon both famous and obscure songs by the Gershwins, the Freed Unit integrated them seamlessly into the story and characters of *An American in Paris*. The heroine, Leslie Caron, is introduced dancing, ballet-style, to "Embraceable You," while costumes, sets, and orchestrations shift, like George's music, between jazzy American and classical European traditions. "I Got Rhythm," by contrast, is presented in a thoroughly American idiom as Kelly dances with kids on a Paris street. Ira Gershwin also added new lyrics to this song that alluded to movie stars from Charlie Chaplin to Hopalong Cassidy and turned the song into an English lesson taught by Kelly to Parisian  kids. He also added a complete new chorus to "'S Wonderful" that provided a Franco-American duet between Georges Guetary and Gene Kelly. Guetary exults "'S *magnifique*!" and "'S *élégant*!" while Kelly responds with "'S what I seek" and "'S what I want!" Finally, they unite in bilingual camaraderie:

> *You've made my life so ting-a-lish;*
> *I'll even overlook your Eng-a-lish!*
> *'S exceptionnel! 'S no bagatelle—*
> *That you should care for me!*

Ira Gershwin's witty wordplay here extends across languages, for, as Gerald Mast observes, "the 'S' stands in as easily for the French 'c'est' as the English 'it's,' which are both contractions in the first place."

An American in Paris provided a new showcase for one of the Gershwins' greatest songs— the last one they worked on together before George's sudden death in 1938. In creating it, the Gershwin brothers evinced the extraordinarily close interplay between lyrics and music that had come to characterize their collaboration. As usual, they started with the music, but in this song, Ira asked George to insert a few extra notes into his melody so that he could work in a simple but critically important word—"and":

> *The radio **and** the telephone*
> ***And** the movies that we know*
> *May just be passing fancies*
> ***And** in time may go…*

"Love Is Here to Stay" was practically thrown away in *The Goldwyn Follies* where it was sung over the radio by Kenny Baker. In *An American in Paris*, however, it received the sumptuous treatment it deserved, sung by Kelly and danced by him and Caron along the banks of the Seine.

No one was more pleased with the film than Ira Gershwin, who thought it rendered tribute to the younger brother he always regarded as the genius in the family. "Everyone connected with the piece has outdone himself," he reflected. "A lot of integrity and ingenuity has gone into the making and I'll be very surprised if this isn't recognized by the critics and public....I think the studio is going to have everything it hoped for when the project started. It's really one of the best ever." For once, the critics, the public, and even the Motion Picture Academy of Arts and Sciences agreed: *An American in Paris* won seven Oscars, including Best Picture—the first musical to be so honored since 1936.

The success of *An American in Paris* prompted Freed to plan another "anthology" musical, this time using his own catalogue of songs with Nacio Herb Brown. Initially, he had thought about doing such a film back in 1949 "as a backstage musical, a remake of an old film called *Excess Baggage* (1928), set in vaudeville" and starring "the 'machine-gun' tap dancer, Ann Miller." But Lerner's success in writing a new screenplay around the songs of the Gershwins prompted Freed to recruit Betty Comden and Adolph Green, two other lyricists and librettists from Broadway. Like Lerner, they had to come up with a screenplay that would integrate the songs into a seamless narrative. As Roger Edens played Freed and Brown songs for them, Comden and Green thought about their historical background. "Many of these songs had been written for the earliest musical pictures made," they realized, "between 1929 and 1931, during the painful transition from silents to sound. And it occurred to us that, rather than try to use them in a sophisticated contemporary story or a gay-nineties extravaganza, they would bloom at their happiest in something that took place in the very period in which they had been written. With this decision made, we began to feel the ground beneath our feet at last."

Their first plan was to write a story about an actor who plays bit parts in silent westerns then suddenly, with the advent of sound, becomes a singing cowboy star. But as they talked with Arthur Freed himself and Douglas Shearer, head of MGM's sound department, they were intrigued by the convulsive effects wrought by the coming of sound: how the whirr of the camera had to be muffled by putting camera and camera operators in an overheated, soundproof box; how stationary microphones had to be concealed in props such as flower vases while actors huddled nearby to make sure the microphones picked up their voices; how such immobile cameras and stationary microphones made the movies stop *moving*. The writers also recalled how actors, who in silent movies had to act with their faces and bodies, now had to act with their voices as well. "We remembered particularly the downfall of John Gilbert, the reigning king of the silent screen in 1928, whose career was finished off by one single talking picture, in which, with his director's encouragement, he improvised his own love scene, insisting on the phrase 'I love you,' repeated many times with growing intensity, exactly as he had done it the year before in front of the silent camera."

To the writers' delight, Gene Kelly, after reading a draft of the script, agreed to play the starring role, even though he had just starred in and choreographed *An American in Paris*. Comden and Green also sided with Kelly and director Stanley Donen in their demand that a dancer, Donald O'Connor, play his buddy Cosmo, rather than Freed's choice of Oscar Levant. After Nina Foch, who had sparkled in *An American in Paris*, did not test well for the part of Lina Lamont, Jean Hagen was given the role. Arthur Freed also cast Debbie Reynolds as the girl Kelly falls in love with. Reynolds "had no particular talent as a singer and no experience at all as a dancer. 'In my opinion,' she said later, 'I was being thrown to the lions.' She was, however, athletic—she had planned to teach gymnastics before she was discovered at a beauty contest in Burbank—and a hard worker. As Kelly put it, she was 'as strong as an ox' and 'a good copyist,' who proved able to master the basics of dancing and put in long hours of demanding physical effort at the 'university of hard work and pain.'"

Reynolds's first song in the film was "All I Do Is Dream of You," which Freed and Brown had written for the 1934 film *Sadie McKee*. Although she does it as a performance number with a bevy of other chorines, the song fits integrally into the story. When Reynolds has a chance encounter with Kelly, playing famous silent movie star Don Lockwood, she affects disdain for movies and expresses her aspiration to become a stage actress. In the next scene, at a Hollywood party, she and other girls pop out of a huge cake to sing the song

in a 1920s "boop-boop-a doop" style as Kelly watches in amusement that a girl he dubs "Sarah Bernhardt" is as much a part of corny, commercial showbiz as he is.

As their romance blossoms, Kelly expresses his love for her in another performance song, "You Were Meant for Me," from *The Broadway Melody* (1929). Because, performer that he is, he cannot directly express his feelings for her in integral song, he must do so in a performance, and as he sets up the song he introduces her to the illusions Hollywood can create. On an empty soundstage, he shows her that 500 kilowatts of electricity can imitate a sunset, wind machines can create a breeze, and then, just as we think that nothing genuinely moving can come out of such artifice, he sings "You Were Meant for Me" in a way that

expresses his love for her innocence despite all the Hollywood claptrap.

One of the few new songs written for the film was "Make 'Em Laugh," since there was nothing in the Freed and Brown catalogue suitable for a knockabout number for Donald O'Connor. When Donen told Freed they needed a new song, Freed asked what kind of a song he wanted. "Well, it should be kind of 'Be a Clown' type number from *The Pirate*," Donen suggested, "because he's trying to cheer Gene up." "Arthur came back with 'Make 'Em Laugh,'" Donen later recalled, "which, in my opinion, is 100 per cent plagiarism." Freed had simply taken Porter's melody, made a few minor changes, and added a new but still very similar lyric. Where Porter had written,

Be a crack jackanapes
And they'll imitate you like apes.

Freed penned,

They'll be standing in lines
For those old honky tonk monkeyshines.

The two songs illustrate the difference between a great lyricist and a very good one.

"Partly we are to blame," Donen explained. "None of us had the courage to say to him, 'For Christ's sake, it obviously works for the number, but it's a stolen song, Arthur.' The only person who might have had the temerity to point out Freed's plagiarism was Irving Berlin, who was on the set when the playback of the song was aired. "Berlin is a tiny little man," Donen recalled, "his head started to move in the direction of the sound. 'Why, why, why—that's "Be a Clown,"' he said, 'I have never heard anything like that in my life!' He then began to sputter and turned to Arthur. 'Who wrote that song?' 'Well, the kids and I all got together and…come on, Irving, that's enough now.' 'The kids and I!' He wasn't going to take the rap alone on that. And Irving Berlin, of all people—one of Cole Porter's closest friends." Still, Donald O'Connor presented the song in a stunning comic dance, bouncing off walls, furniture, and floors, though the many injuries he sustained dragged the filming out over several weeks.

The title song of *Singin' in the Rain* has become one of the most memorable sequences in the history of film. Compared to the stiff performance rendition it received by Gus Edwards in *The Hollywood Revue of 1929*, "Singin' in the Rain"

is one of the most dynamic songs ever filmed. While the other songs are done as performances, the title song is the only dramatically integral song in *Singin' in the Rain*. In it, Kelly gives voice to his joy at being in love with Debbie Reynolds and at the prospect of making a successful sound movie by Donald O'Connor's "discovery" of dubbing. Yet at first Kelly was stymied about how to present the song. "I always hated the Jeanette MacDonald–Nelson Eddy way of going into a song," he said in a critical stab at the operatic stage tradition of bursting from dialogue into song. Instead, Roger Edens came up with a vamp that would ease the transition from talking to singing

in a thoroughly cinematic fashion. "Roger came
up with the solution," Kelly said, " 'Start off with
doodedoodo—doodedoo do.' " Instead of the
static cameras of 1929, the camera for *Singin' in
the Rain* moves dynamically across the set, cran-
ing, tracking, almost dancing with Kelly. The
effect was one of childish abandon so overjoyed

it could find cause for singing even in the midst of a downpour. Kelly asked that
six holes be dug in the sidewalk for water to accumulate in puddles, so that he
could splash in them, "and a lake was dug out in the gutter of the street. In fact,
the whole number, which was shot out of doors on one of the permanent streets
built on the studio back lot (East Side Street), demanded complex engineering to
deliver the right flow of water through a series of pipes for the rain and the downspout." The number stands as a monument to integral song twenty-five years after
the first presentation of song in a feature film when studios decreed a character
had to have a realistic "excuse" to sing. Here Kelly triumphs in integral, expressive
song that hasn't the least excuse, given the weather, for vocal exultation.

The Band Wagon (1953) was the Freed unit's next film built around the songs
of another great team of songwriters—Howard Dietz and Arthur Schwartz.
Beginning with *The Little Show* of 1929, Dietz and Schwartz had written songs
for a handful of sophisticated Broadway revues. Their productivity was always
hampered by the fact that Dietz had a "day job" as vice-president and publicity
head at MGM. In that role, he created the studio's logo—a roaring lion sur-
rounded by the motto "Ars Gratia Artis" ("Art for the Sake of Art"), a design
that reflected his education at Columbia University. Dietz fueled a nationwide
guessing game over who would play Scarlett O'Hara in *Gone with the Wind*, and
he coined such slogans as "MGM—more stars than there are in heaven." When
Clark Gable returned from military service in World War II, Dietz came up
with "Gable's back—and Garson's got him."

"Dietz was our head publicity man, a great friend of mine and a helluva
lyric writer," Freed observed. "I always said to Howard, 'One day I want to do
a picture with your songs.' " It was a tricky undertaking since Dietz, given the
limited time he could devote to lyric writing, preferred to write freestanding
songs for revues rather than integrate them into the story and characters of a
"book" musical. The Freed team would have to create an entirely new dramatic
context for the songs. Given the fact that Dietz and Schwartz had written all of
their songs for the stage, Comden and Green devised a backstager story about
mounting a Broadway musical. But their story, originally called *I Love Louisa*
until Freed managed to buy the rights to use the title *The Band Wagon* from
Twentieth Century-Fox, enlivened the old formula in sparkling fashion.

The very first song, "By Myself," is presented integrally by Fred Astaire. Comden and Green made their main character a former film star who tries to make a comeback in a Broadway show. "We were very nervous in the beginning about Fred's character," Comden recalled, "because it was based in so many ways on his actual position in life. It was not a man down, out and broke, but a man midway in his career, a man thinking of possibly retiring, or continuing to look for fresh fields." Roger Edens thought "By Myself," from the 1937 Broadway revue *Between the Devil*, would establish Astaire's character at the outset. As Astaire gets off the train from California to New York, he sees a group of reporters and thinks they are there to cover his arrival. When he realizes they are there to snap pictures of Ava Gardner, he shrugs off his fading from the limelight and saunters along the train platform chattily singing "By Myself," a catchphrase title that expresses his loneliness but also—as in "I'll do it all by myself"—his resolve to persevere.

The backstager plot thickens as Oscar Levant and Nanette Fabray, playing a husband-and-wife playwriting team, ask Astaire to star in their new musical. It's about a writer of children's books who feels he has sold his soul to the devil because he makes a fortune writing murder mysteries on the side. When they present their idea for the show to Jack Buchanan, who plays a highbrow actor and producer currently starring in *Oedipus Rex*, he sees their story as a modern version of *Faust* and insists they include a prominent ballerina, played by Cyd Charisse. When Astaire demurs at being involved in something so highbrow, Buchanan insists that "Bill Shakespeare" and "Bill Robinson" are both equally

"entertainment." It was for this moment that Freed said to Dietz and Schwartz, "Boys we need another song! In the script this director, Buchanan, is saying that practically anything you can do will work if it's entertaining. I want a 'There's No Business Like Show Business.'" Within an hour, the two songwriters came up with "That's Entertainment" for Buchanan, Astaire, Fabray, and Levant to sing as an egalitarian anthem to every facet of show business:

> *The clown*
> *With his pants falling down,*
> *Or the dance*

That's a dream of romance,
Or the scene
Where the villain is mean;
That's entertainment!

A brilliant "list" song, Dietz's lyric bristles with show business argot and allusions:

The clerk who is thrown out of work
By the boss
Who is thrown for a loss
By the skirt
Who is doing him dirt...
The dame
Who is known as the flame
Of the king
Of an underworld ring,
He's an ape
Who won't let her escape...

The lyric shows Dietz at his most brilliant in handling image and vernacular phrasing—

Some great Shakespearean scene
Where a ghost and a prince meet
And ev'ryone ends in mincemeat

—but also at his most hurried and slapdash—

It can be Oedipus Rex
Where a chap kills his father
And causes a lot of bother.

Even with its lyrical blemishes, however, "That's Entertainment" is one of the great celebrations of show business and functions more as an integral than a performance song. It reflects the show business world of *The Band Wagon*, where Greek tragedy and musical comedy, ballet and tap, *Hamlet* and circus clowns are devoted to the same end—entertainment. Reprised when Astaire leads the cast in jettisoning the *Faust* story and creating a good, old-fashioned musical comedy that triumphs on Broadway, the song again is presented not just as a performance but as an integral number that is central to the plot, characters, and theme of the film.

Compared to this great triumvirate of anthology musicals, original film musicals produced by Arthur Freed in the 1950s were less successful. By 1953 Freed had been at MGM for twenty-five years, fifteen as a producer, during which he had overseen thirty-eight films. Like the advent of sound in the late 1920s, the early 1950s were a time of upheaval in Hollywood. In what was called the "divorcement," courts forced studios to give up their ownership of theater chains, an arrangement that had guaranteed, through "block booking," that whatever movies studios made would be exhibited, since, to get a studio's best films, theaters had to take all of its productions. Now, theater owners were free to choose the pictures they screened, making competition much more rigorous for studios to produce films theaters would *want* to show. Where once studios could carry a staff of songwriters, choreographers, arrangers, and other musical personnel to crank out musicals that would have a guaranteed audience, now each film had to stand on its own. Studios could no longer afford to keep under long-term contract the various people who were needed to put together a musical film.

Even more threatening was the new medium of television, which by 1952 was in ten million American homes, keeping people in their living rooms in the evening rather than enticing them out to the movies. Hollywood fought back with innovations television could not rival—widescreen Cinemascope, stereophonic sound, and 3-D (three-dimensional) films where, with the help of special glasses, the action seemed to leap off the screen and into the audience. While not in direct competition with Hollywood, Broadway musicals had become so successful, along with their original cast recordings made on the new LP (long-playing) records designed for the equally new hi-fi (high fidelity) phonographs, that they augured the safest way of making film musicals. With many of their songs already hits and the cast albums familiar to listeners, a film adaptation that stuck close to the stage original was usually a sure bet. Even though the film versions were often "stagey" rather than cinematic, they pleased audiences who wanted to see a musical they might not have been able to see on Broadway (at a mere fraction of the price).

While most of their previous musical films had been wholly original or very loose adaptations of the stage originals, the Freed Unit at MGM now had to provide the public with faithful film adaptations of successful Broadway shows. Lerner and Loewe's *Brigadoon* (1954) was shot on a huge soundstage that covered forty thousand square feet in a simulation of a Scottish village and its surrounding hills. *Kismet* (1955) followed with its Broadway score, including hit songs such as "Stranger in Paradise," "Baubles, Bangles and Beads," and "And

This Is My Beloved," replicated in the film. *Silk Stockings* (1957) had two new songs by Porter, "Fated to Be Mated" and "The Ritz Roll and Rock," but, as Fred Astaire found in his meeting with the composer during preproduction planning, "Cole has a way of losing interest in the revival of the vehicles he has *already done on the stage.*"

Accelerating the trend toward making Hollywood versions of Broadway musicals were the poor showings of original musical films essayed by the Freed Unit in the 1950s. In *Pagan Love Song* (1950), *Royal Wedding* (1951), and *The Belle of New York* (1952), for example, numbers are staged with spectacular effects that actually detract attention from the song itself. In *Pagan Love Song*, Esther Williams swims in the night sky and sings "The Sea of the Moon" as a lavish water ballet unfolds around her. In *Royal Wedding*, Fred Astaire sings "You're All the World to Me" then dances on the walls and ceiling of his room, a feat made possible by the construction of a set where every object was nailed down inside a box that could be rotated along with the camera. In a variation of the same idea, *The Belle of New York* has Astaire rising into the air when he finds himself in love with Vera-Ellen. When he tells her he is "numb" in her presence, she says when you're in love you should be "elated," and he takes off as he sings "Seeing's Believing," dancing atop the Washington Square Arch as pigeons flutter about him, then soaring into the clouds. In such films it is the spectacle that makes an impact, not the song; their "visual styles and performance energy," observes Gerald Mast, "carry them further than their songs."

Other producers at MGM, however, successfully followed Freed's example and made excellent films where original songs were integral to characters and story. The best of these was *Seven Brides for Seven Brothers* (1954), which might have been even better had it not been restricted in budget from the outset. "*Seven Brides for Seven Brothers* was supposed to be a much more expensive picture than it was," recalled co-star Jane Powell. "But they really wanted to put the money into *Brigadoon*, which they did." Producer Jack Cummings insisted he could pull it off on the relatively low budget, even though it meant using a lot of painted backdrops rather than authentic mountain location shots. "It was a sleeper," Powell recalled. "It was not supposed to be as successful as it was. If it had had a bigger budget, it might not have been what it turned out to be."

The movie was based on "The Sobbin' Women," a story by Stephen Vincent Benét about seven brothers in the mountains of Oregon who, inspired by the eldest's account of the Roman rape of the Sabine women, kidnap girls in a nearby town to be their wives. Benét's folksy story was skillfully adapted by veteran Hollywood writers Albert Hackett, Frances Goodrich, and Dorothy Kingsley; the songs were written by Johnny Mercer and Gene De Paul; and the stunning choreography was staged by Michael Kidd. The chemistry among the creative team made for a magnificently song-and-dance-driven musical film.

The songs of Mercer and De Paul defined the western regional characters, advanced the story, and reveled in dialect. When "Adam" (Howard Keel), the oldest brother, goes into town in search of a wife, he sings a mountain man's forthright serenade to the girl he is determined to find:

> *Bless yore beautiful hide,*
> *You're just as good as lost.*
> *Don't know your name,*
> *But I'm stakin' my claim,*
> *'Less your eyes is crossed.*

Although Keel had as operatic a voice as Nelson Eddy, he talks his way nonchalantly through the song as he strolls through the town, appraising the women he encounters. When he sees Jane Powell splitting firewood and working in a restaurant, he shrewdly offers a proposal of marriage (after apologizing that he doesn't have time for a leisurely eastern courtship). After she consents, however, she finds that she must cook and clean for his unkempt and unmannerly brothers. In scenes reminiscent of Snow White in the home of the Seven Dwarfs, Powell makes the boys wash up and eat in polite fashion. Later, in "Goin' Co'tin,'" she instructs them in dance and etiquette so that they can socialize at a barn raising in town. At this point in the film, Michael Kidd's choreography comes to the fore, first in a spectacular dancing encounter with the town girls—and their beaux—then in a sequence of songs. As Johnny Mercer explained, he and De Paul wrote the songs at Kidd's behest:

> Michael Kidd had this idea of casting seven professional dancers in the leading roles, and this led to some interesting song-and-dance routines like "Lonesome Polecat" and "Sobbin' Women." There you have a classic example of how a songwriter has often to take his cue from his collaborators and, if he's a thorough-bred pro, he'll come up with something that fits the bill and keeps everyone happy. Michael Kidd explained to us his conception of the "Lonesome Polecat" scene—the rhythmic lament of the brothers for their "brides"—and Gene and I went and thought out lyrics and music to match.

Keel's brothers bewail their bachelorhood in a metronomically timed slow ballet as they chop wood and sing:

I'm a lonesome polecat, lonesome, sad, and
blue,
'Cause I ain't got no feminine polecat, vowing
to be true...
Can't make no vows, to a herd of cows...
I'm a mean old hound dog, baying at the
moon...
Can't shoot the breeze, with a bunch of trees...

With little dialogue in between them, one song leads into another as Keel rouses his brothers to action by recounting the story of "The Sobbin' Women" from his wife's copy of *Plutarch's Lives* and urging them to swoop down on the village to make off with their would-be brides. The brothers, their spirits lifted, join in with Keel, singing "Oh, they acted angry and annoyed" as Russ Tamblyn chimes in, "But secretly they was overjoyed." The brothers drive off vowing, "We're going to make those sobbin' women smile!"

After a narrative so wonderfully driven by song, the musical pace slackens as Powell is horrified when the brothers return with the girls just as snow falls to isolate them all for the winter. After sulking in his trapping cabin for the winter, Keel comes to realize, when Powell gives birth to his daughter, that the thought of a man kidnapping *his* child would be horrendous. As spring returns, and the feelings of the would-be brides soften toward the brothers, the nar-

rative again blossoms into song as the six couples celebrate "Spring, Spring, Spring." Johnny Mercer, who some twenty years earlier had balked at supplying multiple refrains for "Too Marvelous for Words," rose to the task by providing each couple with a refrain that catalogued nature's annual fertility rites:

Oh, the barnyard is busy
In a regular tizzy,
And the obvious reason
Is because of the season.
Ma Nature's lyrical
With her yearly miracle,
Spring, spring, spring.
All the henfolk are hatchin'
While their menfolk are scratchin'
To insure the survival
Of each brand new arrival...
Slow but surely the turtle
Who's enormously fertile
Lays her eggs by the dozens,
Maybe some are her cousins...

Although not all the lyrics were used in the movie, the song still provides an exuberant finale of imaginative lyrics that rival nature's own fecundity. Yet while all of Mercer and De Paul's songs function integrally within the film, not a single one became independently popular—a feat that the best Broadway shows by Rodgers and Hammerstein, Lerner and Loewe, and Frank Loesser managed to pull off.

Another MGM producer who took his cue from Arthur Freed was Sol Siegel, whose *High Society* (1956) was Cole Porter's first original film score in ten years. The film opens with Louis Armstrong and his band on a bus bound for the Newport Jazz Festival, singing an expository song, "High Society Calypso," that outlines the back story: Bing Crosby, the wealthy dilettante who runs the festival, "got the blues" cause his former wife, Grace Kelly, who divorced him because she "thought writin' songs was beneath his class," is "gonna marry a square." But Armstrong promises "just trust your Satch to that weddin' and kill that match." Based on Philip Barry's 1939 play, *The Philadelphia Story*, which had been made into a film in 1940 starring Cary Grant and Katharine Hepburn, the story of *High Society* develops through songs.

When, for example, Frank Sinatra and Celeste Holm, playing a reporter and photographer from a slick magazine come to do a story about Kelly's wedding, they vent their envy of the wealth that surrounds them in "Who Wants to Be a Millionaire?" They half-talk, half-sing the banter song in which they affect disdain for caviar, yachts, champagne, and private planes in one of Porter's patented "catalogue" songs. By contrast, the next song is a much simpler, straightforward number that arises out of a meeting between Crosby and Kelly when he thanks her for the first few weeks of their marriage, which have remained the happiest of his life. After his departure, she finds that he has left behind a wedding present, a model of *True Love*, the yacht they had sailed on their honeymoon. As she pushes the boat across her pool, she recalls their honeymoon cruise and, in a flashback, Crosby sings "True Love," with

Kelly joining him, in her weak but charming voice, in the closing refrain. Were it not so bone-simple in its expression of love—"I give to you and you give to me/ True love, true love"—the song would be cloying. With such simplicity, it undoes all the glittering wealth that surrounds them, and even though Crosby and Kelly are on a yacht when he sings it, accompanying himself on a concertina after a simple meal of tomato juice and a sandwich, it expresses the direct and tender affection they have for one another. It became one of Porter's biggest hits, a song, musically and lyrically, so completely different from his usual sophisticated and witty style. Even a connoisseur of song such as music

publisher Max Dreyfus wrote to Porter, "In all my sixty-odd years of music publishing, nothing has given me more personal pleasure and gratification than the extraordinary success of your 'True Love.' It is truly a simple, beautiful, tasteful composition worthy of a Franz Schubert."

The highlight of the film comes as Crosby and Sinatra do their only on-screen duet, "Well, Did You Evah!" a song originally written for the stage production of *Du Barry Was a Lady* (1940). Porter revised the lyric for *High Society*, and Sinatra and Crosby draw upon lines from both the original and revised versions as they banter high society gossip. Sinatra begins with,

> *Have you heard that Mimsie Starr*
> *Just got pinched in the As—tor Bar?*

They chit-chat in between stretches of singing and when Crosby warbles a patented "Ba-ba-babum," Sinatra snaps, "Don't dig that kind of crooning, chum," and Crosby dead-pans, "You must be one of the newer fellas." The song is presented so informally and conversationally that it's not clear when talking turns into singing and back again, forming a seamless interchange of song and dialogue.

Although producers Jack Cummings and Sol Siegel had beaten Arthur Freed at his own game of integrating songs into character and story, Freed ended the decade with *Gigi* (1958), a triumphant swan song. He had closely followed Lerner and Loewe's adaptation of George Bernard Shaw's *Pygmalion* into a Broadway musical. It was Freed, in fact, who suggested a title for the production to a stymied Lerner: "London Bridge is falling down—*My Fair Lady*!" After seeing the out-of-town opening of *My Fair Lady* in Philadelphia, Freed was determined to create an equally lavish and integral musical for the screen. At breakfast the next morning, he told Lerner, "I'm buying *Gigi* and I want you and Fritz to do it for me." "I'd love to write it," Lerner said, "but there would have to be a wait of at least six months." He also pointed out that Loewe had never written music for a motion picture and probably would regard writing for anything but the stage as beneath him. "I'll wait six months," Freed promised, "and you take care of Fritz."

Colette's novella had been the basis of a French film as well as a Broadway play starring Audrey Hepburn (whom Freed initially envisioned in the title role) in 1953. Freed's intention to turn it into a film musical, however, was met with opposition. The Code Office had a litany of objections to a story about a young woman being groomed to become a courtesan, and studio executives put similar objections more pithily: "Why does Arthur want to make a picture about a whore?" As he had with objections to his making *Meet Me in St. Louis*, Freed would answer the naysayers in his own inimitable way—with songs, songs that define character, drive the story, and treat the amoral premise of the film with wit and charm.

As Lerner had predicted, Loewe did not want to do a film—or anything else. Unlike his collaborator, who was always leaping from one project to another, the composer wanted to relax at the gambling tables of Monte Carlo after the success of *My Fair Lady*. The most he would agree to do was read the script when Lerner had completed a draft. Lerner balked at writing lyrics without his regular collaborator, and Freed judiciously let him go off to Europe to work on the script. At Freed's request, Lerner also sounded out Leslie Caron, who had just played in a London stage production of *Gigi*, as well as Maurice Chevalier, whom Lerner had always wanted to write for. Caron was interested in the part but did not want another dancing role and was hesitant about working with Minnelli, whom Freed had slated to direct. Louis Jourdan, in turn, was not interested in doing a singing role and initially turned down the chance to play Gaston. The only part of the puzzle that fell easily into place was Chevalier, who, at seventy-two, agreed to do the role of Honoré, saying "I'm too old for women, too old for that extra glass of wine, too old for sports. All I have left is the audience."

Things began to come together when Loewe was so taken with Lerner's script that he agreed to write the score. When Lerner called Freed with the news, the producer said, "I knew all the time he would come around." He then signed Cecil Beaton, who had worked on *My Fair Lady*, to design sets and costumes, and Hermione Gingold to play the part of Gigi's grandmother (and former lover of Honoré). Then, in what was probably the biggest gamble Freed ever took in his career, he decided that the film would be shot, on location, in Paris. That would mean shutting down the city's major streets, closing Maxim's restaurant for four days, restoring the interior to look as it did in 1900, and opening the huge winter ice palace to shoot a skating scene in what turned out to be a blistering August heat wave.

The first day of shooting was devoted to the opening scene, where Chevalier, as was his custom, talks directly to the camera then sings the film's first song as a crowd of people stroll or ride carriages in the Bois de Boulogne. "With a pioneering spirit, determined to overcome all difficulties," recalled Cecil Beaton, "we met in the Bois that summer morning." But problems with costumes, the movement of the many equestrian and pedestrian extras, and camera technicians prevented even one take. At lunch, Beaton marveled that Freed was unperturbed. "Arthur did not seem worried that the morning had produced no result. 'What's the difference—Vincente's done a lot of planning—it'll work out!' I marveled that the man could behave so philosophically knowing that a day's shooting cost him $40,000." The next day proved even more difficult with poor lighting, windy weather that created clouds of dust, and tightly corseted actresses and extras who passed out in the heat. Only on the third day of shooting, did they get a usable take.

In the finished picture, however, the scene and song come across with effortless grace. The turn-of-the-century setting makes the world of the film seem remote, and Chevalier's direct address to the screen audience in his elderly persona disarms the sexual overtones of his expository song and dialogue. The first people he greets are a married couple with a baby, and he explains that in Paris of 1900, as in all places in all times, most people are married. After a proper bow to the sacredness of the institution, he ever so delicately explains that there are people who "are not married"—mostly men like himself—and people who "do not marry"—mostly women such as the beautiful, elegantly dressed courtesans who drive by in carriages. With that charming observation, he defuses the premise of the story, even commenting with witty irony—and in rhyme—on two such ladies:

> *Here are some of those to behold*
> *For whom the bells have never tolled.*
> *Oh what a poor expense they spare*
> *In those pathetic rags they wear.*

Having touched on the subject lightly and with consummate class, Chevalier then turns to a group of little girls playing in the park, noting that some will grow up to marry and some will be those who "do not marry." Nonchalantly he moves from dialogue into the chatty verse and then the chorus of "Thank Heaven for Little Girls" with its celebration of both childhood and female maturation:

> *Those little eyes so helpless and appealing,*
> *One day will flash*
> *And send you crash-*
> *ing through the ceiling.*

He interrupts the song to introduce Gigi then reprises the bridge and final A-section of the song as the camera follows her from the park to her home.

Just as "Thank Heaven for Little Girls" introduces us to Gigi and the role she is being groomed for, another song, "It's a Bore," quickly follows to introduce "Gaston" (Louis Jourdan), who goes to lunch with his uncle Honoré but complains of the dullness of his life in Paris. In rhymed dialogue and chanted song, the two debate the charms of Paris and other cities, the older Chevalier affirming the excitement

of life—"Don't tell me Venice has no allure"—the younger Jourdan his ennui—"Just a town without a sewer." The exchange impels Jourdan to stop the carriage and, instead of going to lunch at the embassy, get out to call on Gigi and her grandmother, the only place in Paris he finds refreshing.

The next song, "The Parisians," gives Gigi a chance to express her feelings as she is being tutored by her great-aunt (played by Isabel Jeans), a former courtesan, who trains her in the skills of elegant womanliness from table manners to appreciation of fine jewelry. Although Jeans assumes Gigi is ignorant of what she is being groomed for, the girl surprises her by saying she knows that the women in her family are the kind who "do not marry." Jeans recovers by saying, they may marry "at last" and tells Gigi her next lesson will be in learning about cigars—not to smoke herself, as Gigi, in a sudden reversion to innocence, assumes but to select for a male companion. Left to herself, Caron (dubbed by Betty Wand) gives voice to her childish bewilderment over love, sex, and marriage:

> *I don't understand the Parisians!*
> *They think love so miraculous and grand.*
> *But they rave about it*
> *And won't live without it!*
> *I don't understand—the Parisians!*

To render the song cinematically, she rushes out of her aunt's apartment and strides through the park, stopping to speak snatches of the song as she passes statues of nude couples. The song is wittily expressive of her personal confusion and the universal bewilderment of children about sexuality. At its conclusion, she runs into Jourdan, who takes her to the ice palace where he buys her a child's drink and has champagne for himself. They watch his current mistress, played by Eva Gabor, take a skating lesson with a man who, unbeknown to Jourdan, is also her lover.

The charmingly innocent conversation he has with Gigi is contrasted, in the next scene, by the artificial gaiety of his dinner with Gabor at Maxim's. As Jourdan watches Gabor flutter about their table, choosing and lighting a cigar for him, he goes into an impassioned internal monologue, "She's Not Thinking of Me," that is heard on the soundtrack while on screen we merely see him fidgeting and yawning with his usual ennui:

> *Bless her little heart,*
> *Crooked to the core.*
> *Acting out a part,*
> *What a rollicking, frolicking bore.*

Lerner, who was meticulous about his lyrics, frequently leaving a few lines blank when he turned them in to the studio so that he could continue polishing them, held up production for several days until he came up with this rhyme:

> *How she fills me with ennui.*
> *She's so oo-lah-lah,*

So untrue lah-la,
But she's not thinking of me!

Freed was so frustrated by the delay that he ordered musical director André Previn to break into Lerner's hotel room and filch the lyric. Previn refused but told Lerner about Freed's stratagem, and the lyric was expeditiously completed.

As filming progressed, however, so did the budget overruns, close to half a million dollars, and as weather continued to hamper location shooting, MGM summoned Freed to return to Hollywood to finish shooting there. The shift to Hollywood marred songs, particularly the great duet between Chevalier and Gingold, "I Remember It Well," which was shot on a soundstage against a painted backdrop that simulated a sunset. It was a sadly cheapened setting for one of the film's greatest songs, with Chevalier and Gingold talking and singing their way through reminiscences of the last evening of their youthful romance. Chevalier's memory gets things wrong, and Gingold corrects him on each point in gentle stichomythia:

Chevalier: We met at nine.
Gingold: We met at eight.
Chevalier: I was on time.
Gingold: No, you were late.
Chevalier: Ah yes, I remember it
           well.…We dined with friends.
Gingold: We dined alone.
Chevalier: A tenor sang.
Gingold: A baritone.

The exchange continues, and his memory fails him more and more:

Chevalier: You wore a gown of gold.
Gingold: I was all in blue.

Helplessly, he pleads,

Am I getting old?

She lovingly restores his ego with what has to be one of the most heart-wrenching moments in film:

Oh no! Not you!
How strong you were.

How young and gay.
A prince of love in ev'ry way.

And he closes the song with the assurance she has given him in a moving yet
simple repetition of the title phrase:

Ah yes! I remember it well.

It is a thoroughly dramatic, integral, song done in purely Hollywood fashion—
informally, conversationally, more spoken than sung.

The crowning moment of *Gigi* comes with the title song, which emerges
from a comic montage of Gigi being trained by her great-aunt in all the skills
of a courtesan—tasting wine, choosing cigars, selecting gowns—and clum-
sily flubbing each of her lessons. Nevertheless, when Jourdan sees her in her
apartment, not in her Scottish plaid schoolgirl outfit but a sumptuous white
gown with a fashionably high collar, he realizes that she has reached maturity and will soon be eligible to become the mistress of a man of wealth.
After saying she looks like "an organ grinder's monkey," he storms out of
the apartment but returns in a few moments, apologetically, and offers to
take her to tea. It is then that her grandmother, sending Gigi to her room,
informs Jourdan that she now would be compromised were she to be seen
with him in public, given his reputation with women. That "labeling," as
Gingold delicately but with business-minded practicality puts it, would
then ruin her chances to secure a man who would "take care of her." This
exchange truly outrages Jourdan who again storms out of the room and into
the streets of Paris.

The dramatic situation is one of the richest contexts for song, and Jourdan
angrily strides through the city, talking to himself in rhymed patter:

She looked surprisingly mature
And had a definite allure.
It was a shock, in fact, to me,
A most amazing shock to see
The way it clung
On one so young.

After another outburst, he insists she is still a little girl,

Getting older, it is true,
Which is what they always do,

Till that unexpected hour
When they blossom like a flower.

The image of a blossoming flower suddenly gives him pause over a tree-lined stream, and he shifts from rhymed patter to the verse of the title song:

There's sweeter music when she speaks, isn't there?
A different bloom about her cheeks, isn't there?
Could I be wrong? Could it be so?
Oh, where or where did Gigi go?

After more hesitation, he talks his way through the first eight bars of the chorus:

Gigi! Am I fool without a mind
Or have I merely been too blind to realize

Then he ever so gently shifts to singing:

Oh Gigi! Why you've been growing up before my eyes.

From there he alternates between talking and singing in a consummate example of conversational presentation of song in film:

Gigi! You're not at all that funny, awkward little girl I knew!
Oh, no! Overnight there's been a breathless change in you.
Oh, Gigi! While you were trembling on the brink
Was I out yonder somewhere blinking at a star?
Oh, Gigi! Have I been standing up too close or back too far?

In these wonderfully simple lyrics Lerner not only captures Jourdan's realization of his feelings but the universal miracle of a girl's passage to womanhood. At the culmination, Lerner subtly underscores the sexual element in that transition:

When did your sparkle turn to fire?
When did your warmth become desire?

His realization of Gigi's transformation is presented visually through a montage of images of Caron—both as girl and woman—then we see Jourdan in a medium shot against the gushing fountains as he reverses his course and returns to her apartment.

In another film, this extraordinary song would have been the romantic climax, but in *Gigi* it extends the dramatic narrative in song as Jourdan offers to make Gigi his mistress. Although her grand-mother and great-aunt are delighted at the prospect, when Jourdan discusses it with Caron, she tearfully rejects the role of courtesan, fearing the humiliation it will bring and a future when he will tire of her. Once again, he storms out of her apartment and explains his predicament to Chevalier, who advises Jourdan to come to Maxim's  that evening with another woman and promises that by the following day he will have forgotten the whole thing. After Jourdan leaves, Chevalier reflects, as he sits alone with a glass of wine, on the plight of the "poor boy," reasoning that "youth can really do a fellow in." Lerner and Lowe came up with yet another brilliantly integral song for Chevalier that serves as comic relief to Jourdan's anguished aria:

> *How lovely to sit here in the shade*
> *With none of the woes of man and maid.*
> *I'm glad I'm not young anymore.*
> *The rivals that don't exist at all,*
> *The feeling you're only two feet tall.*
> *I'm glad I'm not young anymore.*
> *No more confusion, no morning-after surprise,*
> *No self-delusion that when you're telling those lies*
> *She isn't wise.*

Chevalier talks and sings his way through "I'm Glad I'm Not Young Anymore" then rises and walks off with his characteristic slouch, straw boater tilted rakishly forward, arms fluttering, in an exit that crowns his more than thirty years of nonchalantly rendering song in film.

Despite the fact that not all of the numbers could be shot on location in Paris, that Jourdan is not completely comfortable singing, and that Caron's singing voice had to be dubbed, the extraordinary presentation of integral song made *Gigi* an artistic and commercial success. At a cost of $3,319,355 ($442,159 over budget), it grossed $13,208,725 and garnered nine Academy Awards, plus a special Oscar for Chevalier—more accolades than for any previous musical film. One of those Oscars, most deservedly, went to producer Arthur Freed.

10

Something's Gotta Give

In an industry that thrives by spawning clones of successful films, it is puzzling that other studios did not imitate the films of the Freed Unit at MGM. It may be that it was simply too difficult to create movies that presented excellent original songs expressively and integrally. Such films required talented songwriters, screenwriters, choreographers, directors, performers, and, above all, a producer who, with a songwriter's instinct, could coordinate their efforts to create a film whose narrative was propelled by songs. Paramount's attempt to make such a film in *Aaron Slick from Punkin Crick* (1952), for example, was an abysmal failure. Cast in the mold of such western musicals as *The Harvey Girls*, and stage productions such as *Oklahoma!*, the film's weak narrative has Dinah Shore and Alan Young playing country folk and singing banal songs by Ray Evans and Jay Livingston such as "Marshmallow Moon" and "Purt' Nigh, But Not Plumb." The songs do not define character, emanate from dramatic moments, or drive the narrative; they are merely inserted, here and there, in the story.

After such a failure, Paramount understandably relied more upon the performance convention for presenting song, and, in the first part of the decade, relied as well upon its stalwart Bing Crosby. Crosby made another half dozen films during the decade, including one more "road" picture with Hope, *Road to Bali* (1953), and a blockbuster backstager musical, *White Christmas* (1954). Like *Easter Parade*, *White Christmas* was a combination of Berlin's older songs—including the title song—along with several newer ones, such as "Sisters" and "Count Your Blessings," both rendered as performances. The songs are framed by a Christmas revue Crosby and co-star Danny Kaye stage to help out their former general and his ski resort. *White Christmas* turned out to be the biggest money-making film of 1954, grossing $12 million.

One of the best of the new songs Crosby presented in his 1950s films at Paramount was "In the Cool, Cool, Cool of the Evening" by Johnny Mercer and Hoagy Carmichael, who had written the song for a film called *Keystone Girl*, which was never produced. At a Hollywood party, Mercer and Carmichael played the song, and Frank Capra perked up his ears. "My father heard the song," Frank Capra, Jr. said, "and loved it. He asked Mercer and Carmichael if he could use it in a film he was directing, *Here Comes the Groom*." The film starred Crosby as a roving reporter who adopts two French children but must marry a suitable mother within five days or give them up. With Mercer's folksy dialect ("When the party's gettin' a glow on,/ 'N' singin' fills the air,/ If I ain't in the clink,/ And there's sumpin' to drink,/ You can tell 'em I'll be there"), Carmichael's regional syncopations, Crosby's laid-back persona, and Capra's pleasant discovery that co-star Jane Wyman could sing, "In the Cool, Cool, Cool of the Evening," although not integral to story or character, was presented charmingly. Crosby and Wyman are ex-sweethearts (who, of course, still love each other despite Wyman's engagement to Franchot Tone). They sing the song at night in the Boston real estate office where Wyman works, dancing around desks, opening file cabinets, interrupting the song with spoken quips. After they continue the song in the elevator, past a puzzled cleaning lady in the lobby, and out the door to Wyman's cab, Wyman looks back at Crosby in a shot that suggests she realizes how much fun she has with him. The song won the Academy Award, but because it was not explicitly written for *Here Comes the Groom* (1951), the award caused some controversy. Since it had not been recorded or published before it appeared in the film, however, "In the Cool, Cool, Cool of the Evening" was deemed eligible for the Oscar.

The best of Crosby's backstagers of the decade was *The Country Girl* (1954). The film was based on a successful stage play by Clifford Odets about an alcoholic singer trying for a comeback, his long-suffering wife (played by Grace Kelly), and a tough-nosed Broadway producer (played by William Holden) who mounts a "revolutionary" new musical. In adapting Odets's play into a musical film, writer-director George Seaton concentrated on the dramatic triangle of Crosby, Kelly, and Holden, but minimalized the role of songs in the film. Where the backstager story had once served as merely a clothesline upon which to hang songs, songs now were upstaged by the story. When Ira Gershwin, who was teamed with Harold Arlen to provide the songs, read the script, he realized "the result won't be a musical." Songs take a back seat to the drama, as when Crosby sings "It's Mine, It's Yours" in an audition for the lead in Holden's musical. The sprightly, upbeat song is overshadowed by Crosby's desperate attempt to make a comeback that will help him recover from alcoholism and alleviate the guilt he feels over the accidental death of his son (guilt, he later admits, that is only a crutch he uses to explain the failure of his career). While the film showed that Crosby had real depth as a dramatic actor, it did little to integrate songs into the story or even showcase songs done as performances, such as "The Land around Us," the big number from the musical, which comes off as "an uninspired excerpt from *Oklahoma!*" Crosby, in a cowboy hat, leads his fellow settlers in a song that celebrates the town they will build, envisioning the "post office" here and the "high school" there. The song serves only to highlight the contrast between the pastoral simplicity of small-town life portrayed in the Broadway musical and the harsh realities of New York show business. Crosby's last film for Paramount was a remake of Cole Porter's Broadway musical *Anything Goes* in 1956, in whose original film adaptation he had starred back in 1936, an ironic encore for a star who had done so much to present integral songs in original Hollywood movies.

As Crosby's star faded, Paramount found a new team of comic sidekicks in Dean Martin and Jerry Lewis, a kind of Abbott and Costello duo that could sing. From their first appearance together in *My Friend Irma* (1949), Martin and Lewis went on to make fifteen more films at Paramount before their much-publicized squabbles broke up the act. Most songs in their films were done as performance numbers, but in *Artists and Models* (1955) the presentation of song was more imaginative. Shirley MacLaine and Dorothy Malone are sunbathing on the roof of their apartment building, and MacLaine rubs suntan oil on Malone's back. When Dean Martin comes along, he silently persuades MacLaine to let him take over. As they switch places, MacLaine turns the radio on, telling Malone that the song that comes up, "Inamorata," is one of her favorites. Martin then sings along to the music as he rubs oil on Malone's back, who, unaware of his presence, interrupts the song with quips that compare "Inamorata" and its singer to "That's Amore," Martin's big hit from *The Caddy* (1953).

"Inamorata" gets a much more expressive reprise by MacLaine, who leaves Martin and Malone alone to sing the song by herself in the stairwell. Her rendition introduces a poignant note of romantic yearning rarely seen in Martin and Lewis films. Even before MacLaine can complete the chorus, however, Jerry Lewis enters, and she sings the song to him in comically stentorian fashion as she pirouettes along the banister and stairs. MacLaine's introspective, expressive rendition of "Inamorata," sandwiched between Martin's radio "singalong" performance and her zany serenade to Lewis, is a rare, refreshing instance of song integrated into character and dramatic moment in a Martin and Lewis movie.

Paramount was able to create one musical during the decade that stands with the best "anthology" films of the Freed unit at MGM, largely because it was produced by Roger Edens, directed by Stanley Donen, and starred Fred Astaire. *Funny Face* (1957) was built around songs by the Gershwins but with a handful of new songs, such as "Think Pink," by Edens and screenwriter Leonard Gershe. It was, of course, the Gershwin songs that stood out in the new setting where Astaire plays a fashion photographer, a role modeled on Richard Avedon, and Audrey Hepburn is a drab intellectual bookstore worker he turns into

a high-fashion icon. The most charmingly presented song is "Funny Face," from the 1927 Gershwin stage musical of the same name, which in
the film overcomes Hepburn's antipathy to being
a model. Although she secretly longs to be beautiful, she at first flees from Kay Thompson and

her glamour magazine staff who try to make Hepburn over for their next issue.
She takes refuge in Astaire's dark room, where he sings to her as he develops her
photograph, and she comes to believe in her own beauty. The song thus engineers a character transition—abetted by the visual image Astaire creates—and
advances the narrative in the best tradition of Arthur Freed films at MGM.

Warner Bros. clung to its backstager formula throughout the 1950s, even
filming a remake of *The Jazz Singer* in 1953 with Danny Thomas. The linchpin of
its musical films was Doris Day, who almost always sang songs as performances
rather than as integral expressions of her feelings. She made her film debut in
Romance on the High Seas (1948), playing a nightclub singer on a cruise ship,
and sang several songs by Sammy Cahn and Jule Styne, including "It's Magic,"
which became a big hit. In the 1950s, Warner Bros. featured Day in several films,
most of which had her performing old songs, such as *Tea for Two* (1950), *Lullaby of Broadway* (1951), and *By the Light of the Silvery Moon* (1953). She also
appeared in biopics, such as *I'll See You in My Dreams* (1952), about lyricist
Gus Kahn, and *Love Me or Leave Me* (1955), about Jazz Age singer Ruth Etting
(which was produced at MGM, who had borrowed her, along with her co-star
James Cagney, from Warner Bros.).

The one film Doris Day made at Warner Bros. in which she sang integral
songs was *Calamity Jane* (1953), a clear knockoff of *Annie Get Your Gun* with
Day playing the other legendary female of the old Wild West. The songs, by Paul
Francis Webster and Sammy Fain, also echo numbers from "western" musicals:
"I Can Do without You" is an obvious imitation of the "quarrel song" "Any-
thing You Can Do" from *Annie Get Your Gun*, as "Just Blew in from the Windy
City" is of *Oklahoma!*'s "(Ev'rything's Up to Date in) Kansas City." Still, the
songs drive the narrative and provide expressive moments for the characters.
The film opens with Day in buckskin shirt and pants atop a stagecoach singing "The Deadwood Stage," its "Whip-crack-away" refrain an obvious borrowing from the whip-crack sound effect that made Frankie Laine's recording of
"Mule Train" a huge hit in 1949. The arrival of the stagecoach in Deadwood also
echoes Judy Garland's entrance to "On the Atchison, Topeka & the Santa Fe" in
The Harvey Girls as Day celebrates in song the various goods the stagecoach has
brought to town, then leads the folk—mostly menfolk—in song as she enters
the Golden Garter saloon and leaps onto the bar to order herself a "sasparilly."

Even the performance numbers come off dramatically and integrally. Day heads for Chicago to bring back the renowned "Adelaide Adams," only to return

with Adams's personal maid, played by Allyn McLerie, who passes herself off as the star to get a chance to perform on stage. When she falters in front of the Golden Garter crowd, however, the ruse is exposed and the men jeer her until Day and Howard Keel, as Wild Bill Hickok, persuade the crowd to give her a chance. Bolstered by their confidence in her, McLerie then performs "Keep It under Your Hat" in saucy fashion—dancing through the audience and kicking off the hats of men in the crowd. When she wins local stardom, Keel gazes at a theater poster of her and sings "(My Heart Is) Higher Than a Hawk" in a purely expressive moment.

Day and McLerie sing an equally integral duet, "A Woman's Touch," as they transform Day's ramshackle sod hut into a pretty home. McLerie's tuneful determination to give the house a feminine overhaul is also the first step in transforming Day from gunslinging tomboy to attractive woman. When that transformation is complete, Day sings "Secret Love," in which she realizes

that she has been in love with Keel from the start. In addition to these integral numbers, the whole company, as they ride in buggies to a dance, sing "The Black

Hills of Dakota." Although the treatment of Indians, who largely appear in the film only to be shot at by Calamity, is tasteless, Day remarks to Keel, after the song, that the region is so beautiful that she can understand why the Indians fight so fiercely to keep it. Thus the song, like the title song of *Oklahoma!* celebrates the collective love of the land that binds this community—at least the white community—together.

The Warner Bros. backstager formula, tired as it had become after more than twenty-five years, could still produce an innovative film in *A Star Is Born* (1954), which was to be Judy Garland's great comeback vehicle after years of addiction

and breakdowns. The composer who seemed most appropriate for such a project was Harold Arlen, who had given Garland one of her first big songs in film with "Over the Rainbow." Lyricist Yip Harburg, however, was out of the question. Ever since his first hit, "Brother, Can You Spare a Dime?" (1931), Harburg had been one of the most outspoken liberals in show business. As the influence of the McCarthy-led House Un-American Activities Committee (HUAC) spread during the Cold War, he was one of many writers and performers who were "blacklisted" from working in Hollywood. Instead, Ira Gershwin was brought in to work with Arlen, and Moss Hart was assigned to write the screenplay.

A Star Is Born was to be a musical remake of a successful dramatic film of 1937 (which was, in turn, based on the still earlier 1932 film *What Price Hollywood?*) about an alcoholic movie star who commits suicide after nurturing a young starlet to fame. From the outset, Hart decided to conform to Warner Bros.' conventional presentation of songs as performances but to make them integral to the developing relationship between the young, insecure actress and her adoring but self-destructive mentor. Since Garland would play a singer, she would always have a realistic excuse for bursting into song, either on stage, in rehearsal, or in a private performance. To her co-star, therefore, would fall one of the most difficult assignments in film acting—responding to someone else's singing. Several major actors had been considered for the role of Norman Maine, most notably Cary Grant, but, as James Mason put it, "in the end it came to me and I grabbed it smartly before it slipped away." What probably put off Grant and other stars, surmises film historian Ronald Haver, was the prospect of having to react to Garland in the song sequences with smiles and gestures. Far from being subordinate to Garland, however, Mason was a strong enough actor that his reactions deepened the presentation of each song.

From his considerable experience in writing the "book" for Broadway musicals, most notably *Lady in the Dark* (1941) with songwriters Ira Gershwin and Kurt Weill, playwright Moss Hart knew that a song could express depths of character more powerfully than dialogue, but in Hollywood he was tied to the backstager convention. Still, he wanted the songs to "chart the emotional development of the characters as surely as the speeches and the action advance the surface manifestations of the story." The first song Hart envisioned would introduce Garland and Mason in a performance number that not only estab-lishes their "singer—sung to" relationship but also their mutual dependency. Garland, play-ing a singer named Esther Blodgett, is perform-ing with a band at a Hollywood benefit when Mason, as film star Norman Maine, drunkenly staggers on stage. She manages to save him from

embarrassment by incorporating his antics into her act then deftly escorts him offstage. He, in turn, musters the poise to bring her back onstage for a bow that makes the whole affair seem carefully rehearsed. Later that night Mason seeks her out to thank her for saving him and finds her singing in an after-hours jam session at a local dive. Recognizing her extraordinary talent, the one thing he still respects after all his years in Hollywood, he determines to transform Esther Blodgett into a star—"Vicki Lester."

Well aware of his collaborator's antipathy to writing romantic ballads, Arlen suggested they begin with these first two numbers—a rhythmic song for the Hollywood benefit, then a bluesy torch song Garland would sing in the jazz dive. Moss Hart had suggested that Ira write the "kind of song you can never hear the lyrics to," since the scene of Garland steering the drunken Mason through a dance routine would distract the audience from the lyrics. Amused at the play-wright's suggestion, Ira Gershwin wrote an utterly simple lyric, "Gotta Have Me Go with You," but nevertheless made it subtly integral to the dramatic context by having Garland sing it as she tries to get Mason to "go" offstage with her.

While "Gotta Have Me Go with You" is subordinated to the action on the screen, the next song, the "dive" number, is the central focus of the scene. The

songwriters would have to come up with a great song, one that would reveal Garland's tremen-dous talent to Mason. Arlen unwound what he called one of his "tapeworms"—melodies that were longer and more structurally complex than the usual Tin Pan Alley pattern of a thirty-bar, AABA chorus. It was a chorus of sixty bars in an unusual ABABCAD pat-tern with what Alec Wilder calls a "marvelous use of the fourth interval" at key points in the melody. Arlen had written the melody several years earlier when he was collaborating with Johnny Mercer but was dissatisfied with the flippantly romantic lyric Mercer had come up with:

> *I've seen Sequoia, it's really very pretty,*
> *The art of Goya and Rockefeller City,*
> *But since I saw you, I can't believe my eyes.*
> *You're one of them there things*
> *That comes equipped with wings:*
> *It walks, it talks, it sings,*
> *And it flies.*

Ira Gershwin, however, came up with a new lyric that, Arlen said, "made that melody sound like the Rock of Gibraltar."

The night is bitter,
The stars have lost their glitter.
The wind grows colder
And suddenly you're older.

Gershwin gets his searing, forlorn tone, surprisingly, with feminine rhymes, whose unaccented second syllable usually makes for comic rather than mournful effects.

Although Gershwin always complained that the hardest part of lyric writing was coming up with a title—finding a verbal phrase that will make articulate the abstract emotional meaning of a melody—when Arlen first played the music for this song, Ira leaned over the piano and whispered, "The Man That Got Away." Arlen replied, "I like." Ira's witty transformation of the vernacular catchphrase (the angler's lament for "the one that got away") irked grammarians who, much to Ira's amusement, kept trying to correct it to "The Man Who Got Away."

As Arlen's snaky melody uncoils, Ira stretches out his lyric with driving, internal rhymes:

No more that all-time thrill
For you've been through the mill,
And never a new love will be the same.

Just as skillful as Gershwin's use of rhyme is his juxtaposition of unrhymed and rhymed phrases to reflect the singer's sudden shifts between stoic resolve and desperate longing:

Good riddance, good-bye!
Ev'ry trick of his you're on to.
But fools will be fools—
And where's he gone to?

When Arlen's melody soars in a dramatic wail, Ira drops rhyme altogether for two colloquial compounds linked by alliteration: "There's just no *let-up* the *live-long* night and day." Along with perfectly matching the movement of Arlen's melody, Ira Gershwin was able to make the lyric resonate with the dramatic context of *A Star Is Born*, foreshadowing Mason's alcoholic disappearance after he persuades Garland to leave the band as well as his ultimate "getaway" by committing suicide.

One of the crucial elements in the presentation of "The Man That Got Away" is James Mason's reaction to Garland's performance. Moss Hart's script called for a "slow look of amazement and pleasure" to spread over his face as she sings. "As the number finishes," Hart specified, "the effect on him is electric— he starts to applaud—then drops his hands and keeps staring at the bandstand." Mason does not applaud because he realizes that the song is not done for an audience but for the pleasure of the musicians themselves. Earlier, the bartender had expressed his puzzlement to Mason that musicians who play for hire all evening would then gather after midnight to "jam" for themselves. Mason's face radiantly expresses his shared joy in the practice of art for its own sake, and the film manages to present the song as a performance that transcends the back-stager formula to become something much more integral to character and dramatic context.

Production on *A Star Is Born* was paralyzed by a technological development second only to the advent of "talkies"—the wide-screen process called "Cinemascope." Studios saw Cinemascope as a way to draw audiences away from their tiny television screens and back to the grandeur of the movies. Unfortunately for the presentation of song, Cinemascope transformed the screen into something more like a stage, thus encouraging the movement toward filming successful Broadway musicals in a way that adhered to their stage presentation. Instead of the numerous camera shots that were edited into a sequence of images, actors and sets had to be arranged for a single, stage-like "master shot." One of the appeals of Cinemascope was that it was cheaper to take such a single master shot rather than various crane, dolly, close-up, and other shots of traditional cinematography. The effect on such intimate films as *A Star Is Born*, however, was to blow everything up into gigantic but static proportions. George Cukor, who had originally come to Hollywood as a "dialogue director" to help silent-screen actors cope with the novelty of sound, now found himself the victim of the new wide screen: "We couldn't move the camera up or down, because of distortion, and we couldn't move back and away from the camera...Everything had to be played out on a level plane—if someone were too much upstage, they would be out of focus. And you weren't to come in really close on faces. It was rather like what happened when sound came in— you were supposed to forget everything you'd learned."

Cinemascope had been developed by Twentieth Century-Fox, and, as production began on *The Robe* (1953), the first "epic" film to use the new process, other studios slowed or shut down filming to await the results, just as, some twenty-five years earlier, they had let Warner Bros. experiment with sound in *The Jazz Singer* and *The Singing Fool*. Again, their fear was that if the new process appealed to audiences, their films would immediately seem outdated. Despite the success of *The Robe*, Jack Warner refused to follow other studios in leasing Cinemascope from Twentieth Century-Fox. Instead he was determined to fight back with a wide-screen process of his own, announcing that the first film in "WarnerSuperScope" would be *A Star Is Born*. Both George Cukor and Moss Hart opposed filming such an intimate story on a wide screen, but Jack Warner was insistent. The first results of WarnerSuperScope, especially the scene where Garland sings "The Man That Got Away," strengthened Cukor's hand: not only did the Warner wide-screen process distort the image, it was particularly poor in filming night scenes. Since so many of the scenes in the film took place at night, Jack Warner gave in and announced that *A Star Is Born* would be filmed for a traditional screen.

But at that point, in another echo of the squabblings among the Warner brothers that led to *The Jazz Singer*, Harry and Albert, noting the industry-wide movement to Cinemascope, informed Jack that Cinemascope, not WarnerSuperScope, would be the wide-screen process at the studio. Since *A Star Is Born* was the biggest picture currently under production on the lot, it would be the first Warner Bros. film in the new format. Problems with Cinemascope, along with Cukor's characteristically slow pace of filming and Garland's equally characteristic unreliability, dragged production out for months and ran up costs for a film that, running more than $4 million, was already the most expensive Warner Bros. had yet made.

Then Sidney Luft, producer of the film and then-husband of Judy Garland, wanted to be sure she had a sure-fire "big number" to cement the success of her comeback. Luft was also concerned about the length of the film, which he thought would necessitate an intermission. Garland's big number, he reasoned, could thus be used to climax the first half of the film, marking her full emergence as a star, while the second half would trace the downfall of Norman Maine. Although Ira Gershwin and Harold Arlen provided three different songs for the number, Luft didn't like any of them and Jack Warner concurred. What Luft and Warner wanted was something no songwriters could supply—a "socko" barrage of songs that were *already* proven hits. The highlight of a Judy Garland stage concert, Luft reasoned, came when she sat at the edge of the stage and sang a medley of standards. That, he decided, was what was needed for *A Star Is Born*—an anthology of "Garland's Greatest Hits" and let Moss Hart, Ira Gershwin, and Harold Arlen's painstaking efforts to integrate "performance" numbers with drama and characters be damned.

"Born in a Trunk," a sentimental medley and monologue devised by Roger Edens, took nearly two weeks to film, added another quarter of a million dollars to production costs, and tacked fifteen more minutes onto the film. Cukor, who had no role in the filming of the sequence, objected to it on grounds of length and the fact that it added nothing to the dramatic development of character and plot. Now *A Star Is Born* ran more than three hours—more than

twice the length of an ordinary film. Complaints from theater owners ruled out an intermission, since it would limit "turnover"—the number of showings (and hence box-office receipts) per day. Even without an intermission, it could only be shown five times a day—with the first showing beginning at eight in the morning. Such limited turnover cut into the profits of a film whose production costs had finally run to more than $5 million, making it one of the most expensive films until then ever made. Shortly after opening in September 1954, the losses from the limited turnover made it apparent that in order to have any hope of making the $10 million necessary to offset the $5 million spent making the picture, nearly half an hour had to be carved out of *A Star Is Born*.

Who decided on what was cut remains a mystery, but whoever made the cuts made them not in the usual tiny segments but in wholesale swatches of film. When George Cukor saw the results he was outraged at "the way they just hacked into it…there were other ways of shortening it besides chopping and hacking out vital bits." Among the severest losses were two songs by Gershwin and Arlen, "Lose That Long Face" and "Here's What I'm Here For," the latter their finest ballad in the score. The disappearance of these songs wrecked Moss Hart's intricate plan to advance the narrative by balancing songs with dialogue. What could have been one of the greatest of backstager films suffered from a "socko" Hollywood production mentality. Ira Gershwin consoled himself by saying, "Anyway, La Garland does right by 'The Man That Got Away.'" Even so, the song was passed over for the Oscar for the histrionic "Three Coins in the Fountain" ("Make it mine! Make it mine! Make it mine!") by Sammy Cahn and Jule Styne. Arlen scornfully tacked the Oscar nomination citation to his bathroom wall. For Ira Gershwin, it was his third nomination—and third loss. Reflecting on the fact that his two previous nominations, "They Can't Take That Away from Me" and "Long Ago and Far Away," had also used "away" in their titles, he wryly advised himself to do "away with 'away.'"

While MGM, Paramount, and Warner Bros. continued to present songs in films with varying levels of creativity during the 1950s, other studios either cut back on films that presented songs or relied upon the most timeworn formulas. Twentieth Century-Fox found a successor to Betty Grable—and a counterpart to Doris Day—in Mitzi Gaynor, featuring her in period musicals singing older songs, such as *Golden Girl* (1951), a biopic of nineteenth-century chanteuse Lottie Crabtree, and *The I-Don't-Care Girl* (1953), another biopic, this time of early twentieth-century vaudeville star Eva Tanguay. Like other studios, Twentieth Century-Fox banked on making film versions of successful Broadway shows—*Gentlemen Prefer Blondes* in 1953, *Carousel* and *The King and I* in 1956, and, in 1958, *South Pacific*, probably the most uncinematic and "stagey" film adaptation of any Broadway musical (that also starred Mitzi Gaynor with a dubbed Rossano Brazzi in the role Ezio Pinza had played on the stage). Along with these films, the studio ventured into the teenage musical, safely with *April Love* (1957, even though Pat Boone played a juvenile delinquent!) and more raucously with *The Girl Can't Help It* (1956) with Jayne Mansfield and Little Richard.

The best song to emerge from the studio during the 1950s was written, not surprisingly, for Fred Astaire in the only film he ever made for Twentieth Century-Fox, *Daddy Long Legs*, which gave Johnny Mercer a rare opportunity to write both words and music for a film. Since the mid-1940s, Astaire had been teamed with younger co-stars—Lucille Bremer in *Yolanda and the Thief* (1945), Judy Garland in *Easter Parade* (1948), and Cyd Charisse in *The Band Wagon* (1953). In all of these films, the disparity between Astaire's age and that of his leading lady was a problem. In 1955, teamed with an even younger Leslie Caron in *Daddy Long Legs*, the disparity seemed insurmountable. A script conference dissolved without a solution, and Mercer was asked to try to resolve the problem with a song.

That night, after he went to sleep, something awakened him. "I don't know what woke me up," Mercer said, "I don't know whether I had a problem about that, wanted to write that song, or whether this was a worry that I had about the score I was doing.... I woke up in the middle of the night and wrote the whole thing. Words and music. I went to the piano in the front room, out of bed, and quietly picked it out with one finger. And I wrote it down in my little hieroglyphics, which is my way of writing music. And then finished it the next day."

Whatever sparked the inspiration, Mercer created an extraordinary song, musically and lyrically. Shedding the regional idioms he had used in *Seven Brides for Seven Brothers*, he wrote a classic AABA chorus in Astaire's debonair style:

When an irresistible force such as you
Meets an old immovable object like me...
When an irrepressible smile such as yours
Warms an old implacable heart such as mine...

"Irresistible," "immovable," "irrepressible," "implacable"—it's as if Mercer were leafing through the I-section of one of his favorite dictionaries looking for polysyllabic adjectives that begin with prefixes that contradict or intensify their roots. After starting his A-sections with such erudite terms, he shifts to the vernacular title phrase:

> *You can bet as sure as you live,*
> *Something's gotta give,*
> *Something's gotta give,*
> *Something's gotta give.*

Then in the release, he reverts to Astaire's urbane style:

> *So, en garde, who knows what the fates have in store*
> *From their vast mysterious sky?*

In the final A-section, he goes back to punchy colloquial idioms:

> *Fight, fight, fight, fight,*
> *Fight it with all of our might.*
> *Chances are, some heavenly star-spangled night,*
> *We'll find out as sure as we live,*
> *Something's gotta give,*
> *Something's gotta give,*
> *Something's gotta give.*

Such shifts of tone registered the internal struggle Astaire underwent as he succumbed to Caron's charms, so that his concerns about their age difference, along with those of the audience, were overcome in the resolution of the song.

Although Astaire rendered "Something's Gotta Give" with his usual insouciant blend of talking and singing, filming *Daddy Long Legs* was an ordeal for him. During the course of shooting, his wife, Phyllis, died. Leslie Caron recalled that after a take he would sit down, put his face in a towel, and weep helplessly. Still his casually conversational rendition of the song turned it into an independent hit. The success of the song meant a lot to Mercer, who was beginning to fear that his success as a songwriter was fading since he had not been able to create the enduring Broadway musical that Irving Berlin had with *Annie Get Your Gun*, Cole Porter with *Kiss Me, Kate*, and even fellow Hollywood songwriter Frank Loesser had with *Guys and Dolls*. Not only were these shows hugely successful but many of their songs also went on to independent popularity. With "Something's Gotta Give," Mercer enjoyed a measure of such success; a perfectly integral song that resolved a problem in story and character, it also managed to become a hit at a time when rock 'n' roll was displacing songwriters of his generation. He was especially gratified to receive a note from Frank Loesser praising "Something's Gotta Give" and adding, "It's a real pleasure to see carriage trade writers getting the hits."

After their flurry of making musical films in the previous decade, Columbia, RKO, and Universal cut back musical production severely in the 1950s. The films they did produce featured few original songs. Columbia did routine backstagers such as *Sunny Side of the Street* (1951) and *Cruisin' Down the River* (1953) with mostly older songs, biopics such as *The Eddie Duchin Story* (1956) and *The Gene Krupa Story* (1959), and film adaptations of such Broadway musicals as *Pal Joey* (1957) and *Porgy and Bess* (1959), the latter the last film produced by seventy-five-year-old Sam Goldwyn. One of the few films Columbia made during the decade that presented songs expressively and integrally was *The 5,000 Fingers of Dr. T* (1953), a Stanley Kramer production that was based on an idea by Ted Geisel ("Dr. Seuss"), who also wrote lyrics for the songs. Most of the film is a dream fantasy of a boy, played by Tommy Rettig (star of TV's *Lassie*), who falls asleep as he practices the piano and finds himself in a dungeon where his fiendish teacher, played by Hans Conried, keeps 500 boys and makes them practice round the clock. Except for "The Dressing Song (My Do-Me-Do Duds)." which Conried sings as he dons his regal robes before conducting the boys' "five thousand fingers" in concert, the lyrics lack the verbal sparkle of the Dr. Seuss books.

RKO closed out production in 1957, after a disastrous period, from 1946 to 1955, under the ownership of Howard Hughes. Although most of its own films during the decade were flops, RKO successfully co-produced other films or served as a facility for independent productions. One of the producers who worked with the studio was Samuel Goldwyn, who built several films, such as *Up in Arms* (1944), *Wonder Man* (1945), and *The Kid from Brooklyn* (1946) around Danny Kaye. In these films, Kaye almost always did songs as performances, some of which had been written by his wife, Sylvia Fine, for his earlier stage and nightclub performances. Probably the funniest of her songs was "The Maladjusted Jester" ("And a jester unemployed/ Is nobody's fool") from *The Court Jester* (1956).

In the last film Goldwyn produced at RKO, *Hans Christian Andersen* (1952), however, the songs Danny Kaye sang, by Frank Loesser, were integral and expressive. Loesser, after a long career writing songs for film, had gone to Broadway, where he had written such successful musicals as *Where's Charley?* (1948) and *Guys and Dolls* (1950). By 1952, he was ready to create the same kind of integral score for film, and he got his opportunity with *Hans Christian Andersen*, whose screenplay was written by the equally "integration"-minded Moss Hart. As Loesser's daughter Susan recalled, "Hart and my father worked closely together to weave the script and the songs into a tight, relatively seamless cloth."

After the enormous success of *The Red Shoes* (1948), Goldwyn wanted to produce a film about Hans Christian Andersen that would feature Moira Shearer in a ballet sequence. He first planned to cast Gary Cooper as Andersen, then switched to Jimmy Stewart until Sylvia Fine approached him. "Jimmy's a marvelous actor," she told Goldwyn. "But he's not musical. Why not use Danny? He's very musical, and he's wonderful with children." Goldwyn agreed and commissioned Fine to write the songs. But when, after bringing in some thirty different screenwriters to work on treatments and scripts, Goldwyn settled upon Moss Hart, plans changed again. As Fine recalled, Hart told Goldwyn, " 'Loesser is hot. He just did *Guys and Dolls* and I'm sure he's got another great score coming up.' And so it was Sam and Moss who had to talk to me. Strangely enough, I didn't mind very much—some, but not much. And not because Frank and I were close friends—that had nothing to do with it. It was because of the way he wrote."

Between them, Loesser and Hart created one of those rare films where we move fluidly from song to song. In his native village of Odense, Denmark, Kaye, playing Andersen as a cobbler, runs afoul of the local schoolmaster for telling fanciful stories to the children. As Kaye disconsolately listens to the children chanting their arithmetic lesson ("Two and two are four,/ Four and four are eight...") he sings the wryly satirical "Inchworm," about a practical-minded caterpillar who neglects to appreciate the beauty of the marigolds he traverses. His apprentice Peter (Joey Walsh), who knows the mayor is about to expel him from Odense, urges Kaye to leave for Copenhagen. As the two arrive singing "Wonderful, Wonderful Copenhagen," their song merges into the chants of the various street sellers. Imprisoned for not showing the proper respect for the king's statue, Kaye entertains a little girl who gazes up at his cell window by improvising "Thumbelina" employing his thumbs as puppets. Although "Wonderful, Wonderful Copenhagen" became the best-known song in the film—one adopted by the people of Denmark—it was "Thumbelina" that was nominated for an Academy Award, only to lose out to the theme song from *High Noon*. As Susan Loesser recalls, "My father referred to 'Thumbelina' as an insignificant little ditty, not a real song. Whenever he wanted to make a point about a cheap song, his own or someone else's, he would mention 'Thumbelina.' He never gave himself credit for writing exactly what the scene required: a charming 'little ditty' meant to entertain a small child.... It certainly entertained me.

I was seven when he first performed it for me, and I was enthralled. When he said, 'I could write that junk any day of the week,' I was stunned."

When Peter learns that the Royal Danish Ballet needs a cobbler to create special shoes for its prima ballerina, he arranges for Kaye's release under the custody of the company. There Kaye falls in love with Jeanmaire (who replaced Moira Shearer when Shearer became pregnant) who is married, in a tempestuous union, to the ballet master played by Farley Granger. Kaye resolves to save her from Granger, and that resolve gives rise to two ballads, "Anywhere I Wander," and, in a fantasy sequence where Kaye imagines he marries Jeanmaire, a lilting waltz, "No Two People (Have Ever Been So in Love)."

As expressive and integral as these songs are, Loesser also created "The King's New Clothes" and "The Ugly Duckling," which turn two of Andersen's most famous tales into song. "The King's New Clothes" cleverly turns on the word "altogether," first sung by the king and queen as they believe the tailor who gives the king an "invisible" suit of clothes that only the wise can see:

The suit of clothes is altogether,
But altogether, it's altogether
The most remarkable suit of clothes
That I have ever seen.

As the king parades nude through the town, one little boy who has not been told that only the "wise" can see the clothes, blurts out:

The king is in the altogether,
But altogether, the altogether.
He's altogether as the day that he was born!

Kaye sings and talks his way through "The Ugly Duckling" to cheer up a little boy whose shaved head—the result, he explains, of his doctor's effort to cure an unspecified illness—makes him an outcast. The song's finest moment is actually spoken rather than sung: rejected by the other ducklings, the lonely and forlorn creature is finally spotted by a flock of swans who tell him "You're a very fine swan indeed" to which he replies, with an exquisite off-rhyme, "Me a swan? Aw—go on!"

The song becomes even more integral when the boy's father, a newspaper publisher, summons Kaye to his office to tell him that the tale of "The Ugly Duckling" so lifted the child's spirits that he would like to publish it in the newspaper, along with his other stories, launching Andersen's career as an author. At the same time, "The Little Mermaid," a story he had written to woo Jeanmaire away from Farley Granger, becomes the basis of a successful ballet by the company. Although Kaye has to accept the fact that he can never win Jeanmaire's love, he consoles himself with his emergence as a writer. He reprises "I'm Hans Christian Andersen," a song that has been woven throughout the film, and counterpoints it with "The Ugly Duckling" to describe his own transformation from cobbler to author. As he and his apprentice leave Copenhagen to return to Odense, Peter predicts the fame he will achieve with his tales, making *Hans Christian Andersen* a movie musical that depicts, through song, the portrait of an artist as a young man. To Danny Kaye's credit—and probably the direction by Charles Vidor—he suppressed the flamboyant antics he displayed in his other films to present songs as integral emanations of feeling from a shy, compassionate character.

Through RKO, Walt Disney also produced several animated features, such as *Cinderella* (1950), *Alice in Wonderland* (1951), *Peter Pan* (1953), and *Lady and the Tramp* (1955). In these, the presentation of song continued to pose a problem for Disney. In *Cinderella* and *Alice in Wonderland* the main characters sing integral songs at certain points: Cinderella, upon awakening at the beginning of the film, sings "A Dream Is a Wish Your Heart Makes" to birds and mice as she starts her morning chores. Alice, too, sings "In a World of My Own" before she enters the world of fantasy. While songs move the narrative along in both films, however, as in Disney's films of the previous decade, they are given to minor characters. In *Peter Pan*, Peter doesn't sing at all, a seeming reversion to the "realism" that precluded Pinocchio, Dumbo, and Bambi from singing. Disney's failure to give voice to Peter Pan was underscored in 1954 when a television production of the story featured such wonderfully integral songs as "I Won't Grow Up" and "I'm Flying" by Carolyn Leigh and Moose Charlap. The latter song has its pale parallel in Disney's film as the Darling children take flight with Peter but instead of having the children themselves sing exultantly, Disney has "You Can Fly" sung by an off-screen chorus. Amazingly, the children can, unrealistically, *fly*, but they can't *sing*. Similarly, neither Lady nor Tramp sings in *Lady and the Tramp*, though Peggy Lee sang such delightful songs, which she wrote with Sonny Burke, as "He's a Tramp" and "The Siamese Cat Song" ("We are Siamese if you please…").

These animated films did well: *Cinderella*, for example, grossed $9.25 million, and *Lady and the Tramp* brought in $8.3 million. But Disney also made nonanimated, live-action films that, at far less expense, did just as well. Even the most expensive of these live-action films, *20,000 Leagues under the Sea* (1954), which involved underwater photography, grossed more than $6 million. Why make animated films that featured songs, songs which posed a problem of verisimilitude for Disney, when nonanimated, nonmusical films could be made much more cheaply and do just as well? The animated musical *Sleeping Beauty* (1959) cost so much that, even though it grossed $5.3 million, it put the Disney studio in the red for the first time in ten years.

By contrast, songs in dramatic films of the decade also took on more of an integral rather than "performance" character. In *High Noon* (1952), the title song, by Ned Washington and Dimitri Tiomkin, functions as an internal monologue for Gary Cooper who plays a western marshal torn between facing men out to kill him and running off with his Quaker bride (played by Grace Kelly). Although Cooper himself could not possibly sing in such a dramatic context, the song, sung by Tex Ritter over the titles and opening scene, expresses Cooper's character's consternation and also provides exposition as three gunfighters gather to meet their leader, recently released from prison, on the noon train. As Cooper vainly seeks to find men to stand by him in the looming gunfight, the song comes up again on the soundtrack to give vent to his feelings in what might be called "silent song," since the song expresses Cooper's feelings even though he himself does not sing it:

Do not forsake me, oh, my darlin'
On this our wedding day...

We again hear Ritter's voice singing in the background as Cooper calls on the home of a deputy (played by Harry Morgan) who hides from him, then we hear the song again as Cooper strides toward the church to try to recruit other deputies. When he again fails to find help, he leaves the church and, as he walks through the street, the song comes up yet once more. Under Cooper's characteristic deadpan demeanor, the song expresses his churning emotions in a more effective way than dialogue could. Song thus functions as an interior monologue for a character who not only can not sing but can barely express his feelings in words.

The theme song for *High Noon* is not only unusual for the way it functions in the narrative but also because it was composed by Dimitri Tiomkin, who wrote the musical score for the film. Traditionally, classically trained composers such as Tiomkin wrote scores for films, while songwriters, some with little musical training, wrote the songs. Increasingly in the 1950s, however, the composers who wrote scores also demanded to write the songs, knowing that songs could go on to independent popularity and earn royalties and ASCAP revenues. Tiomkin was one of the first composers who won the right to supply the theme song for a film he scored, and the success of "Do Not Forsake Me" strengthened the case for other composers who wanted to do the same. This encroachment of film scorers upon the turf of songwriters was yet another factor that hastened the demise of the original film musical. In 1945, ten of the fourteen songs nominated for the Oscar originated in full-scale musical films. In 1950, the same pattern held true with four of the five nominated songs coming from a musical film. By 1956, however, only one of the nominated songs was from a musical film, and between 1957 and 1965, only six of forty-five nominated songs originated in a musical film. The rest were "theme" songs, "title" songs, or songs presented as performances in an otherwise dramatic film.

To veteran songwriters, such "background writers," as they termed the film scorers, did not write true songs. Ray Evans and Jay Livingston complained, "They wrote with their heads. . . . They would sit down and write interesting melodies, but they weren't songs. There was no heart, no feeling. You write with your feelings, from your stomach . . . from the heart, it's instinct. They didn't have that. . . . Background composers decided they were going to write all the songs in their pictures [or] they wouldn't score it. . . . It started with Tiomkin, and he said, 'I'm going to write this.' . . . And they killed the music writers. . . . Harry Warren couldn't work after that."

Another film scorer, Alex North, pulled a song from his score for *Unchained* (1955), and Hy Zaret added a lyric. "Unchained Melody," served as another kind of "silent song" to express the yearning of inmates at the Chino, California, prison farm. Chino was one of the first minimum security facilties (on their first day of incarceration, the warden shows them how to put a leather jacket over the barbed wire fence to protect themselves in an escape). Ironically, the ease of escape makes detention even more tormenting than it is in a more traditional prison, and the men are torn between trying to complete their sentences and taking the easy path of escaping back to their loved ones. While the prisoners do not sing themselves, "Unchained Melody," with its images of hungering for a beloved's touch, the wrenchingly slow passage of time, and lonely rivers that long to flow into the arms of the sea, voices their longing as well as their fear that the women they love will turn to someone else in their absence. Sung on the soundtrack of *Unchained* by Todd Duncan (who starred in the original stage production of *Porgy and Bess*), the song became a hit in a recording by Al Hibbler. "Unchained Melody" became a hit again in 1965 in a version by the Righteous Brothers, which was later featured in *Ghost* (1990), where it gave "voice" (in "silent song") to the spirit of Patrick Swayze as he dances, through the medium of Whoopi Goldberg, with Demi Moore.

Another song that expresses the feelings of inarticulate characters is "Rock around the Clock," which is sung at the beginning of *Blackboard Jungle* (1955) as a new high school teacher, played by Glenn Ford, walks through a playground of tough teenagers. In the course of the film, we find that the teenagers have no music of their own to express their feelings, and at one point even turn on jazz, smashing jazz records that belong to a teacher played by Richard Kiley. Throughout the film the teenagers do not sing or even listen to music. Only "Rock around the Clock," played over the opening credits, expresses their anger and defiance in a way they themselves cannot articulate in the film.

Bill Haley and His Comets' rendition of the song had been recorded the year before but had not been a hit. Glenn Ford brought some of his teenage son Peter's records in to the studio to help with the search for the kind of song American teenagers were listening to. When "Rock around the Clock" was selected for use in *Blackboard Jungle*, it was the first rock 'n' roll song to reach the top of the pop charts, igniting the rock 'n' roll revolution. Many teenagers went to see *Blackboard Jungle* only to hear the song, which seemed to express the pent-up emotion of their generation as it was depicted in the film. A Hollywood movie had, once again, given voice to characters who do not sing themselves but whose emotions are made articulate in a song sung "silently" on the soundtrack.

11

ALL THAT JAZZ

The 1960s saw the demise of the hard-won convention—developed by Lubitsch and Mamoulian at Paramount, Astaire and Rogers at RKO, and Arthur Freed and his "unit" at MGM—that ordinary characters could give voice to what they feel at a particular dramatic moment in integral song. For the most part, the only films that have presented song in this fashion in recent years have been aimed at family audiences and couched in fantasy. The best of these were created by Disney, one of the few studios where songwriters remained central to the production of a film musical. As such, they could give song the same integral relation to character and dramatic situation that it had in a Broadway musical. The songs for most Disney films of the last forty years were written by Richard and Robert Sherman, who had started out as pop song writers with hits such as "You're Sixteen (You're Beautiful, and You're Mine)." The Sherman brothers, however, were steeped in the tradition of integral song in film and knew, as Richard Sherman put it, "Writing for character and story is a whole new can of peas.... I think *Wizard of Oz* was a great example of writing story and character and making it happen. It was a classic, of course. And that was one of my inspirations actually. When I said, 'Oh, *The Wizard of Oz*...it's so exciting!' But on second and third and fourth lookings at that film, I realized the first half of it is wonderful musically; the second half is totally without songs. It's underscored. So it was like half a musical, but it was a great picture nonetheless."

Sherman stressed that he and his brother always tried to write songs that were integral to "the story line—more than anything else, *story, story, story*! The characters—that's more important than any melody or any lyric or anything else we do. What's the character about? What's he thinking? What's he feeling? What's he doing? That's the thing that motivates the songs. And if you're a good songwriter, you write something that works for those drives. But those sparks have to come from the stories." Describing Walt Disney as "one of the greatest storytellers of all time," Sherman observed, "We had a tremendous opportunity, my brother Robert and I, from 1960 on to work as storytellers with music."

When Disney invited the Sherman brothers to write songs for *Mary Poppins* (1964), he had them work directly from P. L. Travers's book. "We wrote something like thirty-five numbers for *Poppins* and fourteen were used," Sherman explained. "The reason why we wrote so many songs was because we didn't have a story line. See, all we did was have these books...so we were saying, 'Well, we can take these chapters or this chapter and develop something. And we'd do five numbers and just kept telling stories....The screenplay came later." While Disney gave his songwriters a free hand in creating integral songs, he would let them know what kinds of songs he wanted. "He'd say, 'No, no, that's not saying it the way I feel it.' I mean, he was a very, very exacting individual. But he wouldn't tell you what to write, but he'd sure steer you in the right direction. And he knew what the emotion was that he wanted. And after a while we got to read him."

Once the Sherman brothers had written their songs, Disney would bring in a screenwriter and say, "'The boys have some good stuff here—I want you to now shape it.' And so he would work with us and say, 'We need a number here...but we could take this number and do it here.' Walt was the one that said, 'Well 'Chim Chim Cheree'—that could be the theme number for Bert (played by Dick Van Dyke) because we just have him in this one sequence. Let him be throughout the play. He'd be from the very beginning.' And so Walt made him into a jack-of-all-trades. If you read Mrs. Travers's book, Bert appears in one chapter, 'The Day Out,' when Mary Poppins goes out on her day off, she takes a little excursion into a drawing—picture—with Bert, a sidewalk artist, and they pop in and have tea and have a nice time and they come out. That's what Mrs. Travers gave us. But—'Thank you, Mrs. Travers'—she gave us the opportunity to write one of the great experiences of our lives in that sequence." Sherman explained that he and his brother wrote five songs for that sequence, but "Walt pared it down to 'Jolly Holiday' and "Supercalifragilisticexpialidocious.'"

Despite its length (139 minutes) and the fact that there is not so much a story as a series of episodes involving Julie Andrews as Mary Poppins, the nanny for the children of the Banks family, and Dick Van Dyke as a singing chimney sweep, songs truly do propel the narrative. And the songs are almost all done as integral expressions of character rather than as performances. Indeed, the only performance number is the opening song in which Dick Van Dyke entertains a crowd in a London park by extemporizing lyrics based on their names. Every other song is an expression of personality, and virtually everyone in the film *sings*. Whatever qualms Disney had in earlier films about the "realism" of characters, animated or real, bursting into song, were waived in *Mary Poppins*.

The film opens when Glynis Johns, playing a mother so caught up in the suffragette movement that she has no time to mind her children, enters her home singing an anthem to women's rights, getting her maid and cook to join her in denouncing the stupidity of men. David Tomlinson, as the husband she nevertheless meekly obeys, comes home from work with a song on his lips that serves as exposition, telling the audience that "It's great to be an Englishman in 1910" and listing the virtues of a well-run house where everything is done on schedule. Song and dialogue are then intermixed as Tomlinson dictates an advertisement for a nanny, half talking, half singing his requirements for discipline and rigor. In counterpoint to his stipulations, the children (Karen Dotrice as "Jane" and Matthew Garber as "Michael" Banks) sing their own advertisement, "The Perfect Nanny," for one who will play games, sing songs, and supply sweets. The song-driven narrative continues with the arrival of Julie Andrews as Mary Poppins, who gets the children to pick up the nursery with rhymed dialogue—"In every job that must be done,/ There is an element of fun"—that blossoms into "A Spoonful of Sugar (Helps the Medicine Go Down)," initially sung by her reflection in a mirror. The inspiration for the song came from the son of Robert Sherman, who told his father that children in his school had received the Salk

polio vaccine. Assuming the vaccination was administered by injection, Sherman asked his son if the shot hurt. The boy then explained that the vaccine was dropped on a sugar cube and that made it easier to swallow.

As the song carries Andrews and the children out of the house and to the park, they encounter Dick Van Dyke who introduces another song, "Chim Chim Cheree," as he draws pictures on the sidewalk. Inducing Andrews to use her magic powers to enable the children to "enter" one of his drawings of the countryside, he breaks into yet another song, "Jolly Holiday," with its internal "*jol*ly/ *hol*iday" rhyme, to extol the charms of Mary Poppins. Once inside the imaginary world of his picture, song breaks forth even more abundantly as cartoon characters—penguins, pigs, turtles—talk and sing in an animated sequence that flows from a fox hunt to a horse race, with Andrews, Van Dyke, and the children joining the action by riding carousel horses. Just when it seems the imaginative borders have been pushed as far as they can go, Mary wins the horse race and sings "Supercalifragilisticexpialidocious" to celebrate her victory, another song associated with her that will be reprised throughout the film (at one point she even sings the gargantuan title backward).

As Richard Sherman explained, "We wanted to give the children in the story—again, it came out of story more than anything else—we put the children with Mary Poppins walking down in front of the park and there's Bert...and we said, 'The children have to have an experience with Mary Poppins they'll never forget. So they'll go into this picture with Bert and Mary Poppins, and they'll have an experience they'll never, ever forget.' And how do you express something that's greater than anything you can describe? We said, 'Well. Supercolossal...a supercolossal day, a supercolossal time'...we started *super*...we liked *super*...that was kind of nice, and we said, 'No, it's gotta be more of an obnoxious word.' *Obnoxious*...what do you rhyme? I said, 'English. It should be

atrocious—that's good, there you go!' So we had *superatrocious, obnoxious, adocious*...it sounds smart because you remember when we were kids we used to 'sound smart' when we did these things. We used to make up double-talk words: *dobblecobbleflobblation*—things like that...meaning nothing, but it sounded good. And so we said, 'Well, we said *atrocious* you could sound *precocious* if you said that—that's good. *Super...atrocious...precocious.*' What does that rhyme with? *Docious*—why not? So we had—half the song was there."

Sherman insisted that just as these lyrical ideas had been rooted in the story, they, in turn, inspired his music for the song. "You gotta remember, the words gave us the musical pattern...*califragilistic* is just like we used to say, 'Your galvinator rod is dragging!' We used to yell it to people driving along in the car. And so *galvinator* didn't work with *super...califragilation...califragilistic*. 'Yeah, that's good!' And we put it together. I mean, I'm talking two weeks of slavery to come up with this damn word. Now, it's in all the dictionaries and everything but at the time it was just double-talk. So *supercalifragilisticexpialidocious* became a word for us."

But integral song also grew out of the most tangential of characters and dramatic situations. "Mrs. Travers wrote a series of stories," Sherman recalled, "no actual 'curve' to the storyline of the book, just wonderful incidents with characters. And in one particular place she wrote three pages about a lady who sells bread crumbs at the steps of St. Paul's. That's all it was. It just said, 'She comes every day, and she sells bread crumbs.' And that's all. Didn't have *any* bearing on anything. It just was a little thing. And I remember Bob and I looked at each other that first day when we were reading the book—we read it out loud to each other—being very worried because there's no storyline here. 'What are we going to do?' And we said, 'That could be the symbol of what this whole story is all about!' It could be, my God, a metaphor. We could say, 'Feed the birds, tuppence a bag.' It doesn't take much to give love. It doesn't take much to show a little emotion. A little caring. And then we could have the father who's so busy doing his thing, and the mother so busy that they're not paying attention to the kids, they *need* Mary Poppins to come in. And we got all excited. We said, 'That's the clue to this whole thing. It's right here, right here. This is it!' And I remember vividly that 'Feed the Birds' was an inspiration....God was sitting in the room with us, and we wrote that thing in a hurry. I mean, we had the first sixteen bars anyhow. We really had it. We had that whole feel, and when we had our first meeting with Walt, and we talked about this, and I played it for him, and I talked about 'all around the cathedral the saints and apostles'—I remember we had never seen the place. We had to take some books and find pictures of St. Paul's, and then we saw the statues of the saints and the apostles around it and said, 'Oh God! We're going to put that into the song.' So we had this and said, 'Walt, listen to it,' and when we finished with all the other things we were talking about, he said, 'Play me that bird lady thing again.' So I played and sang it for him. He said, 'That's what it's all about, isn't it?' And we said 'That's right! That's what it's all about!' And he said, 'You guys really think story.' And we said, 'Yes, we do.' Then he smiled and said, 'How'd you like to work here?' And that's the day he put us under contract—an exclusive contract."

In the film, Julie Andrews sings "Feed the Birds" to the children as they watch a poor old woman (played by Jane Darwell) selling bread crumbs at "tuppence a bag" to feed the pigeons around St. Paul's Cathedral. When Mr. Banks takes his children to his office at the bank, he tries to persuade them to open an account with the boy's "tuppence" rather than buy bread crumbs from Darwell. Their disagreement brings in the bank managers, who sing a paean to capitalism that completely bewilders the children. The struggle over the "tuppence" prompts a run on the bank by customers who overhear the quarrel, and the father is dismissed from his position.

That dramatic situation leads to an exchange of song and dialogue between Tomlinson and Van Dyke, the father lamenting the day when Mary Poppins, "with chaos in her wake," led to the loss of his job. Van Dyke replies with an ironic chant about how Tomlinson cannot spare time for his children because

"You've got to grind, grind, grind at that grindstone." He warns the father that one day he will find his children "have up and grown and then they've flown and it's too late for you to give." The song transforms the father, who then confronts his supervisors at his dismissal with a reprise of "Supercalifragilisticexpialido-cious" and walks out of the bank kicking up his heels and singing "A Spoonful of Sugar." Undaunted by his dismissal, Tomlinson leads his children in "Let's Go Fly a Kite," a joyous number muted only by the departure of Mary Poppins, whose work, now that Tomlinson has been transformed—largely by song—into a caring father, is complete.

With its narrative driven by such integral songs, *Mary Poppins*, for Clive Hirschhorn, was "probably the best, most inventive, original screen musi-cal of the decade." For Richard Schickel, its song sequences "have a cinematic excitement entirely missing from most film musicals of recent years and far in advance—as the whole film is—of something like *The Sound of Music*, to which it is superior musically, directorially, thespically and even intellectually." *Mary Poppins* became Disney's greatest commercial success, grossing $45 million and winning five Academy Awards, including Oscars for the Sherman brothers for Best Score and Best Song. Yet for all of its commercial and critical success, *Mary Poppins* was one of the last of a dying breed of original film musicals that pre-sented integral songs. The fact that their story-driven songs for *Mary Poppins* won the Sherman brothers a contract from Disney was an indication that stu-dios that could present original, integral songs—and the songwriters who could write them—had become a rarity in Hollywood. "Nobody else in Hollywood had a contract like that," Sherman added, "not at that time. In the '30s they did it, even into the '40s.... This was the early '60s. It was over. Nobody had staff songwriters anymore. We were the only staff songwriters in Hollywood."

Still, the success of *Mary Poppins* helped to keep the integral tradition of songwriting alive in animated and live-action films aimed at family audiences. Several of these films, such as *Chitty Chitty Bang Bang* (1968), *Bedknobs and Broomsticks* (1971), and *Charlotte's Web* (1973), featured songs by the Sherman brothers, whose presence at Disney maintained the tradition of integrated song long after Walt Disney's death in 1966. Other films with integral songs included *Doctor Doolittle* (1967), *Willie Wonka and the Chocolate Factory* (1971), *Popeye* (1980), *Beauty and the Beast* (1991), and *Tarzan* (1999).

Original film musicals aimed at an adult audience grew rare—and were rarely successful. Ross Hunter's production of *Lost Horizon* (1973), for exam-ple—a musical remake of Frank Capra's 1937 film about airplane crash victims who find themselves stranded in the Tibetan paradise of Shangri-La—is very cautious in its presentation of integral song. During the early part of the film, as characters played by Peter Finch, Sally Kellerman, and Bobby Van, flee a war zone reminiscent of Americans escaping from Saigon, there are no songs whatsoever. After their plane crashes in the Himalayas and they are rescued by residents of Shangri-La, led by a Western-educated host played by John Gielgud, we begin to get songs, by Hal David and Burt Bacharach, "excused" by the remote and fantastical setting.

At first, however, even these songs are done as performances rather than as integral numbers. Peter Finch is intrigued by Liv Ullmann singing "The World Is a Circle" to her class of school children. Then James Shigeta leads a community ritual in "Living Together, Growing Together," another performance song. The film then turns to Peter Finch and Liv Ullmann (dubbed, respectively, by Jerry Hutman and Diana Lee) voicing their interior monologues in "Reflections." The first openly sung integral song does not come until more than halfway through the film, when Sally Kellerman and Olivia Hussey (dubbed by Andrea Willis) debate the merits of living in the larger world as opposed to Shangri-La in "The Things I Will Not Miss." Hussey says she longs to see New York and Paris and escape the rigors of "contemplation," while Kellerman retorts that "contemplation" sounds like a "vacation." Only after Peter Finch has been summoned by the aged High Lama and told he has been brought to Shangri-La to become its leader, does he move from internalized song to openly singing "Question Me an Answer," but by this point such an expressive, integral song seems a strange intrusion into the dialogue of the film. The commercial and critical failure of *Lost Horizon*, along with the fact that not one of its songs became popular, furthered the demise of the original, integrated film musical.

Films that used the anthology convention to present older songs in integral fashion, in the tradition of *An American in Paris* and *Singin' in the Rain*, did not fare much better. Peter Bogdanovich's *At Long Last Love* (1975) featured Burt Reynolds, Cybill Shepherd, and other performers breaking into Cole Porter songs to express what they feel at particular dramatic moments. The film may have suffered from the reverence Bogdanovich felt for classic song and classic film musicals. He was inspired to make *At Long Last Love* after reading a scholarly edition of Cole Porter's songs, and he faithfully presented sixteen songs with all their verses and choruses (even though some of these extra lyrics, especially for witty "catalogue" songs such "You're the Top," were supplied by Porter for Broadway productions where audiences "stopped the show" with their applause and demanded reprises of a song).

Bogdanovich even went so far as to film and record the songs simultaneously, as they would have been in the earliest film musicals before the advent of the prerecording and playback system. "It struck me as a terribly difficult thing to ask an actor to sing something two or three weeks before you shoot it and then not worry about anything when they're doing the scene except getting their lips in synch with what they did three weeks ago. What happens if they feel it differently? You're frozen into something you did in an atmosphere that is not particularly conducive to creativity. You're in a little room with a bunch of musicians sitting out there or you're in a little room with the musicians already having done their work and gone home." Bogdanovich did not bring on a live orchestra to accompany the singers out of camera range, as would have been done in 1929, but rather implanted tiny speakers in the ears of the performers so that they could hear their accompaniment on an electronic piano while the microphones picked up only their voices. Later, after the film was edited, a full orchestral accompaniment was added to each number.

In another attempt to honor the tradition of the classical musical yet "bridge" the technology of the 1930s with that of the 1970s, *At Long Last Love*, while filmed in color, uses black-and-white for most costumes, sets, and props. The most difficult bridge between the two eras, however, came with the presentation of integral song. On the one hand, Bogdanovich eschewed the backstager convention of presenting a song as a performance: "I didn't want to make a musical that was about singing and dancing," he said, "I wanted to make a musical about some people who sing and dance instead of walk and talk." But the line between song presented as a performance and song that emerges integrally from character and dramatic situation keeps blurring. When Burt Reynolds woos Madeline Kahn with "You're the Top," he largely talks his way through the lyric; when Kahn takes a chorus, her powerful voice makes it clear that she is *singing*. When Kahn belts out, a la Ethel Merman, "You're the nose on the great Durante," all Reynolds can do is interject a spoken "Oh, yeah!" The loss of the convention that characters can spontaneously burst into integral song without a realistic excuse is evident when Duilio Del Prete reprises "You're the Top" to Cybill Shepherd; after he concludes, she exclaims "You sing!"—calling attention to the fact that he has just sung a song. Such an acknowledgment would have never occurred in an Astaire-Rogers film or any other integral presentation of song in a film of the 1930s or 1940s. Characters notice songs done as performances in films from that era, but when a character bursts into integral song, the other actors show no surprise.

A far more grim anthology musical was *Pennies from Heaven* (1981), in which Steve Martin plays a sheet-music salesman in 1930s Chicago, whose dreary job and marriage are enlivened by fantasy sequences in which he imagines himself in the glamorous world of the era's movie musicals. Based on a British television series, *Pennies from Heaven* presents songs in a lavish period style that is then juxtaposed to the grim realties of the Depression. The title song, for example, is charmingly sung and danced to by a character who then rapes and murders a blind girl. When Martin is blamed for the crime, he and Bernadette Peters, with whom he has a sordid affair, hide in a movie theater where *Follow the Fleet* is screened. As Astaire and Rogers dance to "Let's Face the Music and Dance," Martin forces himself into the film and performs the song just as he is about to be arrested and "face the music" by going to the electric chair. While disturbing and ambitious, *Pennies from Heaven* was yet another commercial flop that further eroded the prospects of film musicals even when they were created around classic standard songs.

Woody Allen came closer to presenting integral song successfully in his anthology musical *Everyone Says I Love You* (1996), where characters suddenly break into song without any realistic excuse and actors around them take no note of the fact that they are singing. The film opens with Edward Norton casually singing "Just You, Just Me" as he walks with Drew Barrymore. The song articulates his love for her, even though it is recognizable as a classic standard. Throughout the film, actors and actresses, most of whom are not accomplished singers, burst into such songs without any realistic "excuse." Allen blithely presents song in expressive, integral fashion even though the convention for such presentation had virtually disappeared. The fact that the songs that express a character's feelings at particular dramatic moments are well-known standards makes their presentation less jarring. In fact, when Allen himself sings the 1924 song, "I'm Through with Love," his poor singing voice makes him appear more dejected and the song more poignant for its lack of polish and professionalism. Such presentation of song is at once a nostalgic nod to the lost convention of actors bursting into integral song on screen as well as a pushing of that convention to its realistic extreme where even nonsingers can give voice to their feelings in song.

As such integral film musicals dwindled, film adaptations of Broadway musicals increased. Studios had found that it was much safer to make a filmed version of a Broadway show that had already proven to be a success than to hazard a new film musical with original songs. Audiences, moreover, had come to accept the presentation of integral song if they knew that they were watching a screen version of a Broadway musical. During the 1960s, such film adaptations proliferated: *Can-Can* and *Bells Are Ringing* in 1960; *West Side Story* and *Flower Drum Song* in 1961; *The Music Man* and *Gypsy* in 1962; *Bye Bye Birdie* in 1963; *My Fair Lady* and *The Unsinkable Molly Brown* in 1964; *The Sound of Music* in 1965; *A Funny Thing Happened on the Way to the Forum* in 1966; *How to Succeed in Business without Really Trying* and *Camelot* in 1967; *Funny Girl* and *Finian's Rainbow* in 1968; *Sweet Charity*, *Paint Your Wagon*, and *Hello, Dolly!* in 1969.

Cinemascope, as we have seen, reinforced the inherent "staginess" of such productions, as did the attempt to provide audiences with a production that was as faithful as possible to its Broadway original. Such films thus often gave audiences the worst of both worlds—*filmed* versions of *stage* productions, providing neither the thrill of a live performance nor the excitement that cinematography, editing, and other aspects of filmmaking could bring to the presentation of song. What could be more cinematically turgid, for example, than Richard Beymer and Natalie Wood singing "Tonight, Tonight" in *West Side Story*? Set on a tenement fire escape, with virtually no camera movement, the performers' mouths open hugely as they lip-synch to the operatic dubbing of Jim Bryant and Marni Nixon. That such "canned" Broadway shows prospered and even earned critical acclaim is testament to the extraordinary power of musical theater, not to any inventiveness in filmmaking.

The trend began to slow in the next decades, as Broadway itself produced fewer and fewer hit musicals, but still the major musical of any given year was not a Hollywood original but a Broadway retread: *Fiddler on the Roof* (1971), *Cabaret* (1972), *Jesus Christ Superstar* (1973), *A Little Night Music* (1977), *Grease* (1978), *Annie* (1982). A few of these film adaptations of Broadway stage shows tried to be more cinematically engaging, but such "opening out" could undercut the power of a live stage production. As Clive Hirschhorn observes of *Fiddler on the Roof*, filming scenes outdoors and in realistic interiors substituted the "stage show's stylized, Chagall-inspired settings with the real thing." More successfully translated to film was *Cabaret*, which, in a reversal of the usual process of adapting Broadway shows for film, took the integrated songs of the stage production and turned many of them into Hollywood "backstager" performance numbers. When *Cabaret* did present songs beyond the sordid confines of the Kit Kat Club, it could be cinematically stunning, as with "Tomorrow Belongs to Me" which is first heard sung by a cherubic boy's voice over a beer garden scene, but as the camera draws back in a huge crane shot it reveals that the singer is a Hitler Youth. Hollywood's reliance on adaptations of Broadway musicals for the presentation of integral song has continued down to the present with such films as *Evita* (1996), *Chicago* (2002), *Phantom of the Opera* (2004), *Rent* (2005), *Dream Girls* (2006), and *Sweeney Todd* (2007). An ironic countertrend in this same period was that Broadway, facing the paucity of successful musicals, turned to Hollywood to make stage adaptations of such successful film musicals as *42nd Street*, *Victor, Victoria*, and *The Producers*.

While Hollywood relied almost exclusively on filmed versions of Broadway shows to present integral songs, it continued to make backstagers, where songs were done as performances. In many of these films, however, songs were presented with dramatic force, and some of the narratives were driven and united by song performances. In Judy Garland's thirty-fifth and final film, *I Could Go on Singing* (1963), she plays an internationally renowned singer who once had a child with a British doctor, played by Dirk Bogarde. To further her career, she agrees to let Bogarde raise the child and stay forever out of their lives, but when she reaches stardom, only to find it unfulfilling, she tries to establish contact with her son during a London performance tour. Her most moving number is the Howard Dietz and Arthur Schwartz standard, "By Myself." When Garland is told, in a scene in her hotel room, that her hopes for reuniting with her son cannot be realized, she turns and we see her standing in an abstract, red setting. She first sings "By Myself" as an expressive song that articulates her realization that she must go on alone in a reflective, almost-spoken interior monologue. When she reprises the song, however, it gradually becomes a performance number, and we next see her on a stage booming the song out to an invisible audience. The song thus traverses the movement from an expressive, integral song to a performance number done with all stops out.

The backstager formula proved a durable frame for the many films that featured Elvis Presley. By 1965, Presley had made thirteen films—sometimes as many as four a year—that had grossed more than $175 million dollars. Virtually all of the songs in these films were performance-based numbers that had little relation to character or story, but in *Viva Las Vegas* (1964), Presley is heard on the soundtrack singing "I Need Somebody to Lean On" yet he himself is silent as he wanders meditatively through a sparsely populated nightclub so that the song functions as a kind of internal monologue. In the same film, "My Rival" is an old-fashioned integral song that could have come from a musical film of the 1940s as co-star Ann-Margret vents her frustration over Presley's devotion to his racing car.

Perhaps the most bizarre backstager was Mel Brooks's *The Producers* (1968) where Zero Mostel, playing a Broadway producer, persuades his accountant, played by Gene Wilder, to mount a musical show that is bound to be a flop. Mostel's scheme is similar to that in *New Faces of 1937*, where a producer gets financial backing from several "angels," each of whom thinks he is the sole investor in the show. When the show flops, the producer can tell the backers that the show lost money and keep their investments. In both films, however, the show is a smashing success, but *The Producers* has the far more outrageous premise that the show-within-the-film is a musical called *Springtime for Hitler*, a nostalgic celebration of the Nazi leader's romantic life. The title production number is a hilarious throwback to the lavishly staged musicals of the 1930s.

A very different kind of backstager was *Nashville* (1975), a film where songs drive the narrative as powerfully as in any classic musical film. Director Robert Altman got the inspiration to make the film when he heard Keith Carradine perform two of his own songs at a party. One song, "It Don't Worry Me," was a kind of hobo anthem Carradine had written for a movie he was in about riding the rails during the Depression. Although the song captured the gritty feel of the 1930s—"The price of bread may worry some/ But it don't worry me"—it was not used in the film. The other song, "I'm Easy," Carradine had written to impress a co-star in the West Coast production of *Hair*. "I just wanted to get laid," Carradine later admitted. But when Altman heard Carradine sing the two songs, he said, "I knew I wanted to base a whole movie around them, a movie that would simply give me an excuse to put them in."

Originally, Altman planned to use Carradine's two songs along with a group of country-western standards such as "Okie from Muskogee" and "D-I-V-O-R-C-E" but when the rights to such songs proved too expensive, Altman struck upon the idea of having most of his cast of more than twenty major characters write and perform their own songs. Since the movie satirized the emergence of country-western songs as a dominant force in popular music, such songs would reflect the talented but amateurish quality of country music. It also meant that while the songs were all done as "performances," the performers would be creating songs that grew out of their characters and dramatic situations. The film opens in a Nashville recording studio where Henry Gibson sings "Two Hundred Years," a self-congratulatory bit of patriotism on the eve of America's bicentennial. As opposed to the Tin Pan Alley formula chorus of 32 bars, the songs in *Nashville* are based on the nine-teenth-century strophic pattern of verses alternating with a brief refrain, and Gibson's song details in verses his military service to  the country then boasts, in the refrain, "We must be doin' somethin' right/ To last two hundred years" (ironically inviting the audience to reflect on the consid-erably longer lineages of most other countries). In between takes, Gibson berates a long-haired pianist—whom at first, in a most undemocratic elitism, he won't even address directly—then summarily dismisses him as the kind of person who doesn't "belong" in Nashville. He then commands his son to throw Geraldine Chaplin, who plays a BBC reporter doing a documentary on country music, out of the recording studio.

As the son escorts Chaplin into another studio, we hear a gospel song, "Yes. I Do," performed by the Fisk University choir, bizarrely joined by Lily Tomlin in a send-up of how the music industry homogenizes folk traditions. The film cuts back and forth between the two songs, as Chaplin waxes euphoric about how close the black choir members are to their African origins and Gibson performs with an arrogance that undercuts the humble patriotism of his song. To highlight the centrality of the songs in the film, most of the soundtrack is nonmusical, consisting instead of the political ramblings of a third-party presidential candidate from a campaign car that drives about the city, lambasting the preponderance of lawyers in government, urging a tax on church property, abolishing the Electoral College, and other populist issues.

Although every song in *Nashville* is a "performance," each resonates with character and dramatic situation. When Geraldine Chaplin interviews the son of Henry Gibson about his role as his father's business manager, she gets him to confess that he too has aspirations to be a singer and songwriter. He shyly admits that he has written a song, and she asks him to sing it. Opening up to her, he softly croons, "The Heart of a Gentle Woman." In a traditional movie musical, this moment might have led to romance, but Chaplin abruptly cuts him off when she notices that a famous movie star, Elliot Gould, has entered the scene. Although she is not a singer or songwriter herself, Chaplin is as self-centered and aggressive as the denizens of Nashville's country-music world.

The most interesting juxtaposition of performance songs comes near the end of *Nashville* as Keith Carradine sings "I'm Easy" (the song that would go on to win the Oscar), in a nightclub. "Although the song's refrain ("I'm easy") accords with the "image of male rock artists as womanizers" who are "careless of

 others' feelings, using women solely for sex and temporary companionship," the lyrics of the verses, as well as Carradine's "heartfelt performance instill us with some feeling for a character who had, until this time, seemed mostly callous and vain":

It's not my way to love you just when no one's looking,
It's not my way to take your hand if I'm not sure,
It's not my way to let you see what's going on inside of me…

Although the lyric has the amateurish off-rhymes of many country and rock songs (rhyming "games" with "insane"), it registers a romantic quality that adds a tender dimension to the character Carradine plays. Such tenderness comes out dramatically in the following scene where, in bed with Lily Tomlin, he gently lets her teach him a few words of sign language, which she uses to communicate with her deaf children. When she says she must leave, however, he reverts to his crass self, telephoning another woman before she even reaches the door.

During the scene with Carradine in a nightclub, the film cuts to Gwen Welles performing her song, "I Never Get Enough," to an audience of men at a smoker. Where Carradine's song and delivery are slick and professional, Welles is a wretched amateur as a songwriter as well as a performer. Yet both songs sell sex. As Carradine sings, the camera pans across women in the audience,

particularly Tomlin, who clearly are seduced by the song. While the men at
the smoker are appalled by her poor singing, Welles is forced to live up to the
erotic promise of "I Never Get Enough" by
stripping to appease them.

Like so many backstagers of the 1930s
and 1940s, *Nashville* ends with a big, collective performance—but in this case by
country music stars at a political rally.
Ronee Blakely, playing a famous singer suf-
fering from nervous breakdowns, sings several songs then is suddenly assassi-
nated. In a parody of the backstager cliché where the star breaks her leg and
the neophyte must take her place, Barbara Harris, who has been desperately
trying to break into the music business
throughout the movie, gets on stage, grabs
the microphone, and sings "It Don't Worry
Me." "Though she begins by singing tenta-
tively, she resounds finally with a huge and
charismatic voice that encourages not only
the gospel singers to join with her but the
entire audience at the rally." Although it is a

song of political apathy ("You may say that I ain't free/ But it don't worry me"),
"It Don't Worry Me" first quiets, then rouses, the crowd as if it were an inspiring
protest song from the 1960s such as "We Shall Overcome."

Like Woody Allen, Robert Altman, and Francis Ford Coppola (who made
a film adaptation of Broadway's *Finian's Rainbow* in 1968), another major contemporary director, Martin Scorsese, ventured a film musical with *New York,
New York* in 1977. *New York, New York* is firmly cast in the backstager tradition,
with Robert De Niro as a saxophone player in the 1940s and Liza Minnelli as
the singer he relentlessly pursues. The film contains mostly standards, but there
are several new songs, including the title number, by John Kander and Fred
Ebb. In one scene, Minnelli awakens to hear De Niro playing the melody for
"New York, New York" quietly on the piano. He asks if she remembers the song,
which he wrote for her, and she assures him that she does and has been working
on a lyric. Rather than "do" the song, however, they quarrel over his insistence
that she doesn't understand his need to be alone. Throughout the quietly bitter
exchange, he plays snatches of the melody so that the song accompanies their
crumbling relationship. Later, when Minnelli shows him the lyric she has written, De Niro's reaction is a combination of puzzlement and sarcasm. He wonders why she entitles it "New York, New York," and she explains that was where
they met. De Niro, hometown boy that he is, doesn't understand why she repeats

"New York." He then skeptically reads the line "these vagabond shoes are long-ing to stray" and quotes the phrase "top of the heap" in a way that indicates he finds it a cliché. "Is this the final version?" he

asks as he leaves, and she calls out, trying again to please him, "I can change 'top of the heap.'"

We do not even hear the song, however, until they have split and Minnelli has gone on to a suc-cessful recording career as well as film stardom. When she returns to New York, De Niro goes to see her perform in a swank nightclub, and when she sees him in the audience, she dedicates the song to him. She then gives a dynamic perfor-mance of "New York, New York" that signals her maturity as a singer, and the lyric resonates with her own triumphant return to the city. After the performance, De Niro comes to see her backstage where a crowd of friends has gathered. There he

also sees their son, now twelve. In a traditional musical, all these elements would bring DeNiro and Minnelli back together again, and after he leaves, he calls her, and she agrees to meet him outside the theater. As she dons her coat, however, she resists the pull to rejoin him. After waiting for her in vain, he realizes that,

partly through the success of "New York, New York," she has mustered the courage to break with him forever, and as he walks off into the night, the song wells up to end the film.

Although it is driven more by dance than by song, *All That Jazz* (1979) has several imagina-tive song presentations. The best of these come at the end of the movie as Bob Fosse, played by Roy Scheider, lies dying of heart failure in a hospital operating room and imagines the three women in his life are singing to him: his ex-wife vents her anger at him with "After You've Gone;" his current mistress does a variation of "There'll Be Some Changes Made" to try to get him to change his self-destructive habits; and his daughter sings "Some of These Days" but transforms the lyric to emphasize her point that "you're gonna miss *me*, Daddy." Each performance is a grim paean to death with the image of the operating room first on-screen then onstage with Fosse as a director talking to himself on the hospital bed. The three songs form the kind of big backstager performance sequence that typically ended a 1930s Warner Bros. musical. Before the daughter's song, we even get a Berkeley production number by chorus girls singing "Who's Sorry Now?" rotating around his hospital bed sporting huge fans. The daughter's version of "Some of these Days" is the most garish as she is made up and dressed like a vamp, smoking with a cigarette holder, barely able to walk in high heels, an image of her maturity he will not live to see. She's joined by ex-wife, mistress, and chorines in the finale as Scheider comes out of open-heart surgery. He then dies to another performance number, in duet with Ben Vereen, "Bye, Bye Love," whose lyrics are transformed to "Bye, Bye, life…I think I'm gonna die….Bye bye my life good-bye." Scheider then kisses friends in the audience as he takes bows before his death, which has been nothing but a lavish, musical "performance."

Several films of recent years present songs as performances but are not so much backstagers as dramatic films that incorporate songs. In *Dick Tracy* (1990), Madonna sang several original songs by Stephen Sondheim, and in *The Fabulous Baker Boys* (1989) Michelle Pfeiffer sang such standards as "More Than You Know," charmingly, and "Makin' Whoopee," seductively. More intricately woven into the film narrative of *Beaches* (1988) was the song "Glory of Love." Bette Midler's character as a child initially does a cheeky rendition of it at an audition where she befriends the girl who will become her lifelong soulmate. When the friend, played as an adult by Barbara Hershey, has a child, Midler's voice sings "Baby Mine" (from *Dumbo*) on the soundtrack during a montage of the two women preparing for the birth of the baby. After Hershey's character becomes terminally ill and dies, Midler's voice reprises "Glory of Love," now as a more poignant and expressive song than in her childhood audition, as she takes custody of the child, Victoria, and takes her from the house she's lived in. Later, Victoria watches from the wings, smiling, as Midler performs "Glory of Love" on stage, and after the performance, Midler tells Victoria she sang the song the day she met her mother. Woven through the film, the song deepens in significance and cements the relationship of the characters.

The resiliency of the "amateur" backstager convention, derived from all those films where Mickey, Judy, and the high school kids "put on a show" is evident in a film such as *Mr. Holland's Opus* (1995), where Richard Dreyfuss plays a high school music teacher mounting a Gershwin revue as the annual student show. During that staple backstager scene, the audition, we witness the same dreary snatches of classic songs botched by one performer after another. Just when all hope seems lost for finding a student who can sing well enough to play the role of their "ingénue," Jean Louisa Kelly, as "Rowena Morgan," steps onstage and belts out a high school version of Ethel Merman's "I Got Rhythm."

The story takes a deeper twist in the presentation of "Someone to Watch over Me," which Kelly sings in a rehearsal for the revue. While another music teacher proclaims her performance "perfect," Dreyfuss tell the cast to take five, walks to the stage, and asks Kelly, "What do you think the girl's feeling here?"

Kelly looks blankly then, as the possible emotional depths of the song occur to her, she coyly says, "I dunno." "You *have* to know," Dreyfuss snaps, "or you can't sing it. This song is wistful, Miss Morgan. It's about a woman who's alone in a very, very cold world and all she wants more than anything else is to have someone hold her close and tell her that everything's going to be all right. It's about the need for love—*in your gut*." Returning to his seat in the auditorium, Dreyfuss tells the pianist to play the accompaniment in a lower key and Kelly then sings the verse of "Someone to Watch over Me" in a much more moving style, and it is clear that the song expresses her romantic longing for Dreyfuss himself. Over the course of the next few scenes, we see Dreyfuss, in turn, succumbing to his feelings for her. As he sits and works on his opus at home, he writes a section of it that he entitles "Rowena's Theme," and as his wife overhears him play it, she asks who Rowena is. "Huh?" he starts, then stammers, "Legend—a heroine from Norse mythology."

At the climactic performance of the revue, Kelly sings "Someone to Watch over Me" with her eyes riveted on Dreyfuss as he conducts the orchestra, his lips mouthing the lyric back to her in a silent duet of their mutual yearning. His wife, sitting in the audience, is so struck by Kelly's voice that she looks in her program to find out the girl's name and sees "Rowena Morgan." Dreyfuss's lie to her now reveals a symbolic truth—Rowena is indeed a Norse legend, the Lorelei, the siren-like maiden whose song lures sailors to their death on the Rhine (even her last name associates her with another temptress, Morgan LeFay).

Perhaps the most enduring of the "backstager" subgenres has been the musical "biopic" where a contemporary performer portrays a famous singer or songwriter of the past in a film that includes a myriad of performances. Barbra Streisand made her film debut portraying Fanny Brice in *Funny Girl* in 1968, and Bette Midler made hers as a thinly disguised Janis Joplin in *The Rose* in 1979. In the year 2004 alone there were biopics of Cole Porter (*De-Lovely*), Ray Charles (*Ray*), and Bobby Darin (*Beyond the Sea*).

One convention for the presentation of song in film that has been used most innovatively since the 1960s has been that of "silent song," in which, as in *High Noon*, a song heard on the soundtrack at a particular dramatic moment articulates the feelings of character who does not himself sing. *The Graduate* (1967) starred Dustin Hoffman, an actor whose cinematic presence, like that of Gary Cooper, is inimical to bursting into song, yet his very unsuitability for singing made him a perfect vehicle for "silent song." "During the film's opening credits, as we see Hoffman's Benjamin Braddock standing on an airport's moving walkway, the soundtrack plays Simon and Garfunkel's 'The Sounds of Silence.' The song does not merely set a tone for the movie. The melancholy mood and lyrics ('Hello, darkness, my old friend' 'I turned my collar to the cold and damp') indicate Benjamin's loneliness, sadness, and fear, in effect telling us what Benjamin's expressionless face does not." Indeed, the film invites us to understand that the song, while not sung by Hoffman, expresses his character's feelings as much as an integral song would in a traditional musical.

Although "The Sounds of Silence," which plays at two other points in *The Graduate*, seems to express Hoffman's emotions each time it appears, variations in narrative context add nuances to each musical expression. We hear the entire song again during a brilliantly edited montage sequence that shows Hoffman alternately lolling around his parents' home and sleeping in a hotel room with Anne Bancroft ("Mrs. Robinson," the wife of his father's business partner). Again, the mood of the song expresses the character's confusion and dejection, but the lyrics gain new resonance because of the character's alienation from his parents and the affair he is having with an older woman ("In restless dreams I walk alone,/ Narrowed streets of cobblestone"). Moreover, Hoffman's inability to tell anyone his feelings about his alienation are also made articulate in the song ("But my words like silent raindrops *fell*,/ And echoed in the *wells* of silence").

"The Sounds of Silence" is heard again in the last moments of the film after Hoffman, who has fallen in love with Mrs. Robinson's daughter, played by Katharine Ross, persuades her to run away from her wedding. As she and Hoffman sit in the back of a bus, their facial expressions change from jubilation to anxiety over what they have done, and the melancholy song, already expressive of Hoffman's "sadness, loneliness and indecision, works in tandem with the image to help undermine the otherwise happy ending."

Such "silent song" suits Method actors such as Hoffman, "since their performances are often distinguished by failures of speech, their characters' deepest emotions revealed through a rhetoric of pauses, stutters, and lines unsaid." Unlike songs sung by a character in a traditional musical, such "silent song" provides not the relief that comes through musical expression but rather the frustration of a character with inadequate means or occasions to express feelings of alienation and confusion. Such songs were frequently composed specifically for a film so that audiences would not recognize them as preexisting popular songs (though several went on to become popular) but rather imagine them emanating for the first time as a character's silent soliloquy in a movie. Riding a bus to New York, John Voight in *Midnight Cowboy* (1969) expresses himself inwardly, as he cannot do outwardly, with "Everybody's Talking" by Fred Neil and sung on the soundtrack by Harry Nilsson. Paul Newman voices his ebullient feelings—"because I'm free/ Nothing's worrying me"—through "Raindrops Keep Falling on My Head" (Hal David and Burt Bacharach) as he pedals the newfangled velocipede in *Butch Cassidy and the Sundance Kid* (1969). The fact that the song is sung by B. J. Thomas, a performer as little known at the time as Harry Nilsson, contributed to the illusion that the song emanated from the character's thoughts. In *The Thomas Crown Affair* (1968), an even more unimaginable singer, Steve McQueen, is given voice while flying his glider. Taking the visual image of the glider's circling turns and connecting it with McQueen's character's feverishly spinning imagination, lyricists Marilyn and Alan Bergman put intricately sinuous similes to a melody taken from Michel Legrand's soundtrack to create "The Windmills of Your Mind":

> *Round like a circle in a spiral,*
> *Like a wheel within a wheel,*
> *Never ending or beginning*
> *Or an ever-spinning reel.*

The song and its cinematically dazzling presentation comes as close as possible to making Steve McQueen sing.

The Bergmans took the convention of "silent song" a step further in *Yentl* (1983). The film was produced and directed by Barbra Streisand, who, in order to get backing for a movie set in a nineteenth-century European Jewish community, reluctantly agreed to sing in the film. To avoid making a conventional

"musical," Streisand worked with the Bergmans to create a sequence of internal musical monologues that drive the narrative. In her first song, Streisand, alone in her parlor, sings openly about her longing for rabbinical knowledge, but when she enters her sleeping father's bedroom, her lips stop moving, and the song becomes internal, since she cannot voice such unfeminine ambitions in his presence. When she leaves his room and goes to the kitchen, however, she again sings openly. The next day the internal singing resumes when she attends synagogue, and we hear her voice pouring over the singing of the men as she sits, visibly silent, among the women in the back of the temple.

After her father's death, Streisand cuts her hair, dons male clothing, and becomes a rabbinical student. Disguised as a man, she can only express herself, while in the presence of others, through internal, silent song. Such internal song is often poignant, as when she finds herself falling in love with her yeshiva class-mate, Mandy Patinkin (who, despite his magnificent Broadway voice, never sings in the film, openly or silently), expressing internally what she cannot say to him. The convention of internal song also allows for Yentl's ironic commentary on the action in something like a theatrical "aside." For example, she silently sings "No Wonder He Loves Her" as the women of the house fuss over the men—including Yentl—at dinner. As she takes in the inequality of the situation, Yentl satirically asks, in silent song, "So what's not to like about being a man?"

By shifting from openly singing when Yentl is alone to silent song in the presence of others, the Bergmans capture not only the predicament of Yentl but of all "silent" women. At the very end of the  film, when, having shed her male disguise, she sails to America, Streisand moves from openly singing when she is alone in the back of the ship, to internal song as she moves forward among the other passengers, and then, at the song's climax, when she says, "Papa, I have a voice now," she sings openly in the presence of others for the first time in the movie. At first, the other passengers gaze in wonder at her musical outburst, but then, as if acknowl-edging the naturalness of her expression, they accept it as serenely as do extras in an old musical.

Silent song figures in other films, such as *Harold and Maude* (1971), where the songs of Cat Stevens delineate the growing affection between the twenty-year-old Bud Cort and the elderly Ruth Gordon. Similarly, in *One from the Heart* (1982) the songs of Tom Waits give voice to the shifting romantic rela-tionship of Frederic Forrest and Teri Garr. "It Might Be You" by Alan and Marilyn Bergman and composer Dave Grusin is heard on the soundtrack of *Tootsie* (1982) to give voice to both Dustin Hoffman's love for Jessica Lange, a love he cannot express openly because he has disguised himself as a woman to get a role in a soap opera, as well as Lange's father, played by Charles Durn-ing, who, in turn, is falling in love with Hoffman's character. In *When Harry Met Sally* (1989), director Rob Reiner wanted to make a "classic" love story that featured "classic" love songs, so he included such standards as "Love Is Here to Stay" and "Let's Call the Whole Thing Off" to express what Meg Ryan and Billy Crystal are feeling at various points in the narrative. At the climax of the movie, we hear "It Had to Be You," sung by Frank Sinatra as a "silent song" for Billy Crystal as he races through the streets of New York on New Year's Eve after realizing that he has long been in love with Meg Ryan. Even in cartoons, where characters are not constrained from bursting into song, "silent song" rendered unspoken feeling. In *Shrek* (2001), the ogre says nothing, but

John Cale's mournful singing of Leonard Cohen's "Hallelujah" gives a bitterly sarcastic expression to his heartache.

Even without the convention of "silent song," movies continue to incorporate song in ways that give expression to what characters feel at heightened dramatic moments. After a brutal murder scene at the opening of *Goodfellas* (1990), set in 1970, Tony Bennett's "Rags to Riches" comes up on the soundtrack to register Ray Liotta's boyhood dream of becoming a gangster and transport the narrative back to 1950. In an ironic juxtaposition between song and a character's feelings, a gangster played by Michael Madsen mutilates a policeman as he turns up the radio to hear "Stuck in the Middle with You" in *Reservoir Dogs* (1992). After Tom Cruise, playing a sports agent in *Jerry Maguire* (1996), closes a big sports deal, he takes off in his car, hits the radio, and cuts through three different songs until he reaches "Free Falling," which articulates his jubilation. In *Magnolia* (1999), the songs of Aimee Mann reverberate on the soundtrack as we follow the entangled lives of several different characters. At one point, the characters themselves break into song as they listen to "It's Not Going to Stop" on the radio, the song gathering them together in a way the narrative itself does not. While Hollywood's production of full-scale original musicals had declined after 1960, its use of songs in film continued with imagination and vitality.

In 1974, MGM began assembling a series of *That's Entertainment* films, which consisted of song excerpts from its classic musicals. "The implicit message of *That's Entertainment*—delivered as much by the old film clips of spectacular musical numbers as by Fred Astaire, Gene Kelly, and the other aging stars who chattily introduced the numbers—was that they don't film songs like they used to." While MGM could, in these anthologies, take credit for the greatest presentations of integral songs in film, the series does not include the pioneering films of Warner Bros., such as *The Jazz Singer* and *The Singing Fool*, which established the performance convention of presenting song in film. Also ignored was Warner Bros.' revival of that convention with *42nd Street* and the many *Gold Diggers* and other backstager musicals of the 1930s. Also absent from the MGM series were the efforts of Paramount to present songs integrally in films that featured Maurice Chevalier and Jeanette MacDonald. Even more regrettably, MGM's *That's Entertainment* series ignored RKO's Astaire-Rogers films that firmly established the convention that ordinary characters could burst into song, a convention that underlay MGM's own great integral musicals of the 1940s and 1950s.

Perhaps the greatest omission in the *That's Entertainment* series, with its implicit theme that the great era of the integral musical films has passed, is the resourcefulness with which Hollywood has continued to find new ways to present songs—as "silent" expressions of what a character feels at a particular dramatic moment, as "performances" that comment on the narrative, and as innovative juxtapositions between song and story. Indeed, at this writing, the movie *WALL-E* (2008), an animated science fiction romance about robots, is playing in theaters and reviving songs from the 1964 Broadway musical *Hello, Dolly!* which was made into a movie in 1969. In *WALL-E*, a robot (named WALL-E) watches a videotape clip from the movie in which a naïve clerk, played by Michael Crawford, expresses his feelings to a girl, played by Marianne McAndrew, through the song "It Only Takes a Moment," which culminates as the two hold hands and stroll through a park. By replaying the song clip over and over, the robot learns to simulate love by clasping his own fingers together. By watching Crawford and McAndrew, WALL-E also learns about love and humanity. Near the end of the movie, WALL-E's hard drive has suffered damage and the video clip has been erased. WALL-E no longer recognizes the other robot, EVE, he has come to "love," because he has lost his ability to have feelings. It is only when EVE grasps WALL-E's hand and a spark passes through them that WALL-E "awakes" and finds his friend and love again. As WALL-E moves in to be near EVE, Crawford and McAndrew again sing "It Only Takes a Moment."

Writer-director Andrew Stanton recalled the "a-ha! moment" when he realized that the clip from *Hello, Dolly!* of Crawford and McAndrew singing "It Only Takes a Moment" could help him tell his story. "I saw them holding hands and it was like a light bulb going off. Like, that is exactly the best way I could express the phrase 'I love you' from a character that can't say it." *WALL-E*'s new showcasing of the song brought tears to the eyes of songwriter Jerry Herman: "I'm still blown away by the fact that...songs of mine that are close to fifty years old have been used as the underpinning" of *WALL-E*.

Thus the movies continue to present songs in dramatic and moving fashion. True, lyricists and composers no longer provide the extraordinary outpouring of song that movies were blessed with by Cole Porter, Irving Berlin, the Gershwins, Rodgers and Hart, Jerome Kern and Oscar Hammerstein and Dorothy Fields, Yip Harburg and Johnny Mercer and Harold Arlen, Al Dubin and Harry Warren, and the other great songwriters of what has been called the "golden age" of American song. Still, the movies continue to rejuvenate the songs of these great songwriters, as well as the many less-familiar composers and lyricists whose standards constitute the Great American Songbook. Hollywood movies, along with Broadway revivals and jazz and cabaret performances, help keep these great songs alive and kicking, giving America the closest thing we have to a vital repertoire of classical music. Whether they were originally written for Tin Pan Alley, vaudeville, or Broadway, in a movie these great standards become the "songs of Hollywood."

CHAPTER 1

3   "Broadway was the literary...some great songs": E. Y. Harburg, "From the Lower East Side to 'Over the Rainbow,'" *Creators and Disturbers: Reminiscences by Jewish Intellectuals of New York*, ed. Bernard Rosenberg and Ernest Goldstein (New York: Columbia University Press, 1982), 149.

8   "The one advantage...have to say": Donald Knox, *The Magic Factory: How MGM Made "An American in Paris"* (New York: Praeger, 1973), 53.

9   "the film spectator...and harmony nonadventurous": Richard Barrios, *A Song in the Dark: The Birth of the Musical Film* (New York: Oxford University Press, 1995), 110.

10   "many early films...in silence": Rick Altman, *Silent Film Sound* (New York: Columbia University Press, 2004), 89.

11   "As the songs...an upcoming movie": Barrios, 106.

12   "I worshipped Sam...see things coming": Jack Warner, *My First Hundred Years in Hollywood* (New York: Random House, 1964), 57.

12   "one-half of America's...5,000 or less": Douglas Gomery, *The Coming of Sound: A History* (New York: Routledge, 2005), 10.

13   "I agree...money for musicians": Cass Warner Sperling and Cork Millner, *Hollywood Be Thy Name: The Warner Brothers Story* (Rocklin, CA: Prima, 1994), 94–95.

14   "I'll go along...to sing, too": Sperling and Millner, 95.

14   "Okay...the first show": Sperling and Millner, 95.

15   "to the town halls...instrumentalists is ephemeral": Barrios, 22.

15   "a keen ability...and projected image": Barrios, 24.

16   "There is no...life in exchange": Warner, 181.

19   "The foxtrot combines...dance ever has": Mark Grant, *The Rise and Fall of the Broadway Musical* (Boston: Northeastern University Press, 2004), 136.

21   "Leave it in...on their asses": Sperling and Millner, 117–22. Jack Warner, in his memoir, insists that Sam had "Al Cohn write a soliloquy" (Warner, 177).

23   "It was a shock...of a shadow": Sperling and Millner, 131.

23   "Al sits...in sight": "Sam Warner—Now You Has Jazz: The Innovators 1920–1930," *Sight and Sound* (bfi.org.uk/sightandsound/archive/innovators/warner.html, 4/30/03).

23   "The effect on...see about it": Sperling and Millner, 120.

24   "a little kid...his heart out": Sperling and Millner, 141.

24   "How old...take it from there": Harry Jolson as told to Alban Emley, *Mistah Jolson* (Hollywood: House-Warven, 1951), 181.

CHAPTER 2

28   "Will Hays, Czar…of sound films": John Kobal, *Gotta Sing Gotta Dance: A Pictorial History of Film Musicals* (London: Hamlyn, 1971), 25.

28   "His talent…the screen": Bob Thomas, *Thalberg: Life and Legend* (Garden City, NY: Doubleday, 1969), 136–38.

29   "Movies aren't…they're remade": Thomas, 139.

29   "But that set…improve the picture": Thomas, 145.

29   "This is good…all-talkie": Thomas, 123–24.

29   "Winchell proclaimed…to slang": William R. Taylor, "Broadway: The Place That Words Built," *Inventing Times Square: Commerce and Culture at the Crossroads pf the World*, ed. William R. Taylor (New York: Russell Sage Foundation, 1991), 214.

30   "I like your songs better": Thomas, 124.

31   "just the atmosphere…composition of melodies": Isaac Goldberg, *Tin Pan Alley* (New York: John Day, 1930), 230.

34   "The picture song…advertising could accomplish": *Variety* (31 October 1929), 56. Quoted in Katherine Spring, "Pop Go the Warner Bros., & Marketing Film Songs during the Coming of Sound," *Cinema Journal* 48:1 (Fall 2008), 71.

34   "without undue exploitation…song like that": *Variety* (10 July 1929), 49. Quoted in Spring, 77.

35   "This is an experiment…too much money": Thomas, 125.

35   "to get the film…9 or 10 at night": John Kobal, *Gotta Sing Gotta Dance: A Pictorial History of Film Musicals* (London: Hamlyn, 1971), 40–41.

35   "That's not a motion picture…legitimate theater": Thomas, 126.

35   "We don't need…in the lab": Thomas, 126.

38   "learned what not to do": Tom Milne, *Rouben Mamoulian* (Bloomington: Indiana University Press, 1970), 17.

38   "In those days…of a scene": Milne, 25.

40   "But, they said…Mamoulian said, went": Milne, 24–25.

43   "It's not practical…my money with yours": Thomas, 163.

43   "If that's the way…about whores": Richard Barrios, *A Song in the Dark: The Birth of the Musical Film* (New York: Oxford University Press, 1995), 312.

44   "MGM can afford it": Thomas, 164.

45   "I'll never forget…had written": Hugh Fordin, *MGM's Greatest Musicals: The Arthur Freed Unit* (New York: Da Capo Press, 1996), 351.

45   "Revue All Cold…Down on Revues": quoted in Barrios, 186.

45   "The present Hollywood…stage requires none": quoted in Barrios, 212.

45   "the public is…thrown at them": quoted in Barrios, 213.

CHAPTER 3

48   "operettas tended…deadly serious": Richard Barrios, *A Song in the Dark: The Birth of the Musical Film* (New York: Oxford University Press, 1995), 281.

48   "The Warners…a good deal": Barrios, 223.

48   "Before musical plays.…of the stage": Barrios, 224.

49   "his upbringing…the poor Parisian": Scott Eyman, *Ernst Lubitsch: Laughter in Paradise* (Baltimore: Johns Hopkins University Press, 2000), 153.

49   "Dick, that's wrong…you are *right*": Max Wilk, *They're Playing Our Song* (New York: Atheneum, 1973), 101–2.

49   "the comedy of manners…in elegant whispers": Eyman, 15–16.

49   "a small round figure…You are a prince!": Eyman, 154.

50   "If she can sing…the part": Eyman, 155.

50   "crossbreed…casual humorous manner": Eyman, 156.

53   "It can be said…true screen musical": quoted in Ruth Benjamin and Arthur Rosenblatt, *Movie Song Catalog: Performers and Supporting Crew for the Songs Sung in 1460 Musical and Nonmusical Films, 1928–1988* (Jefferson, NC: McFarland, 1993), 126.

55   "I like your…word like that": Wilk, 102

55   "He was the first…or the situation": Wilk, 102.

55   "I work with you…songs integrated": Eyman, 167.

58   "I discovered…poetic stylization": Tom Milne, *Rouben Mamoulian* (Bloomington: Indiana University Press, 1970), 12.

59   "a truly dramatic…and so on": Milne, 12–13.

59   "The curtain rose…like an orchestra": Milne, 13.

63   "charming unexpectedness…superb writing": Alec Wilder, *American Popular Song: The Great Innovators, 1900–1950* (New York: Oxford University Press, 1972), 190–91.

64   "The dramatic action…indigenous to film": John Kobal, *Gotta Sing Gotta Dance: A Pictorial History of Film Musicals* (London: Hamlyn, 1971), 116.

CHAPTER 4

66   "She's just a good…Washington ever did": *42nd Street*, ed. Rocco Fumento (Madison: University of Wisconsin Press, 1980), 13.

67   "I quickly realized…have ever done": John Kobal, *Gotta Sing Gotta Dance: A Pictorial History of Film Musicals* (London: Hamlyn, 1971) 127–28.

67   "surrogate for the average male out front in the stalls": Clive Hirschhorn, *The Hollywood Musical* (New York: Crown, 1981), 60.

67   "We've got these…public see them?": Hirschhorn, 60.

68   "I couldn't figure…the movie business": Roy Hemming, *The Melody Lingers On: The Great Songwriters and Their Movie Musicals* (New York: Newmarket Press, 1986), 255.

68   "that this would not be…hottest composer": Hemming, 256.

69   "always insisted…habit with me'": Hemming, 258.

71   "In *42nd Street*…degree of authenticity": Fumento, 25–27.

74   "For this one…side to side": Richard Barrios, *A Song in the Dark: The Birth of the Musical Film* (New York: Oxford University Press, 1995), 389.

74   "There was nothing…credit for them": Hemming, 263.

76   "my toughest number…the front office": John Kobal, *Gotta Sing Gotta Dance: A History of Movie Musicals* (New York: Exeter Books, 1983), 99.

76   "With Berkeley directing…water you're smiling": Cass Warner Sperling and Cork Millner, *Hollywood Be Thy Name: The Warner Brothers Story* (Rocklin, CA: Prima, 1994), 193.

77   "step-wise…best theater writing": Alec Wilder, *American Popular Song: The Great Innovators, 1900–1950* (New York: Oxford University Press, 1972), 398.

77   "that he had written…from the melody": Hemming, 272.

79   "he would disappear…lyrics in hand": Hemming, 274.

79 "were loyal…best they could": Hemming, 274–75.

80 "that henceforth it…the Production Code": John Mueller, *Astaire Dancing: The Musical Films* (New York: Wings Books, 1991), 55.

80 "invitation to…pussy sometime": Barrios, 410.

80 "forest…swayed prettily": Hirschhorn, 109.

80 "Gone were…his editing": Hirschhorn, 147.

81 "Hollywood seemed to me…fun of it": Philip Furia, *Skylark: The Life and Times of Johnny Mercer* (New York: St. Martin's, 2003), 96–97.

82 " 'I can't do…/Onward!' ": Furia, 94.

83 "always feeling…nitro pills": Furia, 100.

CHAPTER 5

86 "Although many.…could be constructed": Richard B. Jewell with Vernon Harbin, *The RKO Story* (New York: Arlington House, 1982), 10.

86 "The supreme irony…their artistic idiosyncrasies": Jewell, 15.

87 "I am tremendously…this wretched test": John Mueller, *Astaire Dancing: The Musical Films* (New York: Wings Books, 1991), 7.

87 "Come on, Fred…our dance routines": Mueller, 6.

88 "the first time…he get it?": Mueller, 8.

88 "I was amazed…on the screen": Mueller, 51.

89 "I'm a bit…bothered with movies": Mueller, 8.

89 "Although the plot…in the script": Mueller, 9.

90 "Astaire firmly established…one and three": Mueller, 66.

94 "I worked harder…trouble with": Philip Furia, *Irving Berlin: A Life in Song* (New York: Schirmer Books, 1998), 178–79.

95 "No one is taken in": Mueller, 89.

96 "the wholly unexpected…Mata Hari": Alec Wilder, *American Popular Song: The Great Innovators, 1900–1950* (New York: Oxford University Press, 1972), 111.

97 "a contrasting state…white wig": Mueller, 106.

98 "in the repeated…in the other": Mueller, 111.

98 "Kern's haunting music…main strain": Mueller, 111.

98 "This dance on…it was over": Mueller, 112.

99 "RUMORS ABOUT HIGHBROW…TO WRITE HITS": Deena Rosenberg, *Fascinating Rhythm: The Collaboration of George and Ira Gershwin* (New York: Dutton, 1991), 321.

100 "The arresting nature…loving qualities": Wilder, 157.

101 "wondered how long…there it was": Fred Astaire, *Steps in Time* (New York: Harper, 1959), 212–25.

104 "The first says…can get it": Ira Gershwin, *Lyrics on Several Occasions* (New York: Knopf, 1959), 97.

105 "They were going…a Technicolor song": Robert Kimball and Linda Emmet, *The Complete Lyrics of Irving Berlin* (New York: Knopf, 2001), 316.

CHAPTER 6

106 "In 1938…of the United States": Gerald Mast and Bruce F. Kawin, *A Short History of the Movies*, 10th ed. (New York: Pearson Longman, 2008), 267.

106 "fairly wide range...else destroying it": Alec Wilder, *American Popular Song: The Great Innovators, 1900–1950* (New York: Oxford University Press, 1972), 242–43.

107 "The response was...to hear it": Philip Furia and Michael Lasser, *America's Songs: The Stories Behind the Songs of Broadway, Hollywood, and Tin Pan Alley* (New York: Routledge, 2006), 133.

107 "He sings far...a clean-cut sailor": Charles Schwartz, *Cole Porter* (New York: The Dial Press, 1977), 159.

108 "There is radio music...in an hour": Frederick Lewis Allen, *Only Yesterday: An Informal History of the Nineteen-Twenties* (New York: Harper & Row, 1931), 65.

109 "I want them to show...to get laughs": Max Wilk, *They're Playing Our Song* (New York: Atheneum, 1973), 105.

111 "the key word...plot and characters": Herbert G. Goldman, *Banjo Eyes: Eddie Cantor and the Birth of Modern Stardom* (New York: Oxford University Press, 1997), 136.

111 "essentially a visual...suited to radio": Goldman, 162.

112 "That's a goddamned...you write that?": Stefan Kanfer, *Groucho: The Life and Times of Julius Henry Marx* (New York: Knopf, 2000), 56.

112 "I already have...need the music": Kanfer, 134.

113 "Instead of making...only frivolous": Kanfer, 204.

113 "There's music...dumbfounded, staggered": E. Y. Harburg, "From the Lower East Side to 'Over the Rainbow,'" in *Creators and Disturbers: Reminiscences by Jewish Intellectuals of New York*, ed. Bernard Rosenberg and Ernest Goldstein (New York: Columbia University Press, 1982), 140–41. Harburg may have taken his inspiration for "Lydia, the Tattooed Lady" from a scene in *Duck Soup* where Harpo displays his tattoos to Groucho—a girl in a bikini on his arm, his social security number on his bicep, and, as he threatens to drop his pants, one of his grandfather on his posterior.

115 "After Thalberg's death...for the money": Kanfer, 213.

115 "They had been...of his influence": Kanfer, 244.

115 "The amount of work...turkeys is completed": Kanfer, 254.

115 "I had no...just talked fast": Kanfer, 255.

115 "I'm not a stooge...woman in Hollywood": Kanfer, 256.

115 "Your last two...a good picture": Kanfer, 256.

116 "When I say...the way out": Kanfer, 260–61.

116 "It came out...the little guy": Furia and Lasser, 105.

116 "At last...whole picture": Richard Schickel, *The Disney Version: The Life, Times, Art and Commerce of Walt Disney* (Chicago: Ivan R. Dee, 1997), 154.

117 "We will use...destroy it": Schickel, 170.

117 "There's something...about them": Schickel, 215.

120 "I planned to....lesbian accent": Donald Spoto, *Blue Angel: The Life of Marlene Dietrich* (New York: Doubleday, 1992), 74.

121 "I preferred to...more suggestive effect": John Kobal, *Gotta Sing Gotta Dance: A Pictorial History of Film Musicals* (London: Hamlyn, 1971), 190.

122 "'schemed with a way...that we want": *The American Film Institute Catalog of Motion Pictures Produced in the United States: Feature Films, 1931–1940* (Berkeley: University of California Press, 1993), 30.

123 "character story...introduce something new": Twentieth Century-Fox Collection, Archives of the Performing Arts, University of Southern California.

126 "Drop the fat one": David Shipman, *Judy Garland: The Secret Life of an American Legend* (New York: Hyperion, 1993), 57.

CHAPTER 7

130   "was an early...takes revenge": Michael Lasser, "Arthur Freed," *Dictionary of Literary Biography, Volume 265: American Song Lyricists, 1920–1960* (Detroit: Thomson Gale, 2002), 153.

130   "There were a lot...in those things": *American Song Lyricists, 1920–1960*, 157.

131   "I brought in...were *real* musicals": John Kobal, *Gotta Sing Gotta Dance* (London: Hamlyn, 1971), 220.

131   "on a bill...became Judy Garland": Kobal, 257.

131   "Garland and her sister...so much of it": Kobal, 259.

131   "The biggest thing...of Judy Garland": Kobal, 257.

131   "to sing...from the heart": Hugh Fordin, *MGM's Greatest Musicals: The Arthur Freed Unit* (New York: Da Capo Press, 1996), 6.

132   "They love...make a picture": Fordin, 7–8.

132   "Once a year...for prestige": Harold Meyerson and Ernie Harburg, *Who Put the Rainbow in "The Wizard of Oz"? Yip Harburg, Lyricist* (Ann Arbor: University of Michigan Press, 1993), 119.

133   "What can I...are insurmountable": Fordin, 9.

133   "I believe that...the whole script": Fordin, 13.

134   "Arthur had sensed...one emotional idea": Meyerson and Harburg, 120–24.

134   "'Put up your dukes...Bert doing that": Meyerson and Harburg, 125.

134   "not just songs but scenes": Max Wilk, *They're Playing Our Song* (New York: athenaeum, 1973), 224.

135   "I am always...better picture": Meyerson and Harburg, 152.

136   "There is no...to Oz": Fordin, 11.

136   "Harburg and Arlen...'Over the Rainbow'": *American Song Lyricists, 1920–1960*, 157.

136   "'I can't tell you...for Nelson Eddy'": Meyerson and Harburg, 129–131.

136   "'Over the Rainbow...sound has an importance": Meyerson and Harburg, 132–34.

137   "I'm sorry to say...pleaded with him": Meyerson and Harburg, 156.

138   "This score...simple as that": Fordin, 27.

138   "Let the boys...it can't hurt": Meyerson and Harburg, 156.

139   "I asked him...his hotel bill": Kobal, 220.

139   "had the opportunity...the Freed unit": Kobal, 220.

139   "When I arrived...make a musical": Kobal, 220.

140   "It does present...unusual it is": Alec Wilder, *American Popular Song: The Great Innovators, 1900–1950* (New York: Oxford University Press, 1972), 334.

140   "Nothing much happens...or we'll learn": Fordin, 91–94.

141   "Judy came to see me...it's marvelous": Fordin, 95.

141   "'passed-along song...specifically cinematic technique": Jane Feuer, *The Hollywood Musical* (Bloomington: Indiana University Press, 1993), 16.

142   "a device...dominant ninth chords": Wilder, 347.

142   "Hugh and I...song for Judy!'": Fordin, 98.

145   "The mood of the song...leaving the theatre'": Fordin, 99.

146   "I thought it had...it's wonderful": Philip Furia, *Skylark: The Life and Times of Johnny Mercer* (New York: St. Martin's Press, 2003), 156–57.

148   "The lure and love...clown suit": *America's Songs*, 214.

148   "Tears came...have to reprise": Fordin, 205.

148   "It's the best...ever written": Fordin, 205.

149 "privately complained...emotion was nostalgia": Laurence Bergreen, *As Thousands Cheer: The Life of Irving Berlin* (New York: Penguin Books, 1990), 477.

149 "What are we...handle it": Fordin, 226.

149 "Never, never...rug again!": Bob Thomas, *Astaire: The Man, The Dancer* (New York: St. Martin's, 1984), 193.

149 "Let me go...couldn't be fooled": Fordin, 226–27.

150 "You can't put...Write the script": Bergreen, 479.

150 "If Kelly had...was all lighter": *New York Sun* (3 June 1948).

151 "Let's have a 'tramps' number": Michael Freedland, *Irving Berlin* (New York: Stein and Day, 1974), 174.

153 "What are they doing to that poor kid?": Gerald Clarke, *Get Happy: The Life of Judy Garland* (New York: Random House, 2000), 246.

CHAPTER 8

154 "I went home...blues song": William Zinsser, "Harold Arlen: The Secret Music Maker," *Harper's*, May 1960, 44–45.

154 "weak tea...that to John": Alec Wilder, *American Popular Song: The Great Innovators, 1900–1950* (New York: Oxford University Press, 1972), 272.

155 "Jack Warner...of the thirties": Clive Hirschhorn, *The Warner Bros. Story* (New York: Crown, 1979), 209.

155 "I don't want...during the war": Cass Warner Sperling and Cork Millner, *Hollywood Be Thy Name: The Warner Brothers Story* (Rocklin, CA: Prima, 1994), 245.

162 "I told him...for the screen": *The Complete Lyrics of Irving Berlin*, edited by Robert Kimball and Linda Emmet (New York: Knopf, 2001), 349.

163 "in two rather...for a song": *The Complete Lyrics of Irving Berlin*, 351.

163 "We working composers...a "round" song": *Saturday Evening Post*, 14 January 1944.

165 "You don't...this one, Irving": *Liverpool Evening Express*, 27 September 1946.

165 "the set...merely that—a set": John Mueller, *Astaire Dancing: The Musical Films* (New York: Wings Books, 1991), 210.

169 "noted that...not really worked": William G. Hyland, *Richard Rodgers* (New Haven, CT: Yale University Press, 1998), 156.

172 "When we do fantasy...sight of reality": Richard Schickel, *The Disney Version: The Life, Times, Art and Commerce of Walt Disney* (Chicago: Ivan R. Dee, 1997), 200.

172 "the fantastic is...realistic possible style": Schickel, 194.

CHAPTER 9

177 "how pictures start...all Gershwin music": Donald Knox, *The Magic Factory: How MGM Made "An American in Paris"* (New York: Praeger, 1973), 37.

177 "a line here...old song": Edward Jablonski, *Gershwin: A Biography* (Boston: Northeastern University Press, 1987, 1990), 355.

178 "All I knew...in the film": Knox, 40.

178 "We were all...and good drama": Knox, 53.

179 "the 'S' stands...the first place": Gerald Mast, *Can't Help Singin': The American Musical on Stage and Screen* (Woodstock, NY: Overlook Press, 1987), 75.

179 "Everyone connected…the best ever": Jablonski, 355–357.

180 "as a backstage…dancer, Ann Miller": Peter Wollen, *Singin' in the Rain* (London: British Film Institute Publishing, 1992), 31.

180 "Many of these songs…feet at last": Hugh Fordin, *MGM's Greatest Musicals: The Arthur Freed Unit* (New York: Da Capo Press, 1996), 352.

180 "We remembered particularly…the silent camera": Fordin, 352.

181 "had no particular…work and pain": Wollen, 32.

181 "Well, it should…per cent plagiarism": Fordin, 359.

182 "Partly we are…Porter's closest friends": Fordin, 359.

182 "I always hated…doodedoo do'": Fordin, 357.

183 "and a lake…and the downspout": Wollen, 16.

183 "Dietz was our…with your songs": Fordin, 397.

184 "We were very nervous…fresh fields": Fordin, 400.

184 "Boys we need…Like Show Business'": Fordin, 403.

187 "Cole has a way…*on the stage*": Fordin, 444.

187 "visual style…than their songs": Mast and Kawin, 239.

187 "*Seven Brides*…which they did": Philip Furia, *Skylark: The Life and Times of Johnny Mercer* (New York: St. Martin's, 2003), 192.

187 "It was a sleeper…out to be": Furia, 192.

188 "Michael Kidd…music to match": Furia, 192–93.

191 "In all my…a Franz Schubert": Charles Schwartz, *Cole Porter* (New York: The Dial Press, 1977), 256.

192 "London Bridge…*My Fair Lady*!": Fordin, 441.

192 "I'm buying *Gigi*…care of Fritz": Fordin, 441.

192 "Why does Arthur…about a whore?": Fordin, 459.

193 "'I'm too old…is the audience": Philip Furia and Michael Lasser, *America's Songs: The Stories Behind the Songs of Broadway, Hollywood, and Tin Pan Alley* (New York: Routledge, 2006), 261.

193 "I knew all…would come around": Fordin, 458.

193 "With a pioneering…cost him $40,000": Fordin, 469.

CHAPTER 10

201 "My father heard…*Comes the Groom*": Philip Furia, *Skylark: The Life and Times of Johnny Mercer* (New York: St. Martin's, 2003), 190.

201 "the result won't be a musical": Edward Jablonski, *Gershwin: A Biography* (Boston: Northeastern University Press, 1987), 363.

202 "an uninspired excerpt from *Oklahoma!*": Jablonski, , 364.

205 "in the end…it slipped away": Ronald Haver, *A Star Is Born: The Making of the 1954 Movie and Its 1983 Restoration* (New York: Alfred A. Knopf, 1988), 71.

205 "chart the emotional development…of the story": Haver, 57.

206 "kind of song…the lyrics to": Haver, 52.

206 "marvelous use of the fourth interval": Alec Wilder, *American Popular Song: The Great Innovators, 1900–1950* (New York: Oxford University Press, 1972), 286.

206 "made that melody…Rock of Gibraltar": Philip Furia and Michael Lasser, *America's Songs: The Stories Behind the Songs of Broadway, Hollywood, and Tin Pan Alley* (New York: Routledge, 2006), 244.

208 "a slow look...at the bandstand": Haver, 124–25.

208 "We couldn't move...everything you'd learned": Haver, 133.

210 "the way they...out vital bits": Haver, 215.

210 "Anyway La Garland.... That Got Away'": Philip Furia, *Ira Gershwin: The Art of the Lyricist* (New York: Oxford University Press, 1996), 227.

210 "away with 'away'": Ira Gershwin, *Lyrics on Several Occasions* (New York: Alfred A. Knopf, 1959), 48.

211 "I don't know...the next day": Furia, *Skylark*, 200.

213 "It's a real...getting the hits": Furia, *Skylark*, 201.

214 "Hart and my father...seamless cloth": Susan Loesser, *A Most Remarkable Fella: Frank Loesser and the Guys and Dolls in His Life* (New York: Donald I. Fine, 1993), 124.

214 "'Jimmy's a marvelous...wonderful with children": Loesser, 123.

214 "'Loesser is hot...way he wrote": Loesser, 124.

214 "My father referred...I was stunned": Loesser, 127–28.

218 "They wrote with...work after that": Furia, *Skylark*, 216–17.

CHAPTER 11

220 "Writing for character...great picture": Author's interview with Richard Sherman, 2 June 2008 in Beverly Hills, California. All subsequent quotations by Sherman are from this interview.

225 "Probably the best...of the decade": Clive Hirschhorn, *The Hollywood Musical* (New York: Crown, 1981), 381.

225 "have a cinematic...and even intellectually": Richard Schickel, *The Disney Version: The Life, Times, Art and Commerce of Walt Disney* (Chicago: Ivan R. Dee, 1997), 357.

226 "It struck me...and gone home": Miles Kreuger, *At Long Last Love* LP liner notes, RCA ABL 2–0967, 1975.

227 "I didn't want...walk and talk": Kreuger, *At Long Last Love* LP liner notes.

229 "stage show's stylized...the real thing": Hirschhorn, 398.

231 "I just wanted...put them in": Jan Stuart, *The Nashville Chronicles: The Making of Robert Altman's Masterpiece* (New York: Simon & Schuster, 2000), 36–37.

232 "Although the song's...callous and vain": Todd Berliner and Philip Furia, "The Sounds of Silence: Songs in Hollywood Films since the 1960s," *Style* 36:1 (Spring 2002), 29.

233 "Though she begins...at the rally": Berliner and Furia, 29.

236 "During the film's...face does not": Berliner and Furia, 24.

236 "sadness, loneliness...otherwise happy ending": Berliner and Furia, 25

237 "since their performances...and lines unsaid": Berliner and Furia, 26.

240 "The implicit message...like they used to": Berliner and Furia, 19.

241 "a-ha! moment...as the underpinning": quoted in *Minneapolis Star Tribune* (27 July 2008), E8.

CREDITS

LONESOME POLECAT
Music by GENE DePAUL
Lyrics by JOHNNY MERCER
© 1953, 1954 (Renewed 1981, 1982) LOEW'S
INCORPORATED

LOVE IS HERE TO STAY (from "Goldwyn Follies")
Music and Lyrics by GEORGE GERSHWIN and
IRA GERSHWIN
© 1938 (Renewed) GEORGE GERSHWIN MUSIC
and IRA GERSHWIN MUSIC

LULLABY OF BROADWAY (from "Gold Diggers of 1935")
Words by AL DUBIN Music by HARRY WARREN
© 1935 (Renewed) WB MUSIC CORP.

LYDIA THE TATTOOED LADY
Words by E.Y. HARBURG Music by
HAROLD ARLEN
© 1939 (Renewed) EMI FEIST CATALOG INC.

THE MAN THAT GOT AWAY (from "A Star Is Born")
Words by IRA GERSHWIN Music by
HAROLD ARLEN
© 1954 (Renewed) IRA GERSHWIN MUSIC.
and HARWIN MUSIC CORP.

NIGHT AND DAY (from "The Gay Divorcee")
Words and Music by COLE PORTER
© 1932 (Renewed) WB MUSIC CORP.
NOTE: 1944 - French Version by Emelia Renaud
1947 - Spanish Version by Johnnie Camacho

OVER THE RAINBOW (from "The Wizard of Oz")
Music by HAROLD ARLEN
Lyrics by E.Y. HARBURG
© 1938 (Renewed) METRO-GOLDWYN-MAYER
INC.

SOMETHING'S GOTTA GIVE (from "Daddy Long Legs")
Words and Music by JOHNNY MERCER
© 1954 (Renewed) WB MUSIC CORP.

SPRING, SPRING, SPRING
By GENE DE PAUL and JOHNNY MERCER
© 1953 (Renewed) EMI ROBBINS CATALOG
INC.

THEY CAN'T TAKE THAT AWAY FROM ME (from "Shall We Dance")
Music and Lyrics by GEORGE GERSHWIN and
IRA GERSHWIN
© 1936 (Renewed) GEORGE GERSHWIN MUSIC
and IRA GERSHWIN MUSIC

THINGS ARE LOOKING UP
Music and Lyrics by GEORGE GERSHWIN and
IRA GERSHWIN
© 1937 (Renewed) GEORGE GERSHWIN MUSIC
and IRA GERSHWIN MUSIC

TOO MARVELOUS FOR WORDS
Words by JOHNNY MERCER
Music by RICHARD A. WHITING
© 1937 (Renewed) WB MUSIC CORP.

TROLLEY SONG, THE (from "Meet Me in St. Louis")
Words and Music by HUGH MARTIN and
RALPH BLANE
© 1943 (Renewed) METRO-GOLDWYN-MAYER
INC.
© 1944 (Renewed) EMI FEIST CATALOG INC.

YOU MUST HAVE BEEN A BEAUTIFUL BABY
Lyrics by JOHNNY MERCER
Music by HARRY WARREN

YOU'RE GETTING TO BE A HABIT WITH ME

Words by AL DUBIN Music by HARRY WARREN

HAL LEONARD CORPORATION

BE A CLOWN

from THE PIRATE
Words and Music by Cole Porter

GIGI

from GIGI
Words by Alan Jay Lerner
Music by Frederick Loewe

I REMEMBER IT WELL

from GIGI
Words by Alan Jay Lerner
Music by Frederick Loewe

I'M GLAD I'M NOT YOUNG ANYMORE

from GIGI
Words by Alan Jay Lerner
Music by Frederick Loewe

THE KING'S NEW CLOTHES

from the Motion Picture HANS CHRISTIAN
ANDERSEN
Words and Music by Frank Loesser

ONE FOR MY BABY (AND ONE MORE FOR THE ROAD)

from the Motion Picture THE SKY'S THE LIMIT
Lyric by Johnny Mercer
Music by Harold Arlen

THE PARISIANS

from GIGI
Words by Alan Jay Lerner
Music by Frederick Loewe

THAT'S ENTERTAINMENT

from THE BAND WAGON
Words by Howard Dietz
Music by Arthur Schwartz

WALTZ AT MAXIM'S

from GIGI
Words by Alan Jay Lerner
Music by Frederick Loewe

SONY/ATV MUSIC PUBLISHING

BUTTONS AND BOWS

ISN'T IT ROMANTIC

LOVER

MOONLIGHT BECOMES YOU
© 1942 Sony/ATV Harmony.
All Rights by Sony/ATV Music Publishing LLC,
8 Music Sq. W. Nashville, TN 37203.
All rights Reserved.
Used By Permission.

MY OLD FLAME
© 1934 Sony/ATV Harmony.
All Rights by Sony/ATV Music Publishing LLC,
8 Music Sq. W., Nashville, TN 37203.
All Rights Reserved.
Used By Permission.

OH THAT MITZI
©1932 Sony/ATV Harmony.
All Rights by Sony/ATV Music Publishing LLC,
8 Music Sq. W., Nashville, TN 37203.
All Rights Reserved.
Used By Permission.

ONE HOUR WITH YOU
© 1932 Sony/ATV Harmony.
All Rights by Sony/ATV Music Publishing LLC,
8 Music Sq. W., Nashville, TN 37203.
All Rights Reserved.
Used By Permission.

THE SONG OF PAREE
© 1932 Sony/ATV Harmony.
All Rights by Sony/ATV Music Publishing LLC,
8 Music Sq. W., Nashville, TN 37203.
All Rights Reserved.
Used By Permission.

THANKS FOR THE MEMORY
© 1936 Sony/ATV Harmony.
All Rights by Sony/ATV Music Publishing LLC,
8 Music Sq. W., Nashville, TN 37203.
All Rights Reserved.
Used By Permission.

WHAT WOULD YOU DO
© 1932 Sony/ATV Harmony.
All Rights by Sony/ATV Music Publishing LLC,
8 Music Sq. W., Nashville, TN 37203.
All rights reserved.
Used By Permission.

WILLIAMSON MUSIC

BLUE SKIES
By Irving Berlin
© Copyright 1926, 1927 by Irving Berlin
© Copyright Renewed. International
Copyright Secured
All Rights Reserved. Reprinted by Permission.

CHEEK TO CHEEK
By Irving Berlin
© Copyright 1935 by Irving Berlin
© Copyright Renewed. International
Copyright Secured.
All Rights Reserved. Reprinted by Permission.

A COUPLE OF SWELLS
By Irving Berlin
© Copyright 1947 by Irving Berlin
© Copyright Renewed. International
Copyright Secured.
All Rights Reserved. Reprinted by Permission.

IT MIGHT AS WELL BE SPRING
Written by Richard Rodgers &
Oscar Hammerstein II
Copyright © 1945 by WILLIAMSON MUSIC
Copyright Renewed. International
Copyright Secured.
All Rights Reserved. Used by Permission.

LET'S FACE THE MUSIC AND DANCE
By Irving Berlin
© Copyright 1935, 1936 by Irving Berlin
© Copyright Renewed. International
Copyright Secured.
All Rights Reserved. Reprinted by Permission.

TOP HAT, WHITE TIE AND TAILS
By Irving Berlin
© Copyright 1935 by Irving Berlin
© Copyright Renewed. International
Copyright Secured.
All Rights Reserved. Reprinted by Permission

WHITE CHRISTMAS
By Irving Berlin
© Copyright 1940, 1942 by Irving Berlin
© Copyright Renewed. International
Copyright Secured.
All Rights Reserved. Reprinted by Permission.

INDEX

SONG INDEX